Exploring

THE EPISTLES
OF JOHN

THE JOHN PHILLIPS COMMENTARY SERIES

Exploring

THE EPISTLES OF JOHN

An Expository Commentary

JOHN PHILLIPS

kregel
PUBLICATIONS

Grand Rapids, MI 49501

Exploring the Epistles of John: An Expository Commentary

© 2003 by John Phillips

Published in 2003 by Kregel Publications, a division of Kregel, Inc., P.O. Box 2607, Grand Rapids, MI 49501.

Scripture quotations are from the King James Version of the Holy Bible.

Library of Congress Cataloging-in-Publication Data
Phillips, John.
    Exploring the epistles of John: an expository commentary / by John Phillips.
        p.   cm.
Includes bibliographical references.
    1. Bible. N.T. Epistles of John—Commentaries. I. Title.
BS2805.53.P48 2003
227'.94077—dc21   2002154871

ISBN 10: 0-8254-3393-2
ISBN 13: 978-0-8254-3393-1

Printed in the United States of America

10 / 7 6 5

Summary Outline

EXPLORING JOHN'S SECOND EPISTLE

Part 1: A Word of Commendation (vv. 1–4)

Introduction

John wrote for the third generation. Peter and Paul, James and Jude all wrote for the first and second generations of believers. John, however, as a first generation apostle, passed over two generations to write for an increasingly apostate third generation.

For by its third generation, every movement of God needs a fresh touch of the Holy Spirit. The first generation is motivated by *conviction;* great truths have been grasped, and those who have espoused them have a compulsion to spread those truths abroad. They will dare all and die for them. The second generation inherits these truths, but the conviction softens into a *belief.* They believe the truths they have been taught; they debate them, defend them, and disseminate them, but the fire and passion have gone. By the third generation, the belief becomes an *opinion.* The third generation will trade first-generation truth, dilute it, change it, accept counterfeits, and make room for error. And that's why John wrote for the third generation—the third generation needed a fresh revival.

All about him, John saw error and apostasy, the most flagrant deceptions accepted as gospel truth. John likely would have said, "It wasn't like that at all. I was there. I knew Him as well as anyone knew Him. I was one of His chosen twelve. I remember it all as though it were yesterday."

So out of his remarkably retentive memory—quickened, inspired, and energized by the Holy Spirit—John wrote his gospel to remind the church of the essential and eternal deity of Christ. Then he wrote these three epistles to remind his readers of the true humanity of the Lord Jesus.

Three major heresies had made inroads into the church when John wrote toward the end of the first century of the Christian era. The *Ebionites* denied the deity of Christ—to them He was just another created being. The *Docetists* denied the humanity of Christ. Believing that He had not come in the flesh, they taught that He was some kind of phantom who had no corporeal being. The *Cerinthians* denied the union of the two natures of Christ (the human and the divine). Their notion was that "the Christ" descended upon the man, Jesus, at the time of His baptism and departed from Him at the time of His crucifixion. John indignantly denied all three heresies.

Like the apostle Paul, John had a number of characteristic words. Paul's favorite words, for instance, were faith, hope, and love. John's words were light, life, and love. John also made frequent use of the expression *we know.* Moreover, he dwelt in the past—a characteristic of old people—referring to the past some fifty times in his three epistles. The word *beginning* occurs ten times, for that was John's ultimate answer to the heretics. He went back to the beginning, and he says, "I was there!"

Exploring
JOHN'S FIRST EPISTLE

Outline

3. The betrayal of that life (2:3–11)
   a. The test of the Lord's person (2:3–5)
      (1) The claim to know Him put into perspective (2:3)
      (2) The claim to know Him put to the proof (2:4–5)
         (a) The lie test (2:4)
         (b) The love test (2:5)
   b. The test of the Lord's precept (2:6–8)
      (1) A confident expectation (2:6)
      (2) A critical examination (2:7–8)
         (a) The previous commandment (2:7)
         (b) The present commandment (2:8)
            i. The test of new life in Christ (2:8a)
            ii. The test of new light through Christ (2:8b)
   c. The test of the Lord's people (2:9–11)
      (1) The principle stated (2:9)
      (2) The principle studied (2:10–11)
         (a) Loving one's brethren (2:10)
         (b) Loathing one's brethren (2:11)
4. The beauty of that life (2:12–14)
   a. The first round of reasons (2:12–13b)
      (1) Little children: because of their condition in the family (2:12)
      (2) Fathers: because of their concept of the faith (2:13a)
      (3) Young men: because of their conquest of the foe (2:13b)
   b. The further round of reasons (2:13c–14d)
      (1) Little children: because of their progress (2:13c)
      (2) Fathers: because of their perception (2:14a)
      (3) Young men: because of their power (2:14b–d)
         (a) How it is described (2:14b)
         (b) How it was derived (2:14c)
         (c) How it was displayed (2:14d)
5. The boundaries of that life (2:15–23)
   a. The forbidden sphere (2:15–17)
      (1) The love of the world (2:15)
         (a) What it begets (2:15a)
         (b) What it betrays (2:15b)
      (2) The lusts of the world (2:16)
         (a) Its shameful appetites (2:16a)

        (b) Its showy appearance (2:16b)

        (c) Its shallow applause (2:16c)

      (3) The loss of the world (2:17)

        (a) That which is passing (2:17a)

        (b) That which is permanent (2:17b)

    b. The false spirit (2:18–23)

      (1) A word about the time (2:18)

        (a) A past warning about the time Antichrist will come (2:18a)

        (b) A present warning about the time antichrists have come (2:18b)

      (2) A word about the transients (2:19)

        (a) Their departure from the fellowship (2:19a)

        (b) Their disclosure about their faith (2:19b)

      (3) A word about the truth (2:20–21)

        (a) The unction of the Spirit (2:20)

        (b) The understanding of the Scripture (2:21)

      (4) A word about the traitors (2:22–23a)

        (a) The challenge of the Antichrist (2:22)

        (b) The children of the Antichrist (2:23a)

      (5) A word about the testimony (2:23b)

  6. The blessings of that life (2:24–29)

    a. Living in Him (2:24–25)

      (1) The principle involved (2:24)

        (a) He abides in us (2:24a)

        (b) We abide in Him (2:24b)

      (2) The promise involved (2:25)

    b. Learning of Him (2:26–27)

      (1) The unveiling of the seducer (2:26)

      (2) The unction of the Spirit (2:27)

    c. Looking for Him (2:28–29)

      (1) As to the prospect—a truth to be apprehended (2:28)

      (2) As to the present—a test to be applied (2:29)

B. How we show the family life (3:1–24)

  1. New life in Christ (3:1–10)

    a. Our high calling as sons (3:1–2)

      (1) Its commencement in the past (3:1)

   (a) The love that sought us (3:1a–b)

     i. An exclamation (3:1a)

     ii. An explanation (3:1b)

   (b) The love that separates us (3:1c)

  (2) Its continuation in the present (3:2a)

  (3) Its consummation in the future (3:2b–d)

   (a) A hidden mystery (3:2b)

   (b) A holy moment (3:2c)

   (c) A happy meeting (3:2d)

 b. Our holy conduct as saints (3:3–10)

  (1) As to our standing (3:3–5)

   (a) A purifying hope (3:3)

   (b) A present hope (3:4–5)

    God's demands and

     i. The commandments of the law (3:4)

     ii. The character of the Lord (3:5)

  (2) As to our state (3:6–10)

   (a) Sin's blindness (3:6–7)

     i. The vision of Christ (3:6)

     ii. The virtue of Christ (3:7)

   (b) Sin's bondage (3:8)

     i. The Devil and his deeds (3:8a)

     ii. The Devil and his destroyer (3:8b)

   (c) Sin's birthmark (3:9–10)

     i. The divine seed (3:9)

     ii. The Devil's seed (3:10)

2. New love for Christ (3:11–24)

 a. The truth of that love (3:11–18)

  (1) The public execration of that love (3:11–13)

   (a) The message (3:11)

   (b) The murder (3:12)

   (c) The marvel (3:13)

  (2) The personal experience of that love (3:14–15)

   (a) What we know (3:14)

   (b) What we show (3:15)

  (3) The perfect example of that love (3:16)

   (a) The love of the Christ (3:16a)

(b) The love of the Christian (3:16b)

(4) The practical expression of that love (3:17–18)

(a) The callous man (3:17)

i. How he behaves himself (3:17a)

ii. How he betrays himself (3:17b)

(b) The compassionate man (3:18)

i. Not by words alone (3:18a)

ii. Not by works alone (3:18b)

b. The tenderness of that love (3:19–22)

(1) A quiet heart (3:19–21)

(a) A confirming heart (3:19)

(b) A condemning heart (3:20)

(c) A confident heart (3:211)

(2) A quickened hope (3:22)

(a) What prayers are answered (3:22a)

(b) Why prayers are answered (3:22b)

c. The triumph of that love (3:23–24)

(1) The commandment of the Son (3:23)

(2) The confirmation of the Spirit (3:24)

(a) The saint abiding in the Son (3:24a)

(b) The Spirit abiding in the saint (3:24b)

PART 2: GOD'S LITTLE CHILDREN—LONGING FOR HOME WHILE IN THE SPHERE
WHERE THE FATHER IS LOATHED (4:1–5:21)

A. A serious warning (4:1–6)

1. The wicked spirit (4:1–4)

a. The sobering word (4:1)

(1) The requirement (4:1a)

(2) The reason (4:1b)

b. The soundest wisdom (4:2–3)

(1) What is to be demanded by way of confession (4:2)

(2) What will be disclosed by way of confession (4:3)

(a) What the deceiving spirit is not (4:3a)

(b) Why the deceiving spirit is named (4:3b–c)

i. The spirit of Antichrist has been predicted (4:3b)

ii. The spirit of Antichrist is now present (4:3c)

        (1) How we know we love God personally—we love God's people (5:1)

        (2) How we know we love God's people—we love God personally (5:2)

    b. Our attitude toward God's challenge (5:3–5)

        (1) To obey the Word (5:3)

        (2) To overcome the world (5:4–5)

           (a) Victory expected (5:4a)

           (b) Victory explained (5:4b–5)

C. A sufficient witness (5:6–13)

  1. The witness of the Spirit to the Son (5:6)

    a. How He lived out His life (5:6a)

    b. How He laid down His life (5:6b)

  2. The witness of the Spirit to the saint (5:7–10a)

    a. The character of the witness (5:7–8)

        (1) The witness in the heavenly realm (5:7)

           (a) Three voices give separate testimony (5:7a–c)

              i. The Father (5:7a)

              ii. The Word (Christ) (5:7c)

              iii. The Holy Spirit (5:7c)

           (b) These voices give supporting testimony (5:7d)

        (2) The witness in the human realm (5:8)

           (a) Three voices give separate testimony (5:8a–c)

              i. The witness in us (the spirit) (5:8a)

              ii. The witness by us (the water) (5:8b)

              iii. The witness for us (the blood) (5:8c)

           (b) These voices give supporting testimony (5:8d)

    b. The credibility of the witness (5:9–10a)

        (1) It carries its own commendation (5:9)

        (2) It carries its own conviction (5:10a)

  3. The witness of the Spirit to the Scripture (5:10b–13)

    a. What John wrote (5:10b–12)

        (1) The record refused (5:10b)

        (2) The record received (5:11–12)

           (a) A revelation to us (5:11)

           (b) A revolution in us (5:12)

    b. Why John wrote (5:13)

    D. A sinful world (5:14–21)
       1. This world's limits (5:14–15)
          a. God hears us (5:14)
          b. God heeds us (5:15)
       2. This world's lusts (5:16–17)
          a. The seriousness of sin (5:16)
          b. The scope of sin (5:17)
       3. This world's lord (5:18–19)
          a. The wicked one's defeat (5:18)
          b. The wicked one's domain (5:19)
       4. This world's lies (5:20–21)
          a. A last word (5:20)
             (1) Two great feats (5:20a–b)
               (a) The incarnation of the Son of God (5:20a)
               (b) The illumination of the sons of god (5:20b)
             (2) Two great finds (5:20c–d)
               (a) A positive truth (5:20c)
               (b) A positional truth (5:20d)
             (3) Two great facts (5:20e–f)
               (a) A word about the deity (5:20e)
               (b) A word about our destiny (5:20f)
          b. A last warning (5:21)

John was a very old man, feeling the weight of his years and aware that his days on earth were about done. A godly life lay behind him and a very long memory thrilled him. His native land was far away in the land of Israel, although he now lived in Ephesus, a pagan Asiatic city on the edge of the European world. Probably he had come there to escape the Roman war, which had engulfed his homeland and brought about the downfall of Jerusalem, the destruction of the temple, and a virtual end to Jewish national life. If she was still alive, at that time, which is not altogether impossible, we can suppose he brought Mary, the Lord's mother, with him. After all, the Lord had made John her guardian and it is not likely that he would have relinquished that sweet and sacred trust to anyone else.

John had been born at Bethsaida, a fishing village on the Sea of Galilee not far from Capernaum. He had been one of a family of four: his father, a well-to-do fisherman; his mother, Salome, sister to the Virgin Mary; his brother, James, the first apostle to be martyred.

Of all the apostles, John seems to have been closest to the Lord. Not only was he the Lord's cousin, according to the flesh, he was one of the first two disciples called. Along with his brother, James, and his fishing partner, Peter, he had held a privileged position in the apostolic circle (Matt. 17:1; 26:37; Mark 5:37). Further, John is described as "the disciple whom Jesus loved."

He is mentioned three times in the book of Acts (3:1; 4:13; 8:14) in connection with the very early days of the Jerusalem church. After the Jerusalem conference (Acts 15; Gal. 2:9), he disappeared for over forty years, coming back into the spotlight toward the end of the first century to deal with a rising tide of apostasy.

By nature, John had a fiery disposition—the Lord Jesus nicknamed him "son of thunder" (Mark 3:17). But his fiery disposition had been greatly mellowed by the passing of time and by his growth in grace and in the knowledge of God. His writings reveal a tender note, but as these epistles make clear, John would not stand for half measures when it came to revealed truth. He writes in terms of black and white with no tones of gray. As John saw it, everything is true or false, right or wrong, light or darkness, love or hate, life or death. Things are either good or bad. He assumes that his readers have arrived at the same high spiritual plateau on which he himself lived.

It's interesting to note that no Old Testament quotations appear in John's epistles. That, coupled with a reference to idolatry, suggests that when he wrote, John had Gentile converts particularly in mind.

He had lived through a turbulent century. Of the first twelve Caesars, only two had died a natural death—it being suspected that even the great Augustus had been poisoned. Tiberius had degenerated into a fierce and filthy old man; Caligula was a monster, who delighted to murder distinguished citizens by means of poisoned snuff; Claudius was poisoned; Nero launched the Roman Empire on a three-hundred-year persecution of the church, and in the end, he perished while fleeing from those who sought his life. Paralyzed with fear and horror and howling like a dog, he was killed by one of his own attendants. Galbo lasted only a few months and was murdered. Otho committed suicide. Vitellius did not last long. Vaspasian was fonder of money than murder so, as one cynic put it, his victims "rejoiced in having exchanged the agony of being murdered for the luxury of being fleeced." Titus, who completed the siege and sack of Jerusalem, continued in the traditions of his predecessors on the throne in murder and rapine.

Then came Domitian, who was both a savage and a coward, his crimes exceeding those of even Caligula and Nero. He launched the second official Roman persecution of the church—spies and informers lurked everywhere, and there stood "an executioner at every door." Domitian's appearance in the Coliseum was the signal for people to murder one another with sword and spear to heighten the blood lust of the mob.

Such was the Roman world in which John had lived and survived. Such was the world in which the church, assailed by implacable foes from without, was now being threatened by error within. John thus felt compelled to write.

PART 1

God's Little Children—Living at Home in the Sphere Where the Father Is Loved

1 John 1:1–3:24

A. How we share the family life (1:1–2:29)
   1. The beginning of that life (1:1–4)
      a. Some tangible evidence (1:1)

That which was from the beginning, which we have heard, which we have seen with our eyes, which we have looked upon, and our hands have handled, of the Word of life." So much for Docetists and their denial of the humanity of Christ! None knew better than John that Jesus of Nazareth, the living Christ of God, was the eternal, uncreated, self-existing Word made flesh. He was certainly no phantom. John had already put it all in writing in his gospel. Indeed, the first three verses of this letter appear to be a capsule summary of that gospel. But a basic difference can be found between John's gospel and his first epistle: the major emphasis in the gospel is on the essential *deity* of the Lord Jesus Christ; the major emphasis in the epistle is on the essential *humanity* of the Lord Jesus Christ. He was God. He was man. He was both!

Down through the ages, the internal conflicts of the church have often centered on attempts to emphasize the deity of the Lord at the expense of His humanity, or to emphasize His humanity at the expense of His deity. The truth is, He was both God and man in the truest and fullest meaning of the words.

An Old Testament illustration will be helpful. In the tabernacle and the temple, a thick and gorgeous curtain hung between the Holy Place and the Holy of Holies. That veil, which was rent by God's own hand when Jesus died on the cross (Matt. 27:51), symbolized the Lord's person (Heb. 10:19–20). It was made of fine-twined linen dyed red, blue, and purple—colors of great significance. The red spoke of Christ's humanity, for He was "the last Adam" (1 Cor. 15:45), and the name "Adam," like the name "Edom," simply means "red." The blue symbolized His deity, for it is the color of heaven, from whence He came. The purple symbolized the Incarnation—the deity and the humanity of Christ. Take a can of red paint and an equivalent can of blue paint, and pour the one into the other, mix them so that it is impossible to tell where the red ends and the blue begins, or where the blue ends and the red begins, and the color purple is the result—a perfect blending of the red and blue.

Just so with the Lord Jesus. His deity and His humanity were perfectly proportioned and balanced. He was "God manifest in flesh" to such an extent that we can tell neither where His deity ends and His humanity begins nor where His humanity ends and His deity begins. As we trace His life on earth, as recorded in the four Gospels, we never note him acting now as God and now as man. He always acted as God and He always acted as man.

See Him, for instance, as He sat by Jacob's well near Samaria. He was "wearied with his journey" (John 4:6), revealing His humanity. Along came a woman from the nearby town. He asked for a drink because He was thirsty—further evidence of His humanity. But within a few minutes He was telling this woman, a complete stranger, all about her guilty past. Such supernatural insight is evidence of His deity. Where does the one end and the other begin?

See Him in Simon Peter's boat. Again He was tired and went to sleep (Matt. 8:23–27)—evidence of His humanity. Shortly afterward a storm threatened to sink the vessel, but He commanded the howling winds and the heaving waves to be still, producing a total, absolute calm—proof of His deity. Where does the one end and the other begin?

See Him, next, in the stricken Bethany home. His friend Lazarus had just died and been laid to rest. His grieving sisters were inconsolable. John tells us that "Jesus wept" (John 11:35) and that He "groaned in the spirit and was troubled"—evidence of His humanity. A few minutes later He commanded dead Lazarus to come back to life—evidence of His deity. Where does the one end and the other begin?

Far from beginning and ending, the two natures were, in fact, so blended they evince that ever and always He was both God and man—the God-man.

John begins there. He does not introduce himself, nor does he follow Paul's style and sign his letter. Rather, he gets right down to business: "That which was from the beginning," he says. Here, *beginning* refers to the Incarnation, at which the wonderful story of Christ's invasion of our planet begins.

John's gospel begins with similar words—"In the beginning was the Word" (John 1:1). Here, *beginning* does not imply a *start* but a *state*. It does not mean that Christ had a beginning but, on the contrary, is a reference to the Lord's eternal preexistence. This is reinforced as John continues in his gospel with the statement "and the Word was with God, and the Word was God." John then describes the Lord's role in Creation. Here, in his epistle, when John refers to a "beginning," he wants us to envision One who had an eternal preexistence but who, at a specific moment in time, entered into human life on planet Earth. When any other baby is born, it marks the beginning of a new life. When Jesus was born, it signified something quite different; it marked the coming into this world of a person who had existed from all eternity. The Lord Jesus did not have a beginning. He was!

John continues, exclaiming, "We have *heard!* We have *seen* with our eyes! We have *looked upon!* Our hands have *handled!*" The humanity of the Lord Jesus was genuine enough, as well John knew. So much for the "high sounding nonsense" of the Gnostics (Col. 2:8). John had heard Jesus speak many times, had seen Him with his own eyes, and had looked upon Him year after year. John uses two words for seeing. Here the word for "seen" is *horaô,* meaning to see with the physical eye. The claims of the Gnostics notwithstanding, John had been there, and they hadn't; he had seen with his eyes, and they hadn't. The testimony of an eyewitness is far more convincing than the high-flown philosophies of dreamers and speculators. The word used for "looked upon" is *theaomai,* which means to view with attention, to gaze, to look with admiration. John used this word in his gospel when he said, "We beheld his glory" (John 1:14).

But John's witness went beyond hearing and seeing, and looking long and closely. He had also "handled" Jesus. The word John uses is *psēlaphaō,* meaning "to feel" or "to touch." The classic New Testament use of the word is in connection with the Lord's appearing in the Upper Room in His resurrection body. The disciples were alarmed, thinking He was a ghost. He put their minds at ease and laid the imagined "ghost" to rest by inviting them to "handle" Him (Luke 24:39), to assure themselves that He was real, that His body was solid and substantial. He also ate food before them to further convince them that His resurrection body was real. The word John used for "handle" (Luke 24:39) conveys the idea of moving one's hands over a surface, so as to feel its texture. Doubtless, too, John recalled the Lord's resurrection invitation to doubting Thomas to handle Him (John 20:27).

John, perhaps, had in mind the ever closer intimacy he and the other disciples had enjoyed with the Lord during His earthly sojourn. John could remember the first time he had heard Jesus speak, after John's interest in the coming Christ had been kindled by the preaching of John the Baptist. The first words that John ever heard Jesus say, according to the New Testament record, were "Come and see" (John 1:35–39). So John came and heard and saw. Over time, he "looked" upon Jesus thousands of times and was an eyewitness to all that He said and did. John tells us that he could, in fact, have filled libraries with the things he had heard, seen, and observed in regard to Christ during those amazing years of long ago (John 21:25).

John had drawn very close to the Lord and had often touched Him. Earthly monarchs like to keep their distance from their subjects and rarely allow them to come close. Not so Jesus. John, who was the closest to the Lord of all the disciples, actually leaned upon Jesus' breast during the Last Supper (John 13:23).

Little wonder that John had no patience with the heretics who denied the actuality of the Lord's body.

John describes Jesus as "the Word of life," as "the Logos of life." In his gospel he says that "the Word was made flesh, and dwelt among us, (and we beheld his glory, the glory as of the only begotten of the Father,) full of grace and truth" (John 1:14). The Word had adopted a new mode of being and "dwelt" ("tabernacled," "pitched His tent") among men. Moreover, as the tabernacle in the wilderness had been crowned with the Shechinah glory, so the Lord Jesus carried with Him everywhere the aurora of another world, the glory of His Father in heaven.

The Word! Thoughts remain invisible and inaudible until they are clothed in words. With words, what we think and feel and are can be known. And just as our words reveal us, so, too, the Lord Jesus, as "the Word of life," clothes and reveals the great thoughts and feelings of God regarding our sin and our salvation.

John, then, offers tangible evidence.

b. Some transmitted evidence (1:2)

"For the life was manifested, and we have seen it, and bear witness, and shew unto you that eternal life, which was with the Father, and was manifested unto us." God is the author and sustainer of all life, whether it be physical life, spiritual life, or eternal life. The Lord Jesus enjoyed inherent eternal life even before He came to earth. That Christ could give and sustain life was clearly evident at the time He raised His friend Lazarus from the dead. Lazarus had died; his physical life had come to an end, and he had been buried. In talking with Martha, the Lord Jesus made an amazing statement, one that proclaimed Him either to be mad or God: "I am the resurrection, and the life," that is, He claimed to be able to restore Lazarus to *physical* life. He continued, "He that believeth in me, though he were dead, yet shall he live," that is, He had the power to impart *spiritual* life to those dead in trespasses and sins. All they need do is believe in Him. He concluded, "And whosoever liveth and believeth in me shall never die," that is, those who, by believing in Him, are endowed with spiritual life can never really die, because He gives to them *eternal* life, the same kind of life that He, Himself, enjoys, life that will never end (John 11:25–26).

The life Jesus manifested before His family, His disciples, and the world was a supernatural, eternal life, the life of God Himself. That is why He said to the Pharisees who were plotting His death, "Therefore doth my Father love me, because I lay down my life, that I might take it again. No man taketh it from me, but I lay it down of myself. I have power to lay it down, and I have power to take it again. This commandment have I received of my Father" (John 10:17–18). The truth of Jesus' statement was displayed at Calvary. When all the relevant prophecies were fulfilled, He sovereignly dismissed His spirit (John 19:30) and died of His own volition.

"The life was manifested," John recalls. The word he uses for "manifested" is *emphanizō,* meaning "to shine," "to bring to light," "to show plainly." The Lord Jesus, then, has displayed eternal life in terms we can understand. John makes so much of this truth in this epistle that it has been called "the epistle of eternal life." It shows us Him in whom that life was so gloriously enthroned and displayed, and it shows how that life is communicated to us, as well as how others can see that life in us.

For three and a half years John and the other apostles saw the life of God manifested in the life of Christ. They saw One who was absolutely good and wholly without sin, feasting their eyes upon His miracles and lending their ears to His words. They saw One who was completely unselfish, who never lost His temper, was never hasty, thoughtless, or unkind. They watched Him as He "went about doing good," never having to apologize for anything He said or did. He was humble and holy, loving and lowly, and patient and pure. His wisdom, love, and power never ceased to amaze them. He was never at a loss, never taken by surprise, never wrong, and He treated all men alike—rich and poor, powerful and weak, friend and foe—He loved and cared for them all. He had command over demons, disease, and death, could turn water into wine, and make loaves and fishes multiply in His hands. A word from Him and tempestuous winds and waves were hushed to rest. He could walk upon the waves or walk through solid walls and had eyes that could see through all of life's little disguises. He healed people with a word and never lost a case or charged a fee. Speaking the truth without fear or favor, he taught the truth with an unparalleled pungency and potency. He was never deceived, never discouraged, never dismayed. Such was the life He lived. Eternal life was manifested, and John declares himself and the other disciples as witnesses to it all.

   c. Some tested evidence (1:3–4)
    (1) Good news (1:3)

All this is very good news indeed, and John tells us *how true it all is:* "That which we have seen and heard declare we unto you," he says (1:3a). There seems to be a deliberate contrast here between the "we" and the "you," indicating that John picks up the gauntlet thrown down by the cultists and throws it back in their faces. "*We* were there," he says, "*You* weren't. *We* know, *you* don't. *We* saw, heard, studied, and handled. *You* didn't." That is very decisive language. "We really saw and heard what we are writing about," John says.

He further tells us *how tremendous it all is:* "that ye also may have fellowship with us: and truly our fellowship is with the Father, and with his Son, Jesus Christ" (1:3b). John's *gospel* sets forth the life of God in Christ; his *epistle* sets forth the life of God in us. We become partakers of the divine nature (2 Peter 1:4) when we are born again. Thus, the eternal life, which was *inherent* in the Christ, is now *inherited* by the Christian. And that inheritance makes it possible for us to have fellowship with the Father and the Son. Moreover, as we cultivate that fellowship, the life and likeness of Christ in us becomes evident to those around us.

In 1858, David Livingstone, already world famous, returned to Africa to find the source of the Nile. He reached the southern end of Lake Tanganyika in 1867 and moved on toward the interior of central Africa, then dropped out of sight. In 1869 the *New York Herald* sent Henry Morton Stanley on an expedition to find him. After many hardships, Stanley found Livingstone on October 28, 1871, and remained with the famous missionary-explorer until March 1872. These months made a profound impact on Stanley. He said,

> In 1871 I went to him as prejudiced as the biggest atheist in London. To a reporter and correspondent such as I, who had only to deal with wars, mass meetings, and political gatherings, sentimental matters were entirely out of my province. But there came for me a long time of reflection. I was out there away from a worldly world. I saw this solitary old man there, and asked myself, "How on earth does he stop here—is he cracked, or what? What is it that inspires him?" For months after we met I simply found myself listening to him, wondering at the old man carrying out all that was said in the Bible—"Leave all things and follow Me!" But little by little his sympathy for others became contagious; my sympathy was aroused, seeing his piety, his gentleness, his zeal, his earnestness, and how he went quietly about his business. I was converted by him, although he had not tried to do it.[1]

---

1. Henry Morton Stanley, *Dawn,* 16 December 1929. Also Elesha Hodge, "Accidental Missionary," *Christian History* no. 56:40–41.

What H. M. Stanley had seen was the life of God in one of God's own.

We are given this new life in Christ so that we can have fellowship with God and with one another. The word used for "fellowship" here is *koinōnia,* meaning communion, sharing, having things in common. The apostle Paul begins his letter to the quarrelsome Corinthian church by reminding the believers of their common bonds: "God is faithful, by whom ye were called unto the fellowship of his Son, Jesus Christ our Lord" (1:9). He ends his second letter to this church with the often-quoted benediction, "The grace of the Lord Jesus Christ, and the love of God, and the communion *[koinōnia]* of the Holy Ghost, be with you all. Amen" (2 Cor. 13:14).

Fellowship was one of the spiritual pillars of the new-born church. Those saved on the Day of Pentecost "continued steadfastly in the apostles' doctrine, and fellowship *[koinōnia]* and in breaking of bread, and in prayers" (Acts 2:42). Fellowship, however, is a tender plant. It must be nurtured and cared for and protected, or it can easily wither and die. Thus, one of John's chief concerns in this epistle is to cultivate fellowship.[2]

At the very outset, John reminds us that we are brought into no ordinary communion. "Truly," he says, "our fellowship is with the Father, and with his Son." John had come a long way since the days he had trodden the dusty Palestinian pathways in company with Jesus. Those had been indeed happy days of fellowship, climaxing in the Upper Room Discourse (John 13–17). While the disciples enjoyed their communion with the Lord Jesus, however, they were perplexed by His constant references to the Father. Finally, Philip blurted out, "Show us the Father, and it sufficeth us" (John 14:8). But that was just what the Lord had been doing all the time. Now John knew the Father as well as he had known the Son, and he realized that to have fellowship with the Father and the Son was to have fellowship on a very high plane indeed.

(2) Glad news (1:4)

To be brought into fellowship with the various members of the Godhead, and with true believers everywhere, was not only good news, it was glad news. "And

2. Guy King, in his book on 1 John, sees "fellowship" as the unifying principle of this epistle. He titles his book simply *The Fellowship: An Expositional and Devotional Study of 1 John,* and then divides it into fourteen chapters, each expounding a different aspect of John's view of "the communion of the Holy Ghost" (Ft. Washington, Pa.: Christian Literature Crusade, 1954).

these things write we unto you that your joy may be full." John was fully aware of what a dark and dangerous world it was in which they were living. The most horrifying persecutions attacked the church from without and the most heretical persuasions corrupted it from within. John could remember what had happened to Simon Peter when he had stepped out on the waves to walk on the water to Christ. When he took his eye off the Lord, he became overwhelmed by the perils all about him and would have sank beneath the angry billows and perished had it not been for Jesus (Matt. 14:28–31). That day, Peter and John and all the others had learned a valuable lesson: those things that threaten us are already under His control.

"Never mind threatening circumstances," John says. "Get your eye on the Father and the Son and your joy will be full." Joy, however, is not the same as happiness. Happiness depends upon what happens; joy wells up from within and is one of the fruits of the Spirit (Gal. 5:22).

>   2. The basis of that life (1:5–2:2)
>   a. A fact to be considered (1:5)

"This then is the message which we have heard of him, and declare unto you, that God is light, and in him is no darkness at all." Light! What an amazing and wonderful thing light is. Darkness cannot drive out the light, but light can drive out the darkness. There can be no fellowship between light and darkness—and God is light.

The first thing God did in Creation was to "command the light to shine out of darkness" (2 Cor. 4:6). He did so simply by saying, "Light be!" "And light was," the Holy Spirit says (see Gen. 1:3). Physical light bears the image and stamp of its Creator, a God who is, Himself, light. The scholars of ancient and of medieval times knew nothing of the true nature of light. Isaac Newton, in 1666, decided that light consisted of tiny particles, explaining why light traveled in straight lines and cast shadows. In 1678 Christian Huyghens challenged Newton's theory and declared that light traveled in waves. The two theories contended with each other for about a hundred years. Newton also discovered that white light was made up of seven colors—red, orange, yellow, green, blue, indigo, and violet, in that order. Huyghens showed that light waves, when refracted, behaved in an orderly way. The amount of refraction varied with the length of the waves—the shorter the wavelength, the greater the refraction. Violet light, the most refracted, had a shorter wavelength than blue light, and so on. It is this property of light that makes it possible for the eye to detect color. The wave theory held almost complete sway—until Einstein.

In the meantime, scientists were able to calculate the length of light waves and found them to be very small indeed. They were also able to calculate with increasing accuracy the speed of light. In a vacuum (such as space) light travels at 186,282 miles per second, in water the speed of light is 143,000 miles per second, in glass it is 124,000 miles per second, in diamonds it is just 78,000 miles per second.

When Einstein turned his attention to these things, he revived the concept that light consisted of particles. In his view, however, light has the properties of both waves and particles. Einstein discovered, moreover, that the speed of light is constant. In a vacuum, the speed of light never changes, regardless of the motion of its source. It takes light the same time to get from here to there regardless of whether the source of the light is itself moving toward the destination, is stationary, or is moving away from the destination. Einstein called the speed of light a "fundamental constant," and it figured into his famous equation that ushered in the atomic age: $e=mc^2$ (energy equals mass multiplied by the speed of light squared).

Another wonderful property of light is that it cannot be defiled. Even though it passes, say, through a glass of muddy water, light is not defiled. Moreover, light can, and most certainly does, reveal defilement. Also, life as we know it craves light. A plant will always turn toward the light and struggle to reach it.

Such are some of the characteristics of natural, created light. Many of these properties reflect the One who reveals Himself as the Light. He is always the same, He is immaculate and beyond the reach of darkness, He reveals Himself to us in all the diverse beauties of His being. And beneath the sunshine of His smile, life can flourish, take root, and grow. Our desire is toward Him, and He rules over us.

> b. A formula to be considered (1:6–10)
> (1) Beware of darkness (1:6–7)
> (a) Darkness exposed (1:6)

Note here the thrice-repeated formula, "If we say . . . ," which marks John's train of thought at this point in his epistle. The first instance tells us to beware of darkness: "If we say that we have fellowship with him and walk in darkness, we lie, and do not the truth." At once we are confronted with John's love of absolutes—light and darkness, truth and lies. John does not see a twilight zone. He dwells on the equator of moral and spiritual things. When the sun sets on the equator, darkness descends; when the sun rises on the equator, darkness disappears. John was positioned where there is no twilight, just day and night, light and darkness.

In his classical story *The First Men in the Moon,* H. G. Wells portrays the graphic approach of night and darkness on that orb. Mr. Bedford and Mr. Carver had escaped from the Selenites and had before them the urgent task of finding their spaceship—a sphere energized by gravity—before getting caught by the terrifying cold of the lunar winter. The sun had already passed its zenith and was sinking in the west. The explorers had four days before the long moon night began, and they agreed upon a plan. They would mark their starting point by tying a handkerchief on a tall spike. Then they would separate and work out from that center to walk over the crater in which their sphere lay hidden. "We go on seeking until the night and cold overtake us," Carver said, with a glance at the sun. They leaped out in opposite directions, taking advantage of the moon's light gravity to make enormous bounds.

After searching for a long time and awakening after an exhausted sleep, Mr. Bedford felt the growing chill in the air. At last he found the sphere, but by now the temperature was growing very cold. Making sure he did not lose the sphere again, Mr. Bedford began a desultory search for his partner. Locating the handkerchief, he called and called, repeatedly looking at the sun. Now it seemed to be visibly creeping down the sky. At last he found Carver's cap and concluded that he had been recaptured by the Selenites.

As he stood there, stupid and perplexed, something very, very soft and light and chill touched his hand. It was a snowflake, the first snowflake, the herald of the night. By now the sky had darkened almost to blackness and was thick with a gathering multitude of cold, watchful stars. The sun, now touching the crater's rim, was fast sinking out of sight. Everything around stood out against it in a bristling disorder of black shapes. Panic-stricken, Mr. Bedford set out in giant leaps for the warmth and light and safety of the sphere. Before him the sun sank and sank, and the advancing shadow swept to seize the sphere before he could reach it.

John would have us nurture an equal horror of the darkness. No one who walks in darkness, he says, can possibly claim to be in fellowship with the One who is Light.

(b) Darkness expelled (1:7)

John turns now to *the common bond in Christ,* which is the birthright of every believer: "But if we walk in the light, as he is in the light, we have fellowship one with another" (1:7a). To walk in the light means that our lives will be transparent and above reproach. We will harbor nothing shady, nothing we would not want to be seen and known, for light exposes the hidden works of darkness. How can two walk together in fellowship when one has ulterior motives and the other something to hide?

In his book *The Great Divorce,* C. S. Lewis pictures two realms that are forever divorced from one another.[3] The story begins with a gray city in the underworld of the dead. Walking in the rain, the narrator arrives on a long, mean street. Only cheap lodging houses and small shops are to be found, and everything is drab, dingy, and depressing. The streets are empty except for some people who are lined up, waiting for a bus, and who reveal themselves to be common, petty, and quarrelsome. Eventually the bus comes, the narrator boards it, and is taken up an enormous gulf to the world above.

On the bus he converses with various passengers, one of whom had arrived in the gray city by jumping under a train. He explained all about the gray city and how it grew and expanded, people moving away from each other, leaving more and more empty streets. The people built houses and more houses because it at least gave them the illusion of safety. "It will be dark presently," the suicide told him. Worse still, "They" come out once it is dark.

At last the bus reaches the end of its journey. There, everything is full of light, "a cruel light," he calls it, because it shows the ghost people as they really are, ghastly and horrible, withered wraiths of their former selves. And everything in the upper realm is so solid and real, the very grass seems as hard as diamonds to their shadowy feet. One ghost gives immediate voice to the feelings of them all: "I don't like it! I don't like it!" And with that the disturbed ghost-person plunges back into the bus. Then the rest see people coming—bright people, shining ones from "deep heaven." The sight is too much for a few more of the bus people.

And so it goes. But the thing that the ghosts dislike the most is the light. It is the thing that all sinners dislike the most. "And this is the condemnation, that light is come into the world, and men loved darkness rather than light" (John 3:19). John remembered Jesus saying that, but John knew, too, that little chil-

---

3. C. S. Lewis, *The Great Divorce* (New York: Macmillan, 1958), 1, 7, 9, 13, 19.

dren fear the dark. No wonder that *little children* is this old apostle's favorite description of the people of God! We are to embrace the light and walk in the light so that our fellowship one with another might be unbroken.

But what happens if we sin? John comes to that problem at once, mentioning *the cleansing blood of Christ:* "And the blood of Jesus Christ his Son cleanseth us from all sin" (1:7b). That surely has to be one of the most comforting verses in the whole Bible. It is a truth taught from Genesis to Revelation—blood cleanses sin. A skeptic challenged a believer: "How does blood cleanse sin?" he demanded. The believer replied with a counterquestion: "How does water quench thirst?" he asked. The skeptic replied, "I don't know, but I know that it does." "Just so," said the believer, "I don't know how blood cleanses sin, but I know that it does—God says so."

But not any kind of blood. All the animal sacrifices of the Old Testament could neither cleanse nor cancel sin. They could only cover it—sweep it under the rug, so to speak. Isaac Watts (1674–1748) puts it like this:

> Not all the blood of beasts,
> On Jewish altars slain,
> Could give the guilty conscience peace,
> Nor wash away one stain.

The blood of bulls and goats simply pointed forward to Calvary. Every such blood offering was an object lesson for a people still in the kindergarten stage of spiritual development. The shed blood of the Passover lamb, and of the goat on the Day of Atonement, and of the red heifer in the wilderness were pictorial and prophetic enactments of Calvary. It is the blood of Jesus Christ, God's Son, that cleanses from all sin. The Old Testament offerings were accepted only because they were symbols of Calvary. Isaac Watts concludes,

> But Christ, the heavenly Lamb,
> Took all our sins away;
> A sacrifice of nobler name
> And richer blood than they.

The blood of Christ is unique. In some ways it is similar to ours, but in other ways it has no equal.

Blood is a marvelous substance and incredibly complex. The oxygen in our body is carried in the blood stream, chemically combined with hemoglobin to form a solid. Human hemoglobin, the red coloring in the blood cells, is an extremely complex molecule, made up of 3032 atoms of carbon, 812 atoms of hydrogen, 780 atoms of nitrogen, 4 atoms of iron, 880 atoms of oxygen, and 12 atoms of sulfur. Each of these 9520 atoms must be hooked to each other in exactly the right way or hemoglobin does not result.[4] Antibodies in the blood fight and prevent infection, giving us immunity and, further, if blood fails to reach the various cells of the body, death takes place in those cells. When blood ceases to circulate, the body dies.

The blood that flows through an unborn babe's arteries and veins is not derived from its mother. The baby's blood cells are its own, produced within the body of the fetus. Angiogenesis, or blood vessel formation, begins about thirteen to eighteen days into the embryo's life. From the time of conception to the time of birth of the infant, not a single drop of blood passes from the mother to the child. The mother contributes no blood at all.

By means of the Virgin Birth, the Holy Spirit ensured that the Lord Jesus had a truly human body, derived from Adam, but His blood came from quite another source. The Lord Jesus, as man, was conceived by the Holy Spirit (Luke 1:31–35; Heb. 10:4–5)—God was His Father. Consequently, He had divine, sinless, incorruptible blood—so much so that in Acts 20–28 it is actually called "the blood of God." This is the blood that cleanses us from *all* sin, and it is now on the mercy seat in heaven where the Lord took it Himself (Heb. 9:11–14, 19–24). It is there, in the Holy of Holies above, to silence the accuser and justify the believer.

Thank God for that little word *all*. In the Old Testament ritual, on the Day of Atonement, two goats were used. The one was slain and its blood taken by the high priest beyond the veil into the Holy of Holies. There it was sprinkled upon and before the mercy seat where God sat in the Shechinah glory cloud between the figures of the cherubim. Those golden cherubim were so fashioned that their faces were turned inward and downward, so to be forever occupied with the blood upon the mercy seat. The remaining goat was then taken to the high priest, who placed both his hands upon its head. He then confessed over him "*all* the iniquities of the children of Israel, and *all* their transgressions in *all* their sins, putting them upon the head of the goat . . . And the goat shall bear upon him *all* their iniquities unto a land not inhabited" (Lev. 16:21–22, emphases added).

---

4. See Moody Institute of Science movie *Red River of Life*.

Note the fourfold repetition of the word *all,* preceding *iniquities, transgressions, sins.* The word used for "iniquities" is *âvon,* a word that means perverseness and that comes from a root meaning "to be bent," or "crooked"; the word used for "transgressions" is *pâsha,* carrying the idea of revolt and rebellion and having to do with sin against lawful authority; the word used for "sins" is *châtâ,* which means "to miss the mark," "to stumble," or "to come short," referring to sin in thought, word, or deed. Thus, the Day of Atonement represented a thoroughgoing, but symbolic, removal of sin. All that was foreshadowed by the Old Testament type is now fulfilled in Christ—He cleanses us from all sin.

> (2) Beware of deception (1:8–9)
>   (a) Sin denied (1:8)

"If we say we have no sin, we deceive ourselves and the truth is not in us." A man once told me he had not sinned. I said, "I'd like to have a talk with your wife!" To imagine oneself to be without sin must be the ultimate deception.

Before his conversion, the apostle Paul, like the rich young ruler (Matt. 19:16–22), imagined himself to be clothed in a judgment-proof righteousness. He could run his eye down the Decalogue and congratulate himself again and again. "Thou shalt have no other gods before me." Young Saul of Tarsus could say to himself, "I have kept that one!" "Thou shalt not make unto thee any graven image." He could say, "I've kept that one. I've never been an idolater." "Thou shalt not take the name of the Lord thy God in vain." He could say, "I've kept that one." "Remember the Sabbath day to keep it holy." "I've kept that one. I've even done my best to keep all the rabbinical rules about the Sabbath." "Honor thy father and thy mother." "I've kept that one!" "Thou shalt not kill, commit adultery, steal." "I've kept all those!" "Thou shalt not bear false witness against thy neighbor." "I have never done that." Commandment after commandment, all kept! Saul preened himself and thought, "What lack I yet?" And then the arrow of the tenth commandment found the chink in his armor. "Thou shalt have no evil desire" (Exod. 20:1–17). Later on, as the great apostle, he gives us his autobiographical description of what happened: "Nay, I had not known sin but by the law: for I had not known lust except the law had said, Thou shalt not covet." Then "sin revived," he said, "and I died" (Rom. 7:7, 9). He was too honest to go on saying he had no sin, when his sin had found him out.

(b) Sin decried (1:9)

First comes *confession* and then *cleansing:* "If we confess our sins, he is faithful and just to forgive us our sins, and to cleanse us from all unrighteousness." We should note the difference between "sin" (1:8) and "sins" (1:9). The offerings of the Levitical law were divided into two kinds—the sin offerings (made up of the so-called sin offering itself and the companion trespass offering) and the sweet-savor offerings (the burnt offering, the meal offering, and the peace offering). The sin offering related to *sin;* the trespass offering related to *sins.* The sin offering deals with *what we are*—sinners; the trespass offering deals with *what we do*—we sin. The sin offering dealt with the *root*—sin; the trespass offering dealt with the *fruit*—sins. Both offerings were necessary, the sin offering and the trespass offering linked together. We are not sinners because we sin; we sin because we are sinners—just as an apple tree is not an apple tree because it bears apples; it bears apples because it is an apple tree. We do what we do because we are what we are. Sometimes the Holy Spirit has sin in mind, at other times He has sins in mind.

When we trespass against God's law, it is usually by means of specific sins. We say wrong things, or we act in wrong ways, or we adopt un-Christlike attitudes. These sins have to be confessed, first to God and then to those whom we have offended. Moreover, as required under the Mosaic Law of the trespass offering, full restitution must be made together with an additional 20 percent penalty.

We can ask God for cleansing because God is "faithful and just to cleanse us from all unrighteousness." The word John uses for "unrighteousness" is *adikia,* meaning "wrongdoing." God does not cleanse us because He is indulgent and easygoing but because He is faithful and righteous, that is, He is faithful to His promises, and He does what is right. It is right that He should cleanse us because God is just and because Jesus has paid the full price of our *sin* and of all our *sins* at Calvary. God has accepted the blood of Christ as full payment for both our sinful condition and our sinful conduct. And confessing to both our condition and our conduct opens the floodgate of cleansing.

> God will not pardon twice demand,
> First at my Surety's pierced hand
> And then again at mine.

(3) Beware of defamation (1:10)

John returns to those who persist in saying they have not sinned. He points out *the blasphemy* of such a claim: "If we say we have not sinned we make him a liar" (1:10a); and also *the blindness* of such a claim: "and his word is not in us" (1:10b).

God has repeatedly told us in His Word about our sinful condition, and what could be more wicked than to call God a liar. In Romans 1–3 and similar passages, the Holy Spirit thoroughly exposes the sinfulness of the human race. The opening chapters of the epistle to the Romans set before us a court case in which the Holy Spirit acts as the prosecutor of the human race. First is *the summons* (Rom. 1:19–3:8), whereby the *heathen* are brought into court (Rom. 1:19–29) and found guilty of willful blindness, wicked beliefs, and wanton behavior. Nowhere in Scripture is there a more terrible catalog of human wickedness, all climaxing with the practice of sodomy and kindred vices, and with people taking pleasure in those whom revel in vice and violence.

Next, the *hypocrite* is arraigned (Rom. 2:1–16), the man who sits in judgment upon others while secretly doing the same things himself. It is the story of the prodigal son and the elder brother all over again. But the hypocrite's deeds will catch up with him, for one day God intends to publicly judge "the secrets of men."

After this, the *Hebrew* is indicted (Rom. 2:17–3:8). All his special privileges and opportunities are paraded before him, all his advantages of birth and background and Bible truth. Yet so scandalous has his behavior been in the sight of God that the very name of God has been blasphemed among the Gentiles because of him.

Finally, comes *the summation* (Rom. 3:9–20). All humanity is found guilty before God, without exception, without excuse, without escape. Man's vile thoughts, his violent temper, and his venomous tongue are all exposed, revealing that the unregenerate human nature is incurably wicked. As the Old Testament prophet puts it, the heart is "deceitful above all things, and desperately wicked" (Jer. 17:9).[5]

All that deceit and wickedness is proved when a person says that he or she has no sin. Such people prove themselves to be wicked by calling God a liar. "His Word is not in them," John says. Such people refuse to believe the Bible and deny the Holy Spirit's thoroughgoing exposure of the corruption and crookedness and criminality of unregenerate human behavior. The first great work of the Holy Spirit in a human heart, after all, is to convict us of "sin, and of righteousness,

---

5. See John Phillips, *Exploring Romans* (reprint, Grand Rapids: Kregel, 2002).

and of judgment" (John 16:8–11)—of the nature of sin, the need for righteousness, and the nearness of judgment. The person who says he or she has no sin is evidently a person in whose heart the Holy Spirit has not done even His initial work.

> c. A fundamental to be considered (2:1–2)
>> (1) The proposition (2:1a)

"My little children, these things write I unto you that ye sin not." Even though by natural birth we are tainted with sin, sin is not to be the habit of life for the believer. John will repeatedly remind us later in this letter, the believer is a born-again person, regenerated by the Holy Spirit, possessed of a new heart, and a partaker of the divine nature. John wants to lay to rest the notion that sin may be regarded as normal in the life of a believer as it is in the life of the unsaved. He, therefore, adds the words "that ye sin not." It would be an error to say that a believer *is not able* to sin. Romans 7 and all Christian experience prove that to be false. It would be true to say, however, that a believer is *able not* to sin. We have the means of victory over sin at our disposal, the Son of God to be our Savior, the Word of God to be our guide, and the Spirit of God to indwell us and empower us. Paul makes it clear in Romans 6 that the Lord Jesus died not only *for us* but *as us*. As a result, when He died, we died; when He was buried, we were buried; when He was raised, we were raised. Such is His identification with us and our identification with Him. Thus, we already stand, in Christ, on resurrection ground. We who were once dead *in* sin are now dead *to* sin, positionally and so far as God is concerned. But there's more to it than that. The Lord Jesus not only gave His life *for* us, He now gives His life *to* us. As Paul puts it, "Christ in you, the hope of glory" (Col. 1:27).

Our other allies in our constant struggle against sin are the Word of God and the Spirit of God. The Bible is not just another book; it is the living Word of God, full of divine life, power, and authority (1 Peter 1:23–25). The Holy Spirit energizes it and uses it to speak to us, lead us, and inform us (Ps. 119:9–11).

Moreover, the Holy Spirit takes up His permanent residence in the believer's heart. The born-again believer is a person inhabited by God, but how soon we forget that. A whole category of theology in the Bible is devoted to the person and work of the Holy Spirit. He baptizes us, indwells us, fills us, seals us, assures us, and anoints us. What more could we ask than that?

No wonder, then, that John says, "These things write I unto you, that ye sin not."

(2) The provision (2:1b–c)

Note that we have an advocate. John emphasizes here *our advocate's concern:* "If any man sin . . ." (2:1b), and *our advocate's character:* "we have an advocate with the Father, Jesus Christ the righteous" (2:1c). Our advocate! The word is *parakletos,* which John uses five times in his writings (see John 14:16, 26; 15:26; 16:7). The Holy Spirit is said to be "another Comforter."

The Lord Jesus, Himself, is our primary counselor and advocate at the throne of God. When Satan comes into the presence of God, as come he does (Job 1:6–12; 2:1–7; Zech. 3:1–5), he comes as "the accuser" (Rev. 12:12). He does not come to tell lies about us, for he is far too clever to do that, even though, as the father of lies (John 8:44), lies are the idiom of his language. Sad to say, he comes to tell the truth about us. He gets nowhere, however. The accuser is met by the Advocate, and all *He* has to do is raise His pierced hands and Satan is silenced—that is how effective Christ's finished work is. God puts our sins under the blood and beyond the reach of recall.

John here emphasizes the truth of *forgiveness.* It is Paul who develops the parallel truth of *justification.* To ask to be forgiven implies that we have sins we cannot deny, sins that have found us out, sins we cannot contest, sins that prove us to be guilty before God and men. Sins are the basis of a plea for forgiveness. To be *justified,* however, means that I have been exonerated, my standing before the court is perfect, there is no record, it is *just as if I'd* never sinned. The distinction between forgiveness and justification is important.

Forgiveness presumes *guilt*—only a guilty person can be forgiven—a court cannot pardon an innocent man; justification presumes *righteousness.* Forgiveness appeals to the fact that God is *merciful;* justification to the fact that God is *just.* Forgiveness has to do with the fact that God is *love;* justification has to do with the fact that God is *light.* Forgiveness is *conditional,* a circumstance revealed in the Lord's Prayer (Matt. 6:12) and demonstrated in the parable of the unmerciful servant (Matt. 18:23–35). The condition John appends here is, "If we confess our sins . . ." Justification is *unconditional,* absolute, and eternal. Forgiveness relates to what is *wrong;* justification relates to what is *right.* Forgiveness relates to those who are *convicted sinners;* justification relates to those who are *constituted saints.* Forgiveness has to do with our *state;* justification has to do with our *standing.* When we are forgiven, God declares us to be pardoned and, therefore, free from the *penalty* of the Law; when we are justified, God declares us to be righteous and, therefore, fulfillers (in Christ) of the *precepts* of the Law. In forgiveness, the

Law appears in court as our *foe;* in justification, the Law appears in court as our *friend.* When God forgives us, He has our *sin* in view; when He justifies us, He has His *Son* in view. In forgiving us, God accepts the fact that His Son has *explicitly pleaded* for us (Luke 23:34); in justifying us, God accepts the fact that His Son has *exchanged places* with us.

So Satan, obviously, has no case at all against us. When Satan arrives in the presence of God, the Lord silences him at once. Our sins have been sovereignly willed out of existence by a God who controls all the factors of time and space and who has had Calvary in mind from the beginning. Paul puts it this way: "There is therefore no condemnation to them which are in Christ Jesus. . . .Who shall lay any thing to the charge of God's elect? It is God that justifieth. Who is he that condemneth? It is Christ that died, yea rather, that is risen again, who is even at the right hand of God, who also maketh intercession for us" (Rom. 8:1; 33–34).

So "we have an advocate with the Father, Jesus Christ the righteous," the One who takes away our sin and replaces it with His own impeccable righteousness. Still, sin we do, as we know only too well. So forgiveness is available, along with justification, to secure our peace of mind as well as our peace with God. The Lord Jesus, our advocate, secures our release from the guilt and penalty of all our wrong behavior. Hallelujah—what a Savior!

(3) The propitiation (2:2)

John sets before us two aspects of this truth—*the efficiency* of Christ's work: "And he is the propitiation for our sins" (2:2a); and *the sufficiency* of Christ's work: "and not for ours only, but also for the sins of the whole world" (2:2b). This statement agrees with John's famous summary in his gospel: "For God so loved the world, that he gave his only begotten Son, that whosoever believeth in him should not perish, but have everlasting life" (John 3:16).

The word used here for "propitiation" (and in 4:10) is *hilasmos,* expressing the thought of expiation or atonement. We are not called upon to do something in order to placate an angry God. On the contrary, God in His wondrous grace has provided the expiation, the atonement, and the propitiation in the person and work of His Son. Thus, the words used for "propitiation" point to the *ground* upon which God shows mercy to the guilty, namely, the finished work of Christ. The Lord Jesus is both the propitiator and the propitiation.

In writing to the Romans, Paul speaks of both propitiation (*hilasterion,* a word used in the Septuagint to describe the "mercy seat"; Heb. 9:5) and reconciliation (Rom. 3:25; 5:10). With regard to the two concepts, there exists both an affinity and a difference. Propitiation has to do with Christ's work Godward, by which He restores God's favor manward; reconciliation, by contrast, has to do with Christ's work manward by which He removes man's enmity Godward. Such is the *efficiency* of Christ's finished work.

John adds a further note about the *sufficiency* of Christ's finished work. The propitiation that is *efficient* to wipe out all the believer's sins is *sufficient* to do the same for all: Calvary took care of "the sins of the whole world." Paul affirms that Christ "died for all" (2 Cor. 5:14–15), that He died for all men without distinction and for all men without exception. Adequate provision has been made at Calvary to cancel all the sins of all the people in all the ages of time. But while the sacrifice of Christ is commensurate with the need of all mankind, it is only effective for the individual when it is accepted by faith.

> 3. The betrayal of that life (2:3–11)
>   a. The test of the Lord's person (2:3–5)
>   (1) The claim to know Him put into perspective (2:3)

It's easy enough to say that we know someone. Often, though, when we say we "know" someone, we mean that we have met that person or know about that person, but we do not really know that person in depth. A person's acquaintance does not know that person as well as a close friend knows him; a close friend does not know a person as well as that person's spouse and children know him; a person's close family members do not know that person as well as God knows him.

We say that we know the Lord Jesus, but John challenges that. On what level do we know Him? "Hereby do we know that we know him, if we keep his commandments." The kind of knowledge John defines here is that which has so penetrated into the character and personality of the Lord Jesus that trust in Him and obedience to Him is the soul's instinctive response.

John possibly had in mind the Lord's own challenge along these same lines. In the Upper Room, with the shadow of the Cross upon Him and Judas's defection and betrayal before Him, Jesus said to His disciples, "If ye love me, keep my commandments" (John 14:15). The warning was too late for Judas, but it was timely enough for Peter and the others. With the departure of Judas, the Lord talked about His own approaching departure and about the coming of the Holy Spirit. "You love Me? You say you know Me? Then, do what I say!" It's as simple as that. How can we know Him, in all the glory of His stainless humanity, knowing He is absolutely trustworthy, and not do what He says? How can we know Him in all the splendor of His deity, knowing Him to be infallible and infinite, yet at the same time challenge His commands?

"Hereby we do know!" John introduces another of his distinctive and recognizable threads: "If we say . . ." "Hereby we know . . ." "He that saith . . ." John is very fond of picking up such challenging statements and weaving them as attention-getting strands of truth into the fabric of this letter.

The word used for "know" here is *ginōskō,* and it suggests experiential knowledge rather than academic knowledge. It occurs twice in this verse, once in the present-continuous tense and then in the perfect tense. We have the constant, moment-by-moment experience of knowing Him because we have already come to know Him. And we are to know that we know. The aged apostle places this absolute knowledge in stark contrast to the pseudo knowledge that was the boast of the agnostics.

John had known the Lord Jesus very well indeed in the days when He lived on earth, had known Him as a family member (his mother and the Lord's mother were sisters), and as Master and Lord (John was one of His disciples and a member of the inner circle of the disciples). But now, as an old man, the last surviving member of the apostolic circle, with years of meditation and experience upon which to draw, John knew Him better than ever. Our knowledge of Christ, too, is to be just like John's, a living, growing knowledge.

We get to know Him better and better, trust Him more and more, and, consequently, obey Him in all matters great and small. So Polycarp thought. Polycarp was born about the year A.D. 70, is believed to have been a disciple of the apostle John, and became bishop of the church at Smyrna in Asia Minor. The Roman emperor Marcus Aurelius (who had some sort of a reputation as a scholar and a philosopher but who was certainly neither scholar nor philosopher enough to tolerate a superior system of thought, such as Christianity) launched a savage persecution of the church, which was widespread and prosecuted with great cruelty. One of its victims was Polycarp. The old warrior took refuge in a friend's house but was betrayed for a bribe by one of the household slaves. While he was being bound to the stake, the Roman proconsul offered him his freedom if he would honor Caesar and curse Christ. Said the martyr, "Eighty and six years have I served Christ; how can I curse Him, my King and my Savior?" Polycarp was one of those who knew that he knew Him and was willing to be "obedient unto death."

(2) The claim to know Him put to the proof (2:4–5)
(a) The lie test (2:4)

"He that saith, I know him, and keepeth not his commandments, is a liar, and the truth is not in him." So far as John was concerned, it was as simple as that. Obedience to the Lord is what separates the true believer from the false professor.

There are many such tests, for the Lord's commandments are numerous. Those who love the Lord, for instance, respond obediently to the two ordinances He left with the church—baptism and the Lord's Supper. In baptism, we display a great truth—*our death with Him;* at the Lord's Supper, we proclaim a companion truth—*His death for us.* Both ordinances are mandated by the Lord (Matt. 26:26–28; 28:19–20). Active attendance at the gatherings of the Lord's people is another command, sanctified by the practice and teaching of the early church (Acts 2:41–42; Heb. 10:19–25). Cooperation with the Holy Spirit is enjoined (John 14:15–17, 25–26; 15:26–27; 16:12–15; Eph. 5:18–19), as is a thankful spirit (Eph. 5:20). Indeed, much of the New Testament is taken up with the Lord's commandments—some given directly by Him and others given apostolically by the Holy Spirit. John has already taken into account our occasional failures and our temporary lapses from the path of obedience (1:8–2:11). But the general attitude and tenor of the life of the believer is one of obedience, while the general attitude and tenor of the life of the unbeliever is one of disobedience and self-will. The occasional stumbles of a genuine believer do not constitute him or her an unbeliever any more than occasional conformity by an unbeliever to some stated command of the Lord constitutes him or her a believer. Even a stopped clock tells the correct time twice every day!

(b) The love test (2:5)

"But whoso keepeth his word, in him verily is the love of God perfected: hereby know we that we are in him." Our knowledge of God is tested by our obedience, so is our love for God. The person who claims to love God but who does not do what God says is self-deceived. What John has in mind here is the practical outflow of love from the believer's heart toward other people. An illustration will be helpful here.

Corrie ten Boom once saw the man she hated in a church in Munich. The year was 1947, and she had come to a recently defeated Germany from Holland, a country that had known the full rigors of German occupation and Gestapo rule. And she had come to proclaim the message that God loves and forgives. She recognized the man, recognized him at once. How could she ever forget him? He had been one of the most brutal guards at the Ravensbruck concentration camp where she had been imprisoned and where her sister died.

At the close of the service—at which she had been speaking of the love of God and of His willingness to forgive—the man approached her. He wore a brown hat and an overcoat, but her mind's eye saw him as she had last seen him—in his black uniform and wearing the cap with its skull and crossbones. Her blood ran cold.

He came up to her and spoke. "I have become a Christian," he said. She dragged her mind back to the present. "God has forgiven me for all the cruel things I did in that camp. I have come to ask you to forgive me, too."

It seemed to the missionary that time stood still as she struggled with her heart. How could she forgive this man, when her sister's dear, emaciated face came between them. She thought of the cruel death that her sister had died, and a coldness lay an icy hand upon her heart. The man held out his hand, and the seconds seemed like centuries. Then the indwelling Christ prompted the response. She reached out her hand and took his. Warmth, supernatural and sublime, flooded her heart. Tears came to her eyes as she said, "I forgive you, my brother—with all of my heart."[6]

That's what John is talking about—love perfected in the believer, enabling him or her to keep His Word, even to Christlike forgiveness of a cruel enemy (Matt. 6:12–14). We know *Him?* We love *Him?* Excellent. Prove it.

      b. The test of the Lord's precept (2:6–8)
          (1) A confident expectation (2:6)

"He that saith he abideth in him ought himself so to walk, even as he walked." The concept of abiding in Christ is one John first heard from the Master's own lips in His teaching concerning the vine (John 15:4). First came the command: "Abide in me"; then came the accompanying truth: "I also abide in you"; fol-

---

6. Corrie ten Boom, *Tramp for the Lord* (Ft. Washington, Pa.: Christian Literature Crusade; Old Tappan, N.J.: Revell, 1974), 55–57. Reprinted article from *Guideposts* (1972).

lowed by the practical application: "As the branch cannot bear fruit of itself, except it abide in the vine, no more can ye, except ye abide in me." The concept of being "in Christ" occurs about 130 times in the New Testament, which gives us some indication as to its importance. Graham Scroggie points out that Christ is the sphere of the Christian's life, that is, we are not encircled in Christ but "ensphered." A circle would surround us on only one plane, whereas a sphere wraps around us in all directions.[7]

The idea of "abiding" is a favorite one with John. The word he uses for "abiding" is *menō,* meaning "to dwell" or "to remain" or "to continue." It occurs forty-one times in John's gospel and twenty-six times in his epistles. The Lord's own illustration for *abiding* is the best: a branch simply remains where it belongs, attached to the vine. The life of the vine flows through it and makes it possible for the branch to put forth leaves, produce flowers, and bear fruit. The believer is thus placed as a branch in the Vine (Christ) and is expected to simply allow the life of the Vine to flow through him or her. The branch does nothing in or of himself but simply allows the Vine to express Himself through him.

John then abruptly changes the figure from abiding to walking. Walking is one of the first skills we learn in life. We learn to walk before we learn to talk. Walking implies making progress, and John doesn't leave us to wonder long what he means: we are to "walk even as he [the Lord Jesus] walked."

Perhaps John had in mind the day he and Andrew stood by the Jordan with John the Baptist on the lookout for the Messiah. His coming was imminent. Then, suddenly, there He was, and they were "looking upon Jesus as he walked" (John 1:36). The Baptist recognized Him at once: "Behold the Lamb of God!" he said, recognizing Him by His walk. He was the sinless, spotless Lamb of God, and it was evident in every move He made. John and Andrew at once fell in step behind Jesus and, before the day was over, were abiding with Him (John 1:36, 39). Andrew became a soul winner from that hour and John became the Lord's closest friend on earth.

Now a very old man, John can think of no better definition of the Christian life than simply abiding and walking. Abiding in Christ, walking like Him.

> (2) A critical examination (2:7–8)
>> (a) The previous commandment (2:7)

---

7. Graham Scroggie, *The New Testament Unfolded* (London: Pickering & Inglis, 1954), 52.

"Brethren, I write unto you no new commandment, but an old commandment which ye had from the beginning. The old commandment is the word which ye have heard from the beginning." Doubtless John could remember the day when the craftiest lawyers of the nation had sought to trap the Lord Jesus. He had just silenced the Herodians and the Sadducees, and the Pharisees tried next. They put forth one of their cleverest advocates: "Which is the great commandment of the law?" the lawyer said, tempting Him (Matt. 22:35–36).

The rabbis had long since started on that vast work of elaboration of the Law that ultimately evolved into the Talmud. Already their commentaries and rulings and binding traditions had begun to replace the Torah in authority. The scribes divided all 613 commandments of the Mosaic Law into 248 affirmative commandments (the number of the members of the body, as they counted them) and 365 negative ones (one for each day of the year). They saw great significance, too, in there being not only 613 commandments in the Law but also 613 letters in the Decalogue (the Ten Commandments). They greatly elaborated the Law, expanding to the point of absurdity, for instance, the commandments concerning keeping the Sabbath. Some commandments they rated as great, some as small. The dietary laws and the law concerning circumcision were great laws, so were laws concerning the ritual sacrifices and laws dealing with feast days and fast days. But what was *the* great commandment? The lawyer put Jesus to the test.

What was the great commandment? The Lord took His questioner back at once to the great creedal statements of Deuteronomy 6:5; 10:12; 30:6. Then He summarized all man's duty to God and all man's duty to man in two comprehensive statements that were already embedded in the Pentateuch (Lev. 19:18)—"Thou shalt love the Lord thy God with all thy heart, and with all thy soul, and with all thy mind. This is the first and great commandment. And the second is like unto it, Thou shalt love thy neighbor as thyself" (Matt. 22:37–39). The Lord added, "On these two commandments hang all the law and the prophets."

The apostle Paul said much the same thing when he wrote to the Roman church, which was there, at the legislative capital of the world: "Owe no man any thing, but to love one another: for he that loveth another hath fulfilled the law. For this, Thou shalt not commit adultery, Thou shalt not kill, Thou shalt not steal, Thou shalt not bear false witness, Thou shalt not covet; and if there be any other commandment, it is briefly comprehended in this saying, namely, Thou shalt love thy neighbor as thyself. Love worketh no ill to his neighbour: therefore love is the fulfilling of the law" (Rom. 13:8–10).

Such was the old commandment, and such was the great commandment—

love God supremely, love all men sincerely. All the other laws are expositions of these two rudimentary and revolutionary principles. If everyone loved God and other people like that, we would not need the countless laws that tie us up in knots to this day.

(b) The present commandment (2:8)

John now states the new commandment, giving two tests as to whether or not it is being applied—*the test of new life in Christ:* "Again, a new commandment I write unto you, which thing is true in him and in you" (2:8a), and *the test of new light through Christ:* "because the darkness is past, and the true light now shineth" (2:8b).

For the old commandment, sublime as it was, lacked something. Fallen man cannot love God the way God commands him to love Him, and he cannot love his neighbor, either, the way God commands him. What was needed was an incarnation of this love principle. People needed to see it in action in everyday human life. They needed, moreover, to have that new love life implanted in them. In other words, it needed to be *exemplified,* as it was in the Lord Jesus, and it needed to be *experienced,* to be incarnated in them by the miracle of rebirth.

John saw how Jesus lived, the way He reacted, the things He said, the things He did for people, even His enemies. Everything about Jesus was like turning on the light in a dark place. The Old Testament commandments embodied principles, precepts, and propositions that had been discussed and debated for centuries. When Jesus came, all of a sudden, they were personified. The law came to life in Jesus! "We never saw it in this fashion," was the involuntary comment of even the Lord's critics when He forgave the sins of the palsied man, and then healed him to prove He could both forgive and heal (Mark 2:12).

What was new now about the old commandment was its incarnation, first in Christ and then in the hearts and lives of His regenerated people.

John was not particularly interested in theology for theology's sake. Indeed, none of the General Epistles (Hebrews to Jude) are much concerned with ecclesiology or eschatology or other such things. James, the first of the New Testament authors, and John, the last of the New Testament authors, paid little heed to the great doctrines of the church. When James wrote, Pauline ecclesiology was in its infancy, for James wrote before the first church council (Acts 15). In any case, James seems to have been more than a little suspicious of Paul's sophisticated and comprehensive theology of Christ, the Cross, and the church. When

John wrote, Paul had been dead for some thirty years and his books were in general circulation. John saw a need to go back beyond Pentecost, back to Christ Himself.

"The darkness is past!" he exclaims. "The true Light shineth." Love had been incarnated in Jesus. Love shone in all His ways, and what was true of Him is to be true of us.

c. The test of the Lord's people (2:9–11)
   (1) The principle stated (2:9)

"He that saith he is in the light, and hateth his brother, is in darkness, even until now." Love and hate. Light and darkness. As far as John is concerned, these things cannot coexist in the same heart. The aged apostle had come a long way since the day he had wanted to call down fire on Samaria because he felt the Samaritans had insulted the Lord (Luke 9:51–56). Since then he had been to Samaria and, along with Peter, had been instrumental in imparting the Holy Spirit to newly converted Samaritan believers, thereby welcoming old enemies into the Jewish church as first-class members of the mystical body of Christ (Acts 8:14–17).

(2) The principle studied (2:10–11)
   (a) Loving one's brethren (2:10)

"He that loveth his brother abideth in the light, and there is none occasion of stumbling in him." Not that all our brothers in Christ are lovable! We all know some who have crossed us or criticized us, and some even who have done us harm. Others, by nature, we tend to dislike for no apparent reason at all. As the old rhyme puts it,

> I do not like thee, Dr. Fell,
> The reason why, I cannot tell;
> But this I know, and know full well,
> I do not like thee, Dr. Fell.

In his book *A Tuft of Comet's Hair,* F. W. Boreham includes a fine essay on Dr. Fell.[8] He points out that when it comes to disliking people, there are two catego-

---

8. F. W. Boreham, *A Tuft of Comet's Hair,* 2d ed. (London: Epworth Press, 1927).

ries: disliking people for a reason, and disliking people for no particular reason. We dislike some people, for instance, because they are know-it-alls. No matter how fine a sermon you preach, they find something to criticize. No matter how many people applaud your latest book, they pick it to pieces with smug complacency and personal bias. We dislike "noisy people," who sweep over an assembled company with a tidal wave of animal spirits. And we dislike those who are quite the opposite, who seem to have no personalities at all. They bore us with a complete "organ recital" when we ask them how they are. We dislike those who want us to know how well connected they are, who drop names, and are related to famous people. They had lunch the other day with a cabinet minister or the mayor. We dislike those who gush. Even an accidental meeting becomes a state occasion.

Second, and even more troubling, is our dislike of those whom we dislike without reason. People like Dr. Fell.

John has no patience with any of this. He knew Jesus too well to entertain personal dislikes, no matter whether they were rooted in something he could put a finger on or rooted in something vague, a clash of personalities, perhaps, or an unattractive appearance.

John remembered how completely human Jesus was. He had His preferences, finding a kindred spirit, for instance, in the rich young ruler. The moment Jesus met him His heart went out to him (Mark 10:21). So, too, with Martha, Mary, and Lazarus (John 11:5). John, himself, had occupied a special place in Jesus' heart, frequently describing himself simply as "the disciple whom Jesus loved" (John 13:23; 19:26; 20:2; 21:7, 20). Nonetheless, the Lord did not allow preference or prejudice to make a difference in His heart, never allowing human feelings to motivate Him to the extent that He attracted this one and repelled that one. There were no Dr. Fells in Jesus' life. He loved Pilate as much as He loved Peter and would have saved Caiaphas as gladly as He saved Nicodemus.

That is what John remembered, and that was the standard by which he sought to lead his own life. And that is the standard he lays down for all who say they love the Lord.

For, after all, how are unbelievers to know what the Lord is really like unless we ourselves exhibit a true image of Him to one another. We are reminded of the little girl who became increasingly annoyed at the cartoons and caricatures of her famous father, which appeared in the newspapers. One day she took a photograph of her father from the wall and sallied forth to show the newspaper editor and the cartoonist what her father was really like. John expects us to do the same, to show people what Jesus is really like.

(b) Loathing one's brethren (2:11)

"But he that hateth his brother is in darkness, and walketh in darkness, and knoweth not whither he goeth, because the darkness hath blinded his eyes." Darkness does that. The classical biblical example is King Saul, who was jealous of David. The dark chapters of Saul's life began when David won the applause of the nation for going into the valley of death to destroy Goliath, the Philistine giant from Gath. For a while Saul seems to have struggled with his malice and ill will. But it grew until it dominated his whole life, until he forgot everything else, even allowing the administration of the kingdom to fall into ruins. He hated those who loved and supported David, even his own son Jonathan, whom he tried to kill in a fit of rage. He brooded on his dislike, ignoring the growing Philistine threat to his kingdom, his life degenerating into a mad crusade to hunt David down. He made at least two dozen separate attempts on David's life and massacred an entire colony of priests out of suspicion that they had sided with David and helped him to escape. On two occasions when David had Saul in his power and let him go, Saul owned his wrongdoing but was soon back at his old tricks again, planning crusades and campaigns to corner, capture, and kill David.

Saul hated the man who was really his best friend, in the truest sense of the word. He went from one dark episode to another, blind to everything else until, at last, jealousy, fear, rage, and malice took over his entire existence. He ended up in total darkness, consulting a witch and dying as a suicide on his own sword. "He that hateth his brother walketh in darkness," says John. He was right.

4. The beauty of that life (2:12–14)
   a. The first round of reasons (2:12–13b)
      (1) Little children: because of their condition in the family (2:12)

John is still writing about God's people and their place in the family, drawing our attention to the beginning of our family life, to its basis and to its betrayal. Now he turns to the beauty of our family life in Christ as it embraces young and old alike, writing two rounds of comments upon the condition of various members of God's family: "I write unto you, little children, because your sins are forgiven you for his name's sake." That's where family life in the household of God begins—we are born into the family as little children. The most simple, basic, and elementary concept we have as children of God is that of forgiveness of sins. That is indeed a blessed truth, but we eventually must get beyond forgiveness, otherwise we will remain babes in Christ.

In the book of Exodus, for instance, the great theme is the blood of the Passover Lamb. The blood of a lamb was used to redeem the Hebrew people from slavery in the Egyptian house of bondage. The lamb was selected, scrutinized, and slain, and its blood was applied. The sufficiency of the blood of the slain lamb was all the Israelites needed to know to get them out from under Egypt's chains. The sufficiency of the shed blood of Christ, the true Passover Lamb, is all the sinner needs to know in order to free him or her from Satan's chains.

The book of Leviticus is quite different. It begins with chapter after chapter devoted to detailed descriptions of one offering after another. The Israelites had to master this system of offerings. Just so today, those who have been redeemed by the blood of Christ now need to master the whole theology of the Cross. The Old Testament burnt offering, the meal offering, the peace offering, the sin offering, and the trespass offering each made a contribution to an ever-growing revelation about the greatness, costliness, and vastness of the work that would be done by Calvary's Lamb.

All that was needed in order to begin, however, was the rudimentary knowledge that blood had been shed, that it provided shelter from the wrath that was abroad in the land, and that the avenging angel would pass over (hence the word *Passover*) every house where the blood was displayed as required by God. Just so, the saved sinner needs only to know that his or her sins are forgiven. Salvation is based on the Word of God, the work of Christ, and the witness of the Spirit (Rom. 8:16; Heb. 11:4; 1 Peter 1:23; 1 John 2:1–2). Many a sinner has gone to heaven knowing next to nothing about the greatness of God's redemptive plan.

One simple soul found faith in Christ at the end of a service through reading John 3:16. Her counselor had given her a New Testament and marked the verse for her. After she retired to bed that night, however, doubts began to arise about her newly received salvation. She decided Satan was filling her mind with these troublesome thoughts, and she reasoned further that since Satan was said to love darkness rather than light he must be under her bed, the darkest place in the room. She turned on a light, found the marked place in her Bible, put her finger on the verse, and thrust the New Testament under the bed. "Here," she said to the Devil, "read it for yourself!" That was good enough for a start! She would soon need to know much more than that.

Little children are not expected to know very much, whether in a human family or in God's family. In God's family they are forgiven "for his name's sake."

The name of Jesus makes the difference between guilt and grace. So much is treasured up in that name. It is the saving name (Acts 4:12), the sovereign name (Phil. 2:9–11), the satisfying name (John 14:13), the sanctifying name (Col. 3:17).

Remember the story of Ali Baba and the forty thieves? Ali Baba was a poor peasant who happened to discover the cave where a gang of thieves kept their plunder. It was a magic cave, the door to which would open only if the proper password was spoken. The robbers would say, "Open sesame," and the door would open, then close behind them when they had passed the portal. Ali Baba used the password once the thieves were gone and gained entrance to the treasure. The door closed behind him, and the peasant forgot everything in his rapture at finding this vast fortune. He ran the gold and the jewels through his fingers, gloated over the rosy future he foresaw for himself, and filled his pocket with choice samples. He forgot all about time and the peril he would be in if the thieves came back. At last he decided it was time to leave but, to his horror, he could no longer remember the magic word. He wracked his brains, remembering that it was some kind of cereal. He called, "Open wheat!" He called again, "Open barley!" "Open corn!" It was no use. He had forgotten the word.

One thing only a babe in Christ has to remember—the name of Jesus! That name fills the hosts of hell with fear. That name opens the gates of glory, unlocks the vaults of heaven, and is the key to the Father's heart. John impresses upon the "little children" the importance of that name. "I write unto you, little children, because your sins are forgiven you for his name's sake."

(2) Fathers: because of their concept of the faith (2:13a)

"I write unto you, fathers, because ye have known him that is from the beginning." Spiritual maturity, not mere age, is referred to here. Those who have grown up in the faith and become fathers themselves know God in a much fuller and deeper way than do new converts.

As noted in the Old Testament, the enslaved Hebrews needed only to know that a lamb had been slain and blood applied. A redeemed people, however—with the waters of judgment flowing between them and the Egyptians, as well as their old way of life—needed to know very much more than that. Thus, God added other books of the Pentateuch to the book of Exodus. Leviticus, for instance, with its elaborate system of sacrifices and offerings, feast days and fast days, rules, rituals, and regulations, expounded the deeper significance of redemption and gave many marvelous and manifold glimpses of the purposes of God in grace.

In the New Testament we find a similar pattern. First are the Gospels, which record the facts concerning Christ's life, death, and resurrection. In the Epistles, however, all these truths are expanded and expounded and woven into an elaborate theology.

So, from "little children," we need to grow up until we become "fathers." John's word to fathers in the church is "Ye have known!" They were no longer on milk; now they could handle meat. They could enter into the deep things of God, and they could exegete and expound the Scriptures.

(3) Young men: because of their conquest of the foe (2:13b)

"I write unto you, young men, because ye have overcome the wicked one." John's placing young men last in both lists may have been his way of underlining their importance. The young men do the work and fight in the frontline. One does not expect much from little children, nor does one expect the older men to go forth to battle, except in emergencies. Old men give counsel; young men get things done. The old men "dream dreams" (Acts 2:17), while the young men "see visions." The "fathers" live increasingly in the past and are custodians of the great truths, traditions, and triumphs of the church in history. The young men, however, catch the vision of wrongs to be righted, of causes to be espoused, of harvest fields to be reaped, of worlds to be conquered, of foes to be routed in battle.

The aged John admired the young men he had gathered around him. "Ye have overcome the wicked one," he said. The words used for "wicked one" refer to Satan as the supreme author of wickedness in the universe. And the threat of Satan cannot be understated. Satan is pictured as being full of labor and pain in working wickedness, travailing as a woman with child who has come to the birth and is straining to bring forth evil. In the Lord's Prayer, Jesus urged us to ask God to "deliver us from evil" (evil one; Matt. 6:13). In the parable of the sower, the seed, and the soil, the Lord reveals that it is this same Wicked One who snatches away the good seed of the Word of God from the minds of those whose hearts have not been prepared to receive it (Matt. 13:19). Likewise, in the parable of the wheat and the tares, it is the Evil One who sows his counterfeit agents into the world to deceive. These counterfeit ministers, missionaries, and seminary professors are actually called "the children of the *wicked one,*" and that "wicked one" is identified as the

Devil (Matt. 13:38–39). In His high-priestly prayer, the Lord Himself prayed for us that we might be kept from evil (evil one; John 17:15).

John knew of young men who had been kept from the Evil One—they had encountered him and overcome him. As young men are urged to "flee youthful lusts" (2 Tim. 2:22), we are to flee from fornication and from idolatry (1 Cor. 6:18; 10:14) and from the "many foolish and hurtful lusts" that accompany the love of money (1 Tim. 6:9–10). But we are not told to flee from the Devil. He would simply stab us in the back. We are told, in contrast, to submit ourselves to God and to "resist the Devil," and he will flee from us (James 4:7). The word used for "resist" means to withstand, to oppose, to resist. Against this enemy we must stand and fight.

> b. The further round of reasons (2:13c–14d)
> > (1) Little children: because of their progress (2:13c)

"I write unto you, little children, because ye have known the Father." John takes a second look at these three classes within the local church and adds an extra comment for each. The smallest child soon gets to know its father, and in fact, the words "daddy" or "papa" are almost the first words a child learns to speak. The wondrous joy of having a loving human father is one of the most precious things in this world. Greatly to be pitied are those who have never known a father's love.

The concept of God as a Father is rare in the Old Testament. There He is known by other and more distant titles. He is *Elohim* and *Jehovah* and *Adonai*. He is *Jehovah Jireh* and *Jehovah Nissi* and *Jehovah Tsidkenu*. He is *El Shaddai* and *El Elyon* and so on. The Lord Jesus, however, reveals Him as Father, the name by which He called Him in His first recorded utterance (Luke 2:49). It was the name He uttered as men nailed Him to the cross (Luke 23:34), it was on His lips as He bowed His head in death (Luke 23:46), it was the name He spoke in resurrection (John 20:17), and it was the name that was still being spoken by Him on His way to Olivet and home (Acts 1:4, 7).

Over and over again John had heard the Lord Jesus speak about the Father and talk to His Father. It is the final and greatest revelation of God—that He is "the God and Father of our Lord Jesus Christ" (Eph. 1:3). Even babes in Christ can know that God has become their Father (Matt. 6:9), and that they can talk to Him, trust Him, love Him, and obey Him.

Jesus addressed God as "Abba Father" in Gethsemane (Mark 14:36), and the

Holy Spirit teaches born-again believers to address God in the same way (Rom. 8:14–15). The name *Abba* roughly corresponds to our word *daddy*, and is the name whereby a child addresses a father. *Father*, however, is the name used by an adult son. Getting to know God as "Abba Father" (the two names are always used together when used at all) is a sure means of growth in the Christian life. It was an encouraging sign to John that his converts and babes in Christ, his little children, were growing up. "Ye have known the Father," he says.

(2) Fathers: because of their perception (2:14a)

"I have written unto you, fathers, because ye have known him that is from the beginning." Here are the same words that John used in the previous verse. He had nothing to add to that, so he takes the fathers back, back to a dateless, timeless past, a moment he calls "the beginning." *Beginning* was evidently a favorite concept of John's. Thus, he begins both his gospel and his epistle. "In the beginning was the Word," he says, "and the Word was with God, and the Word was God" (John 1:1). That takes us back to the beginning of time, to the moment when Father, Son, and Holy Spirit in omnipotent power and with omniscient genius flung the stars into space, when the angelic sons of God were there and shouted for joy (Job 38:7). What a sight it must have been! He created with effortless ease countless stars and their satellites into vast orbits. Stars and galaxies move at inconceivable velocities and with such precision that an eclipse or the visit of a comet can be pinpointed with mathematical certainty. The galaxies that carpet the night sky were born in fiery wombs, they wax old, and they die. They fill space with their splendor and declare the glory and the greatness of our God. And Jesus was there when it all began, an active partner in Creation's wondrous work.

In his epistle, John goes back beyond the moment of Creation, to "the beginning," an expression that occurs nine times in this epistle. The "beginning" John has in mind in this passage is not the beginning of the gospel, so far as his personal acquaintance with it was concerned. Nor does he refer to his formal introduction to the Lord Jesus by John the Baptist. That might have been the beginning of the gospel for him, but it was certainly not its ultimate beginning. For that we must go back before the beginning of time and to that moment in a dateless, timeless past when God the Father, God the Son, and God the Holy Spirit took counsel together and decided that They would act in Creation. With Their infinite foreknowledge, They knew that if ever They acted in Creation, the day would come when They would have to act in redemption. That was "the beginning" John has in mind here—the moment when the members of the Godhead decided that, at a given point in time and at a certain place in the universe, They would deal with the mystery of iniquity. The second person of the Godhead would assume humanity and provide redemption for a ruined race.

And this was the One John had known, One infinitely greater than the false "Christ" of the cultists. The Docetists, for instance, viewed matter as essentially evil and spirit as essentially good, and taught that there could be no truce between them. They discarded the biblical doctrines of Creation, on the one hand, and of the Resurrection, on the other hand. According to them, the body in which Christ manifested Himself was not really a body of flesh and blood at all; it only seemed to be so.

The heretic Cerinthus postulated a dualistic view of the universe and invented a false Christology. According to him the man Jesus was the natural born son of Mary and Joseph. He was wiser than other men, however, and of greater virtue. According to Cerinthus, "the Christ" descended on this man Jesus at the time of his baptism, and empowered him to perform miracles and to teach people about the Father. This "Christ," Cerinthus said, abandoned the man Jesus just before he died.

John's Lord Jesus Christ was infinitely greater than the Christ of the cultists— then and now. What a pitiful "Christ" the Jehovah's Witnesses preach, for instance. Their "Christ" was Jehovah's first creation, an inferior, temporal being. They identify him (prior to his human existence) with Michael the archangel, and claim that he was crucified but did not rise from the dead; his body was supposedly dissolved in the tomb. He returned to earth as a spirit in 1874, or was it 1914, or was it 1918? The Jehovah's Witnesses are as confused on that issue as they are on so many others.

What a pitiful "Christ" the liberals have! Their "Christ" was not virgin born but was illegitimately born. He performed no miracles, and he was martyred because he was ahead of his times. He did not bodily rise from the dead, and he is not now seated, physically, at God's right hand in heaven, nor is he coming again. Nor is there anything remarkable to them about the Bible, which they view as just another book, one full of errors and contradictions. All these conclusions, hailed as the assured results of so-called "higher criticism," are presented with a great show of scholarship. And they are all false.

The "fathers" to whom John writes would have been deceived by none of this high-sounding nonsense (Col. 1:8). They knew better, because they had "known him that is from the beginning."

(3) Young men: because of their power (2:14b–d)

We note how that power is *described:* "I have written unto you, young men, because ye are strong" (2:14b). We note also how that power was *derived:* "and the Word of God abideth in you" (2:14c). We note, moreover, how that power was *displayed:* "and ye have overcome the wicked one" (2:14d).

The young men were strong, that is the glory of young men (Prov. 20:29). That was the glory of Samson. He could rend a lion, take on a whole army, carry away a city's gates. He was strong! We admire his strength, but he never learned to subdue his lusts. Still, in the end, he triumphed gloriously, and his name rings in history to this day. John's young men were strong. The word used for "strong" is *ischuros,* which relates to physical strength but which can also be rendered "mighty." John's use of the word here focuses on the young men's spiritual strength, as is indicated by the immediate context.

The young men derived this strength from the Word of God, the one weapon we all have at hand and the one that Satan fears. John's young men were not taken in by the cultic errors being peddled around Ephesus by Satan's emissaries. They knew how to wield "the sword of the Spirit" (Eph. 6:17), exposing the subtle lies of the enemy.

Throughout history, God has had His strong young men. Martin Luther was twenty-seven when he marched down the stairs of the *Scala Sancta* in Rome, realizing that salvation was by faith not by works. He was thirty-four when he nailed his monumental Ninety-five Theses to the door of that Wittenburg church.

George Müller was twenty-seven when he moved to Bristol, sure that God wanted him to open an orphanage strictly on the basis of faith. With no money in hand, he was committed to telling his needs only to God.

John Bunyan was thirty-two when he was jailed for preaching without the permission of the established church. In that prison he wrote his immortal *Pilgrim's Progress.*

William Booth was thirty-six when he founded the Salvation Army. He threw himself into the dens and stews of London's East End to rescue the poor, the wretched, and the despised.

David Brainard was twenty-five when he set out to convert the American Indians. He was only twenty-nine when he died.

William Carey was still in his teens when he could read the Bible in six languages. He was thirty-two when he went to India and launched the modern missionary era.

Such are God's strong young men. The world is a better place because of them and the church more glorious for all eternity.

> 5. The boundaries of that life (2:15–23)
>   a. The forbidden sphere (2:15–17)
>   (1) The love of the world (2:15)

The world—our enemy. One of our enemies. The Wicked One is enemy number one; the flesh is enemy number two; the world is enemy number three. The love of the world is, indeed, a very great peril. John tells us what *a love of the world begets:* "Love not the world, neither the things that are in the world" (2:15a). Doing so creates a vicious cycle— a love of the world begets a love of the things of the world, and a love of the things of the world begets an increasing love of the world. The word used here for "world" is *kosmos,* which has a considerable range of meaning in the New Testament. It can signify, for instance, the world as created by God, a place of great beauty and order. So used, the word stems from a root that carries the idea of something carved and planed and polished. It can also mean the world of human beings for whom Christ died (1:2). But in the sense John uses the word here, *the world* represents human life and society with God left out, human life and society as organized by Satan and in whose lap it lies (5:19). The world is the Devil's lair for sinners and his lure for saints. Thus, the world is one of God's enemies—it murdered His Son, and it hates His people.

The world is typified in the Old Testament in various ways—Egypt and its culture, Babylon and its cults, and Assyria and its cruelty are all Old Testament types of the world. The Bible story began in Babylon in Mesopotamia from whence Abraham came. The home of idolatry, Babylon represents this world's *false religion.* Egypt, representing this world's *foolish wisdom,* was a land of pyramids and of a people obsessed with death and ways to circumvent it. It was a land of great splendor and of many skills, in all of which Moses was learned. But it knew not God. The Pharaohs spent vast fortunes on their tombs, only to have them plundered and their mummies carted off to the world's museums to be gawked at by thoughtless millions. Assyria, with its fiendish cruelty and its love for waging ruthless war, represents this world's *fearful wickedness.*

Abraham no sooner escaped the world, as represented by Babylon, than he fell headlong into the world as represented by Egypt (Gen. 12:1–2, 10–20). It was a painful experience.

We are to "love not the world" or its "things." Such was the bane of the rich fool of the Lord's parable (Luke 12:15–21)—the man was rich, but he was not rich toward God. He loved things, but ended up leaving them all behind. And the key to the parable is "things" for things are the very essence of the trap set for us by the world. Its technique is to so focus our attention on this world so that we forget the world to come. That was the essential difference, right at the beginning of the human story, between the descendants of Cain (Gen. 4:17–24) and the descendants of Seth (Gen. 5:1–32). Cain's kind of people lived for this world and what it had to offer. They built a great antediluvian society filled with the fruits of art, science, and industry—and lost it all in the Flood. Seth's kind of people lived for the world to come—into which they were gathered, one by one, when their days on earth were done.

That, too, is what went wrong in Solomon's life. In his early days he lived for God and walked with God. Over time, however, he greatly expanded his harem and lived increasingly like an Oriental despot. The affairs of this world and the deceitfulness of this world's riches engulfed him, and in the end he made a shipwreck of his life, spending his last days wringing his hands over a misspent life. The book of Ecclesiastes reveals Solomon's despair, wailing over having lived for so long for the wrong world.

John tells us also *what a love of the world betrays:* "If any man love the world, the love of the Father is not in him" (2:15b). Those who live for this world betray a serious lack of understanding that this world is the enemy of God. John could still hear the earnest voice of the Lord Jesus as it rang through that Jerusalem upper room, praying that His loved ones might be protected from the world, from its attacks and from its attractions. His sheep had been given to Him "out of the world" (John 17:6) so that now we, as God's people, are *in* the world but no longer *of* the world.

The Lord said bluntly, "I pray not for the world" (John 17:9), so entrenched was its enmity. Thus, how can we love and admire a system that hates our Beloved? Moreover, the Lord was anticipating an imminent departure from the world: "Now I am no more in the world, but these are in the world, and I come to thee" (John 17:11). The world's animosity toward the Lord Jesus would soon be transferred to His people.

"While I was with them in the world," He said, "I kept them in thy name" (John 17:12). That was nowhere more evident than in Gethsemane when the Romans, the rabbis, and the rabble came to arrest Him. He at once gave Himself up and secured the disciples' escape. "The world hath hated them, because they are not of the world," He continued, "even as I am not of the world" (John

17:14). Doubtless, many in high places would have rejoiced to make a clean sweep of the disciples as well as getting rid of their Master.

Still, the Lord did not pray for His disciples to be immediately raptured: "I pray not that thou shouldest take them out of the world, but that thou shouldest keep them from the evil" (John 17:15)—from the Evil One, that is, he who is the prince and god of this world. Satan would indeed attack them and their heirs and successors in the world from that day to this. The very gates of hell itself, however, cannot prevail against His church (Matt. 16:18).

The presence of His own in a world that hates them is for a purpose: "As thou hast sent me into the world, even so have I also sent them into the world," Jesus declared (John 17:18). They are heaven's ambassadors to the lost people of this world, having the task to evangelize and win out of the world a people for His name.

We can see, then, why coming to terms with *this* world betrays a sad state of soul. When the world puts on its friendly faces, it is often more to be feared than when it puts on its frowning face. Either way, it is our foe, and coming to terms with it is treason and betrays a cold heart.

(2) The lusts of the world (2:16)

There are three of them, beginning with the world's *shameful appetites:* "For all that is in the world, the lust of the flesh . . . is not of the Father, but is of the world" (2:16a). We all have legitimate drives and desires placed in our hearts by an all-wise Creator, and the world knows how to whet our appetites and inflame them into lusts. Satan fans them into flames and they become roaring infernos, destructive to ourselves and to those around us.

The first temptation that Satan presented to the Lord Jesus in the wilderness, when He was at the end of His physical endurance and famished with hunger, appealed to the flesh. Satan challenged Jesus to turn stones into bread and put an end to His gnawing hunger. For fleshly temptations do not necessarily come from sexual desires. Consider, too, that there in the wilderness, the Lord Jesus was in the absolute center of God's will—being hungry! The Devil sought to seduce the Lord away from His allegiance to His Father by persuading Him that if God loved Him, He would provide for His physical needs, and if He failed to do so, He would be perfectly justified in taking matters into His own hands. Something else is to be considered, as well—if Jesus had transformed the stones into bread and eaten it, the bread would have killed Him; a long fast has to be broken with liquids not solids.

We can learn, then, that indulging "the lust of the flesh" does not necessarily mean climbing into bed with another man's wife or indulging some pornographic or perverted desire. It can mean simply satisfying a legitimate desire in an illegitimate way. The lust of the flesh is one of the world's devices for weaning us away from complete trust in the goodness and faithfulness of God.

The second lust of the world is its *showy appearance:* "For all that is in the world . . . the lust of the eyes . . . is not of the Father, but is of the world" (2:16b). The world knows how to catch our eye and draw us into this, that, or the other form of lust. The Devil, in other words, knows how to package and merchandise his wares so that they appear attractive.

Satan used "the lust of the eye" with great effect in the temptation of Eve: "When the woman saw that the tree was pleasant to the eyes" (Gen. 3:6), she succumbed to its allure. It was much the same with Adam in his turn. Satan was too clever to try to deceive Adam with the kind of twisted logic he used on Eve. Indeed, he did not tempt Adam at all. He faded into the background and allowed Eve to tempt him. She stood there before him in her lost condition, desirable and persuasive, and he saw her, ruined by the Fall, and loved her notwithstanding all. She held out the forbidden fruit and, Adam, like Eve, followed his eyes into sin.

It was the same with the foolish young man whom Solomon watched from his window. The brief twilight of the Middle East had settled over the street where the wanton woman lived. She was a bold-faced hussy, and she seduced the fellow with her words—but what words! She painted alluring pictures with words, describing how she had picked him out from among all the others passing by. Then she talked about her bed, about its coverings of tapestry, its carved legs, the fine linen that covered it, the aloes, myrrh, and cinnamon that breathed their fragrance all about it. Then when the picture danced with allure in his mind's eye, she moved on to the heady draft of pleasure that could be his if he came with her. He could drink and drink again until the dawn. These painted pictures did their work, and no doubt, she made full use of her physical attractions to reinforce her alluring words. He went with her, "as an ox goeth to the slaughter," added Solomon (Prov. 7:22).

We cannot help but wonder how Solomon knew so much about the woman, and why he sat there by his window, moralizing, when he had all the authority of the law and all the power of the throne behind him to put a permanent stop to her activities. He evidently had watched her at work many times before. "She hath cast down many wounded, yea many strong men have been slain by her," he

confides to us. It would seem that Solomon himself, for all his poems and proverbs, found the woman alluring. The lust of the eye was as fatal to him as it was
to the young man he described. He apparently enjoyed watching the woman ply
her trade, finding her as attractive as she was deadly.[9]

The third lust of the world is its *shallow applause.* "For all that is in the world
. . . the pride of life, is not of the Father, but is of the world" (2:16c). Pride is the
ultimate sin, the original sin, the sin that transformed brilliant Lucifer into the
very Devil himself (Isa. 14:9–14; Ezek. 28:12–19). There can be pride of place,
pride of race, and even pride of grace. It can take many forms. What do we take
pride in? That is the quarter from which this particular danger is likely to come.
As F. F. Bruce points out, there can even be a form of pride that apes humility.
The loathsome Uriah Heep, in Dickens's masterpiece *David Copperfield,* exuded
this most objectionable sort of pride—pride in his humility.

When David first met Uriah Heep, he shook hands with him, and it was an
unpleasant experience in itself. "I rubbed mine afterwards," David Copperfield
confesses, "to warm it, and to rub his off." What follows is a typical exchange
between the two, with David as the speaker:

> "You are working late tonight, Uriah," says I.
>
> "Yes, Master Copperfield," says Uriah.
>
> As I was getting on the stool opposite, to talk to him more conve-
> niently, I observed that he had not such a thing as a smile about him,
> and that he could only widen his mouth and make two hard creases
> down his cheeks, one on each side, to stand for one.
>
> "I am not doing office-work, Master Copperfield," said Uriah.
>
> "What work, then?" I asked.
>
> "I am improving my legal knowledge, Master Copperfield," said Uriah.
> "I am going through Tidd's Practice. Oh, what a writer Mr. Tidd is,
> Master Copperfield!"
>
> My stool was such a tower of observation, that as I watched him
> reading on again, after this rapturous exclamation, and following up the
> lines with his forefinger, I observed that his nostrils, which were thin
> and pointed, with sharp dints in them, had a singular and most uncom-
> fortable way of expanding and contracting themselves; that they seemed
> to twinkle instead of his eyes, which hardly ever twinkled at all.

---

9. See John Phillips, *Exploring Proverbs* (reprint, Grand Rapids: Kregel, forthcoming).

"I suppose you are quite a great lawyer?" I said, after looking at him for some time.

"Me, Master Copperfield?" said Uriah. "Oh, no! I'm a very 'umble person."

It was no fancy of mine about his hands, I observed; for he frequently ground the palms against each other as if to squeeze them dry and warm, besides often wiping them, in a stealthy way, on his pocket-handkerchief.

"I am well aware that I am the 'umblesh person going," said Uriah Heep, modestly; "let the other be where he may. My mother is likewise a very 'umble person. We live in a 'umble abode, Master Copperfield, but have much to be thankful for. My father's former calling was 'umble. He was a sexton."

"What is he now?" I asked.

"He is a partaker of glory at present, Master Copperfield," said Uriah Heep. "But we have much to be thankful for. How much have I to be thankful for in living with Mr. Wickfield!"

I asked Uriah if he had been with Mr. Wickfield long.

"I have been with him going on four year, Master Copperfield," said Uriah, shutting up his book, after carefully marking the place where he had left off. "Since a year after my father's death. How much have I to be thankful for, in that! How much have I to be thankful for, in Mr. Wickfield's kind intention to give me my articles, which would otherwise not lay within the 'umble means of mother and self!"

"Then, when your articled time is over, you'll be a regular lawyer, I suppose?" said I.

"With the blessing of Providence, Master Copperfield," returned Uriah.

"Perhaps you'll be a partner in Mr. Wickfield's business, one of these days," I said, to make myself agreeable, "and it will be Wickfield and Heep, or Heep late Wickfield."

"Oh, no, Master Copperfield," returned Uriah, shaking his head, "I am much too 'umble for that!"

He certainly did look uncommonly like the carved face on the beam outside my window, as he sat, in his humility, eyeing me sideways, with his mouth widened, and the crease in his cheeks.

"Mr. Wickfield is a most excellent man, Master Copperfield," said

Uriah. "If you have known him long, you know it, I am sure, much better than I can inform you."

I replied that I was certain he was; but that I had not known him long myself, though he was a friend of my aunt's.

"Oh, indeed, Master Copperfield," said Uriah, "Your aunt is a sweet lady, Master Copperfield."

He had a way of writhing when he wanted to express enthusiasm, which was very ugly; and which diverted my attention from the compliment he had paid my relation, to the snaky twistings of his throat and body.[10]

Besides pride of humility, however, is another form of pride—pride of scholarship. This kind of pride is exhibited by those, for instance, who tell us that "thoughtful people" can no longer accept the plenary, verbal inspiration of the Scriptures.

Frederic William Farrar was a scholar of great repute in his day—Dean of Canterbury, honorary chaplain to the Queen, canon of Westminster, and later Archdeacon of Westminster and Chaplain of the House of Commons. Farrar was an intellectual of the highest order, as well as a popular preacher, and his two-volume *Commentary on the Life of Christ* makes fascinating reading.

That did not prevent him from falling into the trap of thinking that scholarship was essential to understanding the Scriptures. In his introduction to his two-volume commentary on the books of Kings, he tells us that he accepted without reservation the conclusions of the so-called "higher criticism," which was coming into its stride in his day.

Of the destructive theory, he says, "I do not see how there can be any loss in the positive results of . . . Higher Criticism."[11]

Our blessed Lord, with His consummate tenderness, and divine insight into the frailties of our nature, made tolerant allowance for inveterate prejudices. "No man," He said, "having drunk old wine straightway desireth new; for he saith, The old is good." But the pain of disillusionment is blessed and healing when it is incurred in the cause of insincer-

10. Charles Dickens, *David Copperfield* (Franklin Center, Pa.: Franklin Library, 1980), 205, 213–15.
11. F. W. Farrar, *The First Book of Kings* (reprint, Minneapolis: Klock & Klock, 1981), 10.

ity. There must always be more value in results earned by heroic labour than in conventions accepted without serious inquiry. Already there has been a silent revolution. Many of the old opinions about the Bible have been greatly modified. There is scarcely a single competent scholar who does not now admit that the Hexateuch is a composite structure; that much of the Levitical legislation, which was once called Mosaic, is in reality an aftergrowth which *in its present form* is not earlier than the days of the prophet Ezekiel; that the Book of Deuteronomy belongs, in its present form, whatever older elements it may contain, to the era of Hezekiah's or Josiah's reformation; that the Books of Zechariah and Isaiah are not homogeneous, but preserve the writings of more prophets than their titles imply; that only a small section of the Psalter was the work of David; that the Book of Ecclesiastes was not the work of King Solomon; that most of the Book of Daniel belongs to the era of Antiochus Epiphanes; and so forth.[12]

In defending his love affair with the critics of his day, he says,

When we study the Bible it is surely one of our most primary duties to beware lest any idols of the caverns or of the forum tempt us "to offer to the God of truth the unclean sacrifice of a lie."[13]

Presumably he is referring to those who still hold to the inerrancy of Scripture and to its plenary verbal inspiration. He speaks of "the *ex cathedra* assertions of ignorant readers, though they are often pronounced with an assumption of infallibility, are not worth the breath which utters them."[14] He appeals to St. Jerome, who "complained in his day there was no old woman so fatuous as not to assume the right to lay down the law about Scriptural interpretation."[15]

One of the many books Dean Farrar wrote was a commentary on the book of Daniel, in which he espoused all the outlandish claims of the higher critics. Doubtless, Farrar would have considered Sir Robert Anderson an untrained nonprofessional in matters of biblical exposition. Sir Robert, however, had a mind as keen as Farrar's. A highly placed professional in Britain's famed Scotland Yard,

---

12. Ibid., 11–12.
13. Ibid., 13.
14. Ibid., 6.
15. Ibid., 7.

Anderson was also a brilliant student of the Scriptures. He refuted Farrar's commentary in a book titled *Daniel in the Critic's Den* and wrote a half-dozen other books that have been a help to God's people for years—including his book *The Silence of God,* a Christian classic.[16]

Because Anderson repudiated higher criticism, Farrar would have dismissed him as not being a "competent scholar." But among the Bible-believing, evangelical Christian who reject the soul-deadening theories of the liberal are many competent scholars—including, for instance, F. F. Bruce who, among many other great accomplishments, memorized the entire New Testament in Greek.

John, who faced the "intellectuals" in his day, was a humble former fisherman, but he knew more than all of the critics put together. The intellectualism and high-sounding nonsense (Col. 2:8) of the Gnostic cultists of John's day has a modern counterpart in the pronouncements of the higher critics. They exhibit the same "pride of life" in a more religious form. John said that all this kind of thing is "not of the Father, but of the world." And doubt it not—the same kind of pride that is found in those who seek to destroy the Bible can be found in the hearts of those who vehemently defend it.

(3) The loss of the world (2:17)

John contrasts two things—*that which is passing:* "And the world passeth away" (2:17a); and *that which is permanent:* "But he that doeth the will of God abideth for ever" (2:17b).

The "world," as a planet, is but a transitory fixture in space; its future, looking at things from the standpoint of modern science, is tied to that of the sun. The sun itself is a moderate star, said to be approaching middle age, powered by nuclear fusion, its energy derived, for the most part, from the conversion of hydrogen into helium. Although it is consuming itself at a prodigious rate, it is so vast that it has consumed only a few hundredths of 1 percent of its original mass. More significant than its conversion of mass to energy is the likelihood that about half the sun's hydrogen mass in the core (the only place where fusion can take place) has already been converted into helium. Once it has consumed the remainder (five billion years from now, according to astrophysicists), the sun will become a red giant and eventually a frigid cinder. In the process of becoming a red giant, it will expand to one hundred times its present diameter and, in so

---

16. Sir Robert Anderson, *The Silence of God* (reprint, Grand Rapids: Kregel, 1952); idem, *Daniel in the Critics Den* (reprint, Grand Rapids: Kregel, 1990).

doing, will vaporize the earth.[17] So, even from the standpoint of secular science, the world is in the process of passing away. Scripture confirms this—except that it does not give it the optimistic five billion years to meet its doom. The apostle John confirms Peter's warning that the earth is to be destroyed in a nuclear-type holocaust (2 Peter 3:10–13; Rev. 21:1), this catastrophic disaster to close the soon-coming millennial reign of Christ. The world is truly passing away and is hastening toward its fiery end at breakneck speed.

This climax will also bring an end to the "world" as a God-rejecting, Bible-denying, Christ-hating, Spirit-despising, Christian-persecuting, soul-destroying place. The individual living on earth today, and going in for the things that the world (as a system) has to offer, faces the end much sooner than that. Death will put an end to the appeals of the world, and "after death the judgment," God says (Heb. 9:27). For the Christ-rejecting, world-loving unbeliever, there awaits the Great White Throne (Rev. 20:11–15); for the believer there awaits the judgment seat of Christ (Rom. 14:10; 1 Cor. 3:12–15; 2 Cor. 5:10).

No wonder John urges us to "do the will of God," for "he that doeth the will of God abideth for ever." Since the Christian is an heir of the world to come, he or she should hold lightly the desirable and legitimate things that the world *(as a place)* offers and vigorously reject the sinful things that the world *(as a system)* offers.

It is significant that half the book of Genesis is taken up with the stories of two men—Abraham and Jacob—both of whom exemplified the pilgrim character of God's people in relation to this world. Abraham's symbol was a tent and an altar, his tent portraying his attitude toward this world, his altar speaking of his attitude toward the world to come. He confessed himself to the sons of Heth to be "a stranger and a sojourner [pilgrim] among them" (Gen. 23:4), and in this he stands in contrast with sin-cursed Cain, the man who founded this world's system and who lamented that he was "a fugitive and a vagabond in the earth" (Gen. 4:12).

Jacob's symbol was a staff, a fact of which he reminded the Lord when he prayed that he might be delivered from the vengeful hand of Esau, already marching to meet him with a force of four hundred men (Gen. 32:10–11). Our last glimpse of Jacob reveals the old patriarch as he prepares for his last pilgrimage. His boys are gathered around his bed and heaven is opening up before him. We see him, thus, leaning on his staff and blessing his boys (Gen. 49; Heb. 11:21).

---

17. See *Voyage Thro' the Universe—the Sun* (Alexandria, Va.: Time-Life Books, 1990), 48–49.

Truly "the world passeth away, and the lust thereof." We grow old and feeble and either lose our appetite at last for the pleasures and treasures of the world or try to hang on to them more tenaciously than ever. But, either way, they have no power in the hour of death. In contrast, "He that doeth the will of God abideth for ever." John would have us keep eternity's values in view.

> b. The false spirit (2:18–23)
> > (1) A word about the time (2:18)

John has written about *the forbidden sphere,* this present and passing evil world. Now he turns our attention to *the false spirit* that pervades the world. John reminds us, first, of *a past warning* about the time—*Antichrist will come:* "Little children, it is the last time: and ye have heard that antichrist shall come." The early church, and the apostles themselves, tended to use the expression "the last time" or "the last days" or, as perhaps here, "the last hour" as a generic term for the time between the Lord's departure to heaven and the time of His coming again (Rev. 1:1). They generally anticipated the return of the Lord in their own lifetimes.

We now have the full blaze of the entire Old and New Testaments to draw on for our more comprehensive understanding of end-time events, as well as the light of two thousand years of human history since Pentecost. Obviously, the Lord did not come in the lifetime of the apostles. Indeed, Peter knew, almost from the start, that the Lord would not come in his lifetime (John 21:18–19; 2 Peter 1:14). Moreover, a rumor circulated in the early church that the apostle John would live until the Lord returned. John knew, however, that this popular belief was based on a misunderstanding of the Lord's words (John 21:20–23).

A vast and comprehensive body of eschatological teaching is contained in the Bible, and John was thoroughly at home in the Old Testament, especially in the apocalyptic writings of Daniel and Zechariah. He knew by heart the Lord's Olivet Discourse (Matt. 24–25) and must have been thoroughly conversant with the prophetic teachings of Paul, especially as developed in his two Thessalonian letters.

That there is to be a personal Antichrist is evident from any number of Scriptures, including John's own book of Revelation. This person will appear on earth after the rapture of the church (1 Thess. 4:13–5:11; 2 Thess. 2:6–8), but his coming has been foreshadowed in history, especially in the activities of Antiochus Epiphanes, the "little horn" of Daniel 8:9. The activities of the Antichrist himself are foretold in Daniel 7:8—where there, too, he is referred to as a "little horn"—

and further described in Daniel 11. The Antichrist has numerous names and titles in Scripture: "the man of sin" and "the son of perdition," as well as "the wicked one" (2 Thess. 2:3, 8). In Revelation he is often referred to as "the beast" (Rev. 13:1–10; 17:3–18). He will unify the West by reviving the old Roman Empire, and he will eventually take over the whole world for a short while, initiating the Great Tribulation and launching an all-out war against the Jews and the converts of the Jewish evangelists of Revelation 7. He will meet his end at the hands of the returning Christ at the Battle of Armageddon (Matt. 24; Rev. 16:12–15; 19:11–21).[18]

Much of this had already been written into the prophetic Scriptures when John wrote this epistle and, as we can see now, looked some two thousand years into the future. The New Testament authors, when they added their inspired contribution to the prophetic Word, had no idea that the church age would last so long.

The assumption of first-century believers that the Lord's return might be in their lifetimes was not at all unreasonable. We might legitimately ask, What would have happened if the Jews had accepted Christ instead of rejecting Him? Presumably, in that case, the Lord would have been handed over by Judas to the Romans, and He would have been crucified and buried and raised again as foretold. The emphasis would then have been on the kingdom and not the church. Nero would have been the Antichrist and the Neronic persecutions would have blossomed into the Great Tribulation; Armageddon would have been fought and the Lord would have returned to inaugurate the Millennium—and it would all have been over a thousand years ago!

The Lord, however, in several of the kingdom parables cautioned against a too-optimistic view of His swift return. The "evil servant" in the Olivet Discourse, for instance, said, "My lord delayeth his coming," and then allowed his unregenerate character to express itself (Matt. 23:48–51). Note also the parable of the wicked steward, who acted in the same way for the same reason (Luke 12:45–46). In Mark's account of the Lord's prophetic discourse, the Lord Himself said He would be "as a man taking a far journey" (Mark 13:34), implying He would be gone for some considerable time.

Many have seen a similar hint in the parable of the Good Samaritan. Having saved the poor wayfarer, he took him to an inn and took care of his welfare until

---

18. See John Phillips, *Exploring the Book of Daniel* (reprint, Grand Rapids: Kregel, forthcoming); idem, *Exploring Revelation* (reprint, Grand Rapids: Kregel, 2001); idem, *Exploring the Future* (reprint, Grand Rapids: Kregel, 2003).

his return. The two "pence" he gave to the innkeeper represent two days' wages, and the two days of his anticipated absence may well represent the two-thousand-year delay between Pentecost and the Lord's return (Luke 10:35). So, then, John reminds his readers of a coming time when *the* Antichrist will come, the one foretold in many a past warning.

John turns next to *a present warning* about the time—*antichrists have come:* "Even now are there many antichrists; whereby we know it is the last time"—the "last time" in the sense that "God . . . hath *in these last days* spoken unto us by his Son" (Heb. 1:1–2, emphasis added), and in the sense that all the time between the Lord's ascension and return is "the last time."[19]

So, then, John was alarmed. At the end of the apostolic age he saw an embattled church beset by persecution from without and subversion from within. It seemed to him that the final end was in sight, but beyond John's immediate horizon was a vast, unimagined vista. The church would continue on earth century after century, and the gates of hell would not prevail against it.[20]

What John was seeing in the burgeoning Gnostic heresy was just an initial and partial and illustrative fulfillment of end-time events. It is quite a common thing for Bible prophecies, especially Old Testament prophecies, to have both a near and far fulfillment—the near one being partial and incomplete but similar to the final and complete fulfillment to take place later on. We are at the other end of church history now—and Gnosticism is back. "There are many antichrists" in the world, and we "know that it is the last time." Cults are multiplying, charismatic leaders come and go. Some of these are so convincing that their followers willingly commit suicide on a mass scale by taking poison together or by being immolated in a fiery holocaust. Apostasy is again rampant in the church, that "falling away first" of which Paul warned is evident everywhere (2 Thess. 2:3). The harlot church is getting ready to embrace her groom, the Antichrist (Rev. 13, 17), and the false christs are everywhere preparing the way for the Antichrist, as the Lord foretold (Matt. 24:4).

(2) A word about the transients (2:19)

Note that in John's day—as is now and as so often has been in history—the cultists once belonged to a local church. John has two things to say about such—

---

19. See appendix 1, "Gnosticism Unveiled," taken from *Great Leaders of the Christian Church,* by Elgin Moyer (Chicago: Moody, 1951), 36–41. Used by permission.
20. Ibid.

their departure from the fellowship: "They went out from us, but they were not of us" (2:19a); and he mentions *their disclosure about their faith:* "For if they had been of us, they would no doubt have continued with us: but they went out, that they might be made manifest that they were not all of us" (2:19b).

The people in view here were not simply backsliders but apostates. There's a difference. Dig deep into the heart of a backslider and you'll find Christ. Backsliders are never happy in their wayward condition, and although they may die in that condition—as Elimelech did—backsliders are as often as not restored, as Naomi was (Ruth 1:1–3, 6–7). Dig beneath the surface of an apostate, however, into the dark depths of his or her heart, and you'll find the Devil, who delights in these founders and followers of Christ-dishonoring cults.

Classic examples of apostates are given in Hebrews 6:4–8; in 2 Peter; and in the little epistle of Jude. An apostate is a person who at one time responded to the initial work of the Holy Spirit—which is to convict of sin, righteousness, and judgment to come (John 16:8–11). The apostate was once enlightened by the Holy Spirit to an understanding of the person, work, and claims of the Lord Jesus, and may even have made some kind of a profession of faith and joined a local church fellowship. But, as Simon Peter told Simon Magus (Acts 8:18–23), "the root of the matter" is not in the apostate at all. He or she turns away from the truth to support and propagate a lie.

"They went out from us," John says, "because they were not of us." Likely, John had in mind the night in which the Lord Jesus was betrayed. There sat Judas, with the blood money in his pocket, playacting the role of a genuine believer. "One of you will betray me," Jesus said. "Is it I?" cried each one around the table in turn. "Is it I?" echoed Judas, clutching at those accursed coins. "Who is it?" John asked Jesus. "The one to whom I give the sop," Jesus replied. A special mark of honor at a banquet was for the host to give a coveted portion to one of the guests. The Lord had already appealed to the conscience of Judas (John 13:18–21), and now He appealed to his heart (John 13:26). For having dipped that special portion in the sauce, He deliberately handed it to him.

It was a vain appeal. No sooner had Judas eaten that special morsel than "Satan entered into him." Up to that point he had been possessed by evil thoughts; now he was possessed by the Devil (John 13:27), and Jesus instantly dismissed him from the table and from the room. Further appeal was useless. Jesus sent him about the terrible business of treachery and betrayal upon which he had already embarked (John 13:27). John watched the whole thing, and he reminds us that immediately upon receiving the sop, Judas went out. "And it was night," is John's closing comment on this terrible example of apostasy (John 13:30).

How dark! Who can measure the darkness of an apostate's heart? Jesus Himself warned, "If therefore the light that is in thee be darkness, how great is that darkness!" (Matt. 6:23).

> (3) A word about the truth (2:20–21)
>   (a) The unction of the Spirit (2:20)

"But ye have an unction from the Holy One, and ye know all things." The word used for "unction" here is *chrisma,* from which the title *Christ* stems, and which means "the anointed One." True believers have the Holy Spirit to be their all-sufficient, inerrant, and infallible guide into all truth. John remembered the Lord remarking upon this in His Upper Room Discourse. The promise, that "the Comforter . . . shall teach you all things, and bring all things to your remembrance, whatsoever I have said unto you" (John 14:26), anticipates the writing of the Gospels. "But when the Comforter is come, whom I will send unto you from the Father, even the Spirit of truth, which proceedeth from the Father, he shall testify of me: and ye also shall bear witness, because ye have been with me from the beginning" (John 15:26–27)—that looks ahead to the writing of the book of Acts. "Howbeit, when he, the Spirit of truth, is come, he will guide you into all truth: for he shall not speak of himself; but whatsoever he shall hear, that shall he speak: and he will shew you things to come" (John 16:13)—that foretells the writing of the Epistles and the Revelation.

It is a maxim of Bible Study that "God is His own interpreter," that is, the Bible is self-contained and self-explanatory. Thus, we need not go outside of the Bible to understand the Bible—for God gives us the "unction" of the Spirit. The "anointing" of the Holy Spirit is the birthright of every child of God, and it is the Holy Spirit who unlocks for us the wonders of the Word.

The cultists of John's day claimed to belong to a special inner circle that had been initiated into truths and mysteries beyond the reach of the rank and file of the church. "Nonsense!" says John. All we need to know is in the Bible. The Holy Spirit wrote every word of it and is both able and willing to unveil even its deepest mysteries to those who patiently and prayerfully wait upon Him to lead them into all truth. We, too, must beware of "prophets" and others, with so-called "charismatic" gifts of tongues and knowledge and prophecy, claiming to have extrabiblical revelations. Our attitude to such should be one of extreme skepticism. A friend of mine talked to a Mormon who claimed that Joseph Smith was a latter-day prophet and that the *Book of Mormon* was a second New Testament. My friend asked the Mormon, "What does he prophesy? If it's in the Bible, I don't need it; and if it's not in the Bible, I don't want it!"

Often, in our Bible study, we come across things we don't understand. But if we are diligent and patient, if we apply sound hermeneutical principles to the text, and if we are not wedded to some preconceived notions and to arbitrary and erroneous schemes of interpretation, sooner or later the evasive, difficult passages will appear in their true light, and the imagined difficulty or supposed error will be resolved.

Bible study can be likened to doing a ten-thousand-piece jigsaw puzzle—without a picture! The first need is to sort out the pieces—the straight-edged pieces here, the red ones there, the blue ones somewhere else, the green ones off by themselves. Then it's a good idea to get the edging pieces put together so that the size and proportions of the puzzle can be seen. Soon the red pieces fall into place and reveal the sides of a barn, the tree pieces begin to line up, parts of the sky emerge. All of a sudden the man with the dog takes shape. The more pieces we put in, the clearer the picture becomes. Sometimes whole areas of the puzzle suddenly come together. Occasionally, however, we force a piece in where it does not belong. And that is fatal. Then nothing around it will go in, and it is not until we see our mistake that further progress can be made in that area.

If we are willing to be so painstaking over a mere puzzle, how much more we should be willing to take time and effort over Bible study. The Holy Spirit rewards such diligence, not only in opening up to us the Scriptures but also in protecting us from the delusions and excesses of those who are in error.

(b) The understanding of the Scripture (2:21)

"I have not written unto you because ye know not the truth, but because ye know it, and that no lie is of the truth." Thus, Paul could say to his beloved friends at Philippi, "To write the same things to you, to me indeed is not grievous, but for you it is safe" (Phil. 3:1). And Peter could remind believers facing apostasy, "I will not be negligent to put you always in remembrance of these things, though ye know them, and be established in the present truth. Yea, I think it meet, as long as I am in this tabernacle, to stir you up by putting you in remembrance; knowing that shortly I must put off this my tabernacle . . . Moreover, I will endeavour that ye may be able after my decease to have these things always in remembrance" (2 Peter 1:12–15). There is safety in repeating truth that we have already learned. As the old hymn puts it:

> Tell me the story often
> For I forget so soon.
> The early dew of morning
> Has passed away at noon.[21]

There is new truth to be learned. But those who love the Lord never get tired of hearing the eternal truths of the gospel repeated over and over again. Who will ever get tired of such grand old texts as John 3:16; or Romans 10:9; or Isaiah 53? Henry Moorehouse preached night after night in Moody's Chicago Tabernacle on John 3:16, and the great evangelist himself was stirred to the depth of his being. A truth does not have to be novel to be endearing. After all, it was the worldly-wise, sophisticated Greek philosophers on Mar's Hill who "spent their time in nothing else, but either to tell or to hear some new thing" (Acts 17:21). Well, Paul had something new and notable to tell them, and they laughed him out of court.

John, then, was in good company when he wrote to confirm his readers in some grand old truths.

"No lie is of the truth," he added—no matter how clever, sensational, and appealing that lie might be. Here we have one of John's absolutes. Lies and truth are mutually exclusive. Lies come from Satan, since he is the father of lies (John 8:44), and the person who will not bow to the truth automatically embraces a lie. Moreover, truth is narrow and recognizes only one absolute, whereas error is varied and can accommodate almost anything.

Here, for instance, is a mathematical truth, one we learned in the earliest grade in school: "Twice one is two!" That is the truth. It is narrow, dogmatic, and exclusive. Error, by contrast, is broad. Error can say, "Twice one is three," or "Twice one is ten," or "Twice one is a million." Error is broad-minded, as wide as the world, willing to accept almost anything. Truth, however, is narrow, unable to compromise.

What is true of a mathematical truth is true of any other truth. It is true of divine truth, for instance. Error can embrace a vast variety of religious propositions. Truth is confined to what the Bible says (John 17:17). "No lie is of the

---

21. Catherine Hankey, "Tell Me the Old, Old Story," in *Sacred Songs and Solos,* comp. Ira D. Sankey, rev. and enlarged (London: Marshall, Morgan & Scott, n.d.), 1131.

truth." There are many subtle, attractive, and persuasive lies in the world. The Devil is very clever in inventing them and men are very zealous in propagating them. Still, when all is said and done, a lie is a lie and not the truth. The theory of evolution is a lie—albeit a very popular one—and it is promoted by a vast number of very clever people. It contradicts the Bible, however, as to the creation and fall of man; therefore, it is a lie. All the cults teach lies, all the world's religions deny Christ and propagate lies—even though those who proclaim them are passionately convinced that they have embraced the truth.

"No lie is of the truth." That is the Holy Spirit's own verdict, and He is "the Spirit of truth" (John 15:26).

(4) A word about the traitors (2:22–23a)

John elaborates on the particular kind of lie he had in mind. He sets before us *the challenge of the antichrist:* "Who is a liar but he that denieth that Jesus is the Christ? He is antichrist, that denieth the Father and the Son" (2:22); and he sets before us *the children of the antichrist:* "Whosoever denieth the Son, the same hath not the Father" (2:23a).

That is the ultimate lie—to deny that Jesus is the Christ, to deny that He is the Son. That is the very essence of falsehood, the great lie of Satan and of his firstborn son, the Antichrist. All those whom, having once been enlightened, turn around and deny this twin truth, partake so deeply of the spirit of the Antichrist that the Spirit of the living God calls such ones "antichrists."

Some lies are mere factual errors, but other lies reveal the utter rot and decay of the innermost soul. The greatest fact in the history of the universe is that the great, eternal, uncreated, self-existing second person of the Godhead entered into human life by way of a virgin's womb at a place called Bethlehem nigh on two thousand years ago. It is a lie of lies to deny that. The greatest fact in the history of our planet is that the living God, Creator of the universe, Lord of all the galaxies of space, was encompassed "within the span of a virgin's womb" and was born as a man among men. It is a lie of lies to deny that.

It is the greatest truth in all the annals of time and eternity that God, having become man and robed Himself with human flesh, lived a sinless life in a sin-cursed world. That He lived as no one else has lived; that "never man spake like this man"; that "he went about doing good"; that no one, not even His bitterest foe, was ever able to accuse Him of sin; that He was pronounced guiltless and sinless by a Roman governor and dying thief alike—it is a lie of lies to deny that.

It is the greatest truth of all time that this One whom angels worshiped, who could have summoned a dozen angel legions to put an end to all His foes, who had Himself the power to turn water into wine, the power to multiply a little lad's lunch into a banquet for ten thousand, the power to still the surging seas, to cleanse lepers, and to raise the very dead—that very One submitted to the horrors of death upon a cross. It is a lie of lies to deny that.

It is the most wondrous, glorious truth in the Word of God that He was not only sinless and faultless but holy—holy as God is holy—yet He "bare our sins in his own body on the tree" (1 Peter 2:24). He died "the just for the unjust, that he might bring us to God" (1 Peter 3:18). This is so eloquently expressed in the hymn, "I Stand Amazed in the Presence," written by Charles Gabriel:

> He took my sins and my sorrows.
> He made them His very own;
> He bore my burden to Calvary
> And suffered and died alone.[22]

More—He who knew no sin was made sin for us that we might be made the righteousness of God in Him. It is a lie of lies to deny that.

It is the grandest truth ever to excite the interest and curiosity of the angels that this all-glorious One not only died as a victor, with the shout of a conqueror on His lips, but He sovereignly dismissed His own spirit. Not only was He buried, not only was no taint of corruption or decay allowed to touch His sleeping form, but He arose in triumph over sin, death, and the grave. It is a lie of lies to deny that.

It is the most glorious truth ever proclaimed on earth and in heaven that "this same Jesus," Son of Man and Son of God, both Lord and Christ, arose bodily from the tomb. And still more—in that same body He ascended on high, entered into heaven, and sat down on the throne of God at the right hand of the Majesty on high, and that He sits there in a human body, God over all, blessed forevermore. It is a lie of lies to deny that.

It is the grandest truth on mortal tongue, and the grandest truth that angels ever sung, that He is now not only our great High Priest and our advocate with the Father, but He is coming again, coming to reign on earth in the very scene of His rejection. All creation is waiting on tiptoe, anticipating that day. A vast bib-

---

22. C. H. Gabriel, "My Savior's Love," in *Inspiring Hymns,* comp. Alfred B. Smith (Grand Rapids: Singspiration Music/Zondervan, 1951), 85.

lical eschatology anticipates that day. "I will come again!" He said. "He will so come in like manner as ye have seen him go," said the angels to the astonished disciples on Olivet's brow.

John had little patience with those who turned their back upon such great truths as these. He had one scalding word for those who denied and distorted them—"antichrists"! They have a christ, in the cults, but he is not "our Lord Jesus Christ"—to borrow Paul's great phrase (Rom. 16:17–18). He is not the Christ of the Bible; he is a christ of their own making, the opposite in every way to our Lord Jesus Christ.

(5) A word about the testimony (2:23b)

"But he that acknowledgeth the Son hath the Father also." You cannot have the one without the other. Thus, whenever we make mention of the Son, we bear testimony to the fact that there is a Father. John's entire gospel was designed to, among other things, bear testimony of the unique relationship that exists, and always has existed, between the Father and the Son. John had obtained his grasp of the great truths connected with this relationship from listening to the Lord Jesus Himself. If anyone ought to know the scope and significance of this intimate and eternal relationship, it must be the Lord Himself. John, his memory of Jesus' teaching quickened by the Holy Spirit (John 14:26), wrote all these things down, inerrantly and infallibly. Surely Jesus, and John writing under direct inspiration of the Holy Spirit, knew the truth of these matters. Cerinthus and his crowd, and his spiritual heirs and assigns throughout history, wrested the truth to their own destruction.

6. The blessings of that life (2:24–29)
    a. Living in Him (2:24–25)
        (1) The principle involved (2:24)

Two things—*He abides in us:* "Let that therefore abide in you, which ye have heard from the beginning. If that which ye have heard from the beginning shall remain in you . . ." (2:24a). Moreover, *we abide in Him:* "ye also shall continue in the Son, and in the Father" (2:24b). This whole concept of abiding stems from the Lord's teaching concerning the vine and the branches (John 15). How well the aged apostle remembered that long and intimate talk the Lord Jesus had with His own in the Upper Room just before His death. The Lord talked about the mystical union that exists between Himself and His own, the same mystical union that exists between the Father and the Son. The Lord Jesus as man made Himself available to His Father as God in a moment-by-moment, ever continuing relationship. And the Father as God made Himself available, likewise, to the Lord Jesus as man. Now we, as believing men and women, make ourselves available to the Lord Jesus as God in a similar moment-by-moment, ever continuing relationship. And the Lord Jesus as God makes Himself available, likewise, to us as believing men and women. The Lord Jesus claimed that what He said and what He did as man was the result of this mystical relationship with the Father. He expects that what we do as men and women will be the result of a similar mystic relationship with both Himself and His Father.

The Lord vividly illustrated this relationship, identifying Himself as the Vine and His true followers as the branches. The branches of the Vine have a threefold responsibility—to cling, to climb, and to cluster. The branches can do this only as they "abide" in the Vine, and any attempt to live a life independent of the Vine is doomed to failure. It is only as the life of the Vine is expressed through the branches that the Vine and the branches can bear fruit. Thus, a relationship of mutual dependence exists between the Vine and the branches. Since the human factor enters into it, on our side of the mystical and marvelous relationship, the Lord talked about the need for pruning the unproductive, or only partially productive, branches. This way there can be fruit, more fruit, and much fruit.

(2) The promise involved (2:25)

"And this is the promise that he hath promised us, even eternal life." There can be no question of a genuine believer's losing his or her salvation. The relationship of Vine and branch is as real in the Lord's illustration as is the relationship between the Head (Christ) and the members of His mystical body (believers) in Paul's illustration (1 Cor. 12:12–27). As we look at a growing vine we see one whole. We cannot say, "Here is where the vine ends and the branches begin," or "Here is where the branches end and the vine begins." The vine and the branches are one continuous whole, sharing the same life, working toward the same goal.

Similarly, each believer shares in the life of Christ, which is the deathless, eternal life of God. That is the very kind of life He imparts to us—eternal life, the heritage of every blood-bought child of God. The promise is sure, wholly unconditional and absolutely guaranteed by the Father, the Son, and the Holy Spirit. We can pillow our heads upon that great truth (John 10:27–30; Rom. 8:16–17, 33–39).

b. Learning of Him (2:26–27)
    (1) The unveiling of the seducer (2:26)

"These things have I written unto you concerning them that seduce you." Some of the heretics were attractive people with charming, charismatic personalities. Some were scholarly and sophisticated. Some were golden-tongued orators, possessed of considerable powers of persuasion. John unmasked them as the seducers they were. Their goal was to lead people astray into error. The best antidote, however, was to abide in Christ and to know the anointing of the Holy Spirit.

(2) The unction of the Spirit (2:27)

"But the anointing which ye have received of him abideth in you, and ye need not that any man teach you: but as the same anointing teacheth you of all things, and is truth, and is no lie, and even as it hath taught you, ye shall abide in him." The Holy Spirit, says John, will not lead us astray.

It is an axiom of sound exegesis that "God is His own interpreter," that is, we do not need to go outside the Bible in order to understand the Bible. Still, people tend to import their own preconceived notions into their efforts to understand God's Word. They add all sorts of odds and ends of information they have picked up here and there, some of it not always reliable. Often they employ fanciful, even far-fetched methods of interpretation and sometimes incorporate downright error into their resulting "theology." Nowhere are these things more evident than in the way some people handle such specialized areas of Bible knowledge as typology, prophecy, and the parables. One popular writer says, for instance, that the creatures that come up out of the Abyss (Rev. 9:1–11) are helicopters! Since when did helicopters come up out of the bottomless pit? The Abyss is a prison house for malignant and powerful evil spirits (Rev. 20:1–3). The scriptural explanation is that these locustlike creatures of terrible appearance and appetite are evil spirits, presently and mercifully (for the human race) incarcerated by God. Scripture interprets Scripture.

There are three ministries of the Spirit directed toward the world. First, He has a *reproving* ministry (John 16:7–11) to convict the world of sin, of righteousness, and of judgment to come, of the *nature* of sin, of the *need* for righteousness, and of the *nearness* of judgment. He has, second, a *regenerating* ministry (John

3:1–8) as the Lord explained to Nicodemus. The Spirit also has a third *restraining* ministry (2 Thess. 2:3–8), acting through the church as the great hinderer to prevent the premature advent of the personal Antichrist.

Toward the believer, the Spirit exercises a sevenfold ministry. First, He *baptizes* us, that is, He *situates* us, makes us members of the mystical body of Christ, which is the church (1 Cor. 12:13). This mystical bonding between the Christian and the Christ brings each member of the body under the direct control of the Head, and it is the unique feature of the church age.

He also *sustains* us with the *gift* of the Spirit (Acts 2:38; Rom. 8:8). Since the Christian life is a supernatural life and can be lived only by Christ Himself, that life is imparted to us by His Holy Spirit, given to us for that purpose. The various names, titles, and characteristics of the Holy Spirit all portray the Lord Jesus. Thus, the Spirit of God is the Spirit of truth (John 14:17), faith (2 Cor. 4:13), grace (Heb. 10:29), holiness (Rom. 1:4), wisdom (Eph. 1:17), power, love, a sound mind (2 Tim. 1:7), life (Rom. 8:2), and glory (1 Peter 4:14). These characteristics of the Lord Jesus are imparted to us by means of the gift of the Spirit.

A third ministry of the Spirit is that He *sanctifies* us by *indwelling* us and making our bodies His temple (1 Cor. 3:16; 6:19). We must not defile our bodies and, indeed, we cannot habitually do so without reaping the Holy Spirit's displeasure.

The Spirit, too, *secures* us, and that security is, indeed, the significance of the *seal* of the Spirit (Eph. 1:13). A seal is the symbol of a completed transaction. We speak in legal jargon of agreements being "signed, sealed, and delivered," the terms of the contract, thus, becoming binding on both parties.

Fifth, the Holy Spirit *separates* us, for we have the *earnest* of the Spirit (Eph. 1:14). In North America, when a person makes an offer on a piece of property that the person wants to purchase, he or she is required to give some "earnest money" as a token that the person is in earnest, that he or she means business. Another idea behind that of the earnest is that of an engagement ring. Once a young woman accepts an engagement ring, she advertises that her affections, her life, and her future all belong to her beloved. She is separated, set apart, for him.

The Spirit exercises a sixth ministry in that He *strengthens* us by *filling* us (Eph. 5:18). Throughout the book of Acts, we see the believers repeatedly being filled with the Spirit to empower them to witness for Christ and to present Christ, by life and testimony, to a lost world. That we "be filled" is in the imperative mood— it is a command; it is in the passive voice—it is the Holy Spirit who acts, not us;

and it is in the present continuous tense—"be ye being filled." It is something that must go on and on until we get to glory.

Finally, the Spirit *shows* us. He *anoints* us. Throughout the Old Testament period, prophets, priests, and kings were anointed for their specialized ministry (Lev. 8:10–12; 1 Sam. 16:1–13; 1 Kings 19:16). In the Old Testament, the Spirit of God came upon people, like Samson (Judg. 14:5–6) and endued them with power to accomplish extraordinary tasks. One of the titles of the Lord is "the Christ" (the Anointed), for all that was implied by the Old Testament anointing with oil or with the Spirit was consummated in Him.

There was never a time when the Lord Jesus was not filled with the Spirit. He was anointed, however, at His baptism when the Holy Spirit came down and abode upon Him (Matt. 3:16). In the power of that anointing, He vanquished the Devil, using the Word of God with extraordinary power (Mark 4:1–11). In the power of that anointing, He took the Scriptures into His hands in the Nazareth synagogue, turned to Isaiah 61:1—which spoke of the Messiah's anointing—and claimed to be that Messiah. His skill with the Scriptures is demonstrated not only in His ability to find the place He needed but in His closing the book in the middle of a phrase (Luke 4:16–21).

Now we, too, have an anointing (unction) from the Holy Spirit so that we can handle the Scriptures with authority and accuracy, knowing how to bring appropriate passages to bear upon the lives of those to whom we minister.

John's expression here—"need not that any should teach you"—must be taken in context. It obviously does not mean that we can afford to ignore what the Holy Spirit has taught others, for the gift of the teacher is one of the gifts of the Holy Spirit (Eph. 4:11–13). We are all indebted to the great work done by others in opening to us the Scriptures. We are grateful, too, for those who explore for us the vast treasure of the original languages and for those who reveal to us the significance of the geographical and cultural backgrounds of various parts of the Bible. We praise God for those who taught us how to apply sound hermeneutic principles to the Word of God and, thus, to "rightly divide" the word of truth (2 Tim. 2:15). At the same time, we are supremely thankful for the Spirit of God, who not only inspired the sacred Scriptures but who also illuminates them.

The expression "need not that any should teach you," in its context, is a reference to the false teachers who were posing as great exegetes of the Word of God, who claimed that people must listen to them and learn of them, because they had the truth. They were, in actual fact, cult leaders, outside the fellowship, beyond the pale of genuine Holy Spirit illumination and able only to lead people astray.

c. Looking for Him (2:28–29)

We are not only living in Him and learning of Him, we are looking for Him. As to *the prospect*, there is *a truth to be apprehended:* "And now, little children, abide in him; that, when he shall appear, we may have confidence, and not be ashamed before him at his coming" (2:28).

There are two future comings—the Lord's coming in the air to receive His bride, the church; a later, and final, coming to the earth to reign. The first of these we call the *appearing*, the second we call the *advent*. First He is coming *for* us; then He is coming *with* us. Our meeting with the Lord in the air will be followed by our appearance before the judgment seat of Christ (1 Cor. 3:11–15; 2 Cor. 4:10), and such is what John has in mind in verse 28. How sad to be ashamed when we are thus reviewed.

John remembered the Lord's own teaching about these things. In the Olivet discourse, He portrayed a wise and a wicked servant (Matt. 24:45–51), and in His parable of the talents He contrasted the diligent servants and the dilatory one (Matt. 25:1–30).

The sure way to guarantee being unashamed before the Lord at His return is to "abide *in* Him." That is the way to win His approval when the time comes for us to eternally abide *with* Him.

The Old Testament contains pictures of New Testament truth, and in Genesis 24 we catch a glimpse of the anticipation of the church in meeting Christ. The father (Abraham) sent his servant (a type of the Holy Spirit) to find a bride for Isaac. He discovered that bride in distant Mesopotamia, and her heart responded at once to the question, "Wilt thou go with this man?" "I will!" she said.

Then came the journey home. We can picture Rebekah as she plies the servant with questions, wanting to learn all she can about the beloved so as to prepare her heart for the day when she meets him face-to-face.

We picture her *learning* of him. She must have had a thousand questions about the father's well-beloved son, and the servant delighted to fill her mind with thoughts of him. He would not talk much about himself but would direct her thoughts to Isaac. He would tell her all about Moriah and how Isaac became obedient to death and how he did always those things that pleased the father.

Then, we picture her *longing* for him. As the journey wore on, her life in Mesopotamia would become increasingly a thing of the past, Isaac would become more and more real. She would think upon his name (Laughter) and how he filled his father's heart with joy. Thoughts of him would fill her own heart with joy until, at last, her every thought would be of him.

Finally, we picture her *looking* for Isaac. The servant made her increasingly aware that the journey was almost over and that Isaac would be coming to meet her. She began to give more attention to her toilet and her dress so that, should he come unexpectedly, he would find her ready and with nothing of which to be ashamed.

If that was so in that far-off day, and in that Old Testament type, how much more it should be characteristic of us today. John would have us "abide in Christ," fill our thoughts with thoughts of Him, fill our hearts with eager expectation. For the long journey is almost over. Jesus is coming again. Coming suddenly. Coming soon. The Lord's "be ye therefore ready" is echoed in John's "be not ashamed at his coming."

John adds one more thought. As to the *present,* there is a *test to be applied:* "If ye know that he is righteous, ye know that everyone that doeth righteousness is born of him" (2:39). We know, beyond any shadow of a doubt, that He is righteous, for from the cradle to the grave He was wholly free from sin. In describing the Lord's priesthood, the writer of Hebrews declares that He is "holy, harmless, undefiled, separate from sinners, and made higher than the heavens" (Heb. 7:26). He stands in contrast with ordinary priests, who had to offer sacrifice for their own sins before they could minister on behalf of others (v. 27).

The Lord Jesus challenged His contemporaries to point out one sin of which He had been guilty (John 8:46), and they could find none. On the contrary, they had to hire false witnesses to get even the semblance of a charge against Him (Matt. 26:60). The Roman governor, a shrewd trial lawyer, declared himself unable to find any fault in Him at all (Luke 23:4, 14). The dying thief, impressed at last by the superlative goodness of the crucified Christ, rebuked his fellow malefactor for his senseless abuse of the Lord: "This man hath done nothing amiss," he declared (Luke 23:41). God Himself declared from heaven His own unqualified endorsement of Christ's life (Matt. 3:17; 17:5). Peter, who had known Jesus as well as had John, added his testimony: "He did no sin" (1 Peter 2:21–23).

We know that He is righteous, and we know also that we are not righteous. God's verdict on human life is blunt: "There is none righteous, no, not one . . . there is none that doeth good, no, not one . . ." (Rom. 3:10–18). Paul scours his Old Testament to document this verdict with the Holy Spirit's own words (Pss. 5:9–10; 14:2–3; 19:7; 36:1–2; 53:2–4, 13–18; 140:3; Eccl. 7:20; Isa. 59:7–8).

Thus, when we meet someone that "doeth righteousness," we automatically know that he is "born of him." That is why the Lord Jesus impressed upon

Nicodemus, a respected Jewish religious leader, his need to be born again (John 3:1–10). In developing this theme, the book of Romans teaches us that righteousness is *imputed* to us when we become His (Rom. 4:1–8), and it is *imparted* to us by the indwelling Holy Spirit (Rom. 8:1–4). It is through the miracle of regeneration that it becomes possible for ruined sinners of Adam's fallen race to "do righteousness."

> B. How we show the family life (3:1–24)
>   1. New life in Christ (3:1–10)
>   a. Our high calling as sons (3:1–2)
>   (1) Its commencement in the past (3:1)

Having told us how we *share* the family life, John now shows us how we *show* the family life, and he compares, for instance, our new life in Christ (3:1–10) with our new love for Christ (3:11–24). He compares also our high calling as sons (3:1–2) with our holy conduct as saints (3:3–10).

First John 3:1–3 is one of the superlative passages of Scripture. Virtually inexhaustible, it reveals new depths of meaning every time we come back to it.

Our new life in Christ commenced in the unfathomable past with the love that sought us: "Behold, what manner of love the Father hath bestowed upon us, that we should be called the sons of God" (3:1a–b). Here is a love beyond all human comprehension.

Love is not a mere emotion that God feels, nor is it simply something God thinks about and then does. Love is what God is (4:8). It is thus that He reveals Himself in both Old and New Testaments. The first mention of love in the Bible is in Genesis, where God said to Abraham, "Take now thy son, thine only son, Isaac, whom thou lovest, and get thee into the land of Moriah, and offer him there for a burnt offering" (Gen. 22:2). The second mention of love occurs two chapters later: "And Isaac took Rebekah and she became his wife; and he loved her" (Gen. 24:67). From the standpoint of Old Testament typology, then, the first mention of love in the Bible is the love of the Father for the Son, and the second mention of love is the love of the Son for His bride. From the standpoint of eternity, that sums up the whole story. God is love.

The word used for "manner" in the passage at hand is *potapos,* a word primarily meaning "from what country," then "of what sort."[23] Truly there is no coun-

---

23. W. E. Vine, *Vine's Expository Dictionary of New Testament Words,* 1 vol. (London: Oliphants, 1952).

try on earth characterized by such love as that which God embodies and displays in heaven and throughout His vast creation. God's love is thus unique, there being nothing like it, nothing to which it can be compared. One rendering of this passage is "Consider the incredible love the Father has shown" (3:1, J. B. Phillips).

God's love permeates our planet despite the fact of sin and death. Life would be meaningless without love, which reveals itself in all sorts of ways. A father's love for his child is a very protective kind of love, a love that provides and plans and expects little in return. The love of a mother for a child can be very fierce as well as wonderfully tender, often displayed in the wild by animals caring for their young. The love of a child for his or her parents is a charming and beautiful manifestation of love. The love of a brother for a brother has deep bonds, for "blood is thicker than water," as we say. The love of a friend for a friend can be even greater than that of a brother (Prov. 18:24), a love that is illustrated in Jonathan's love for David (1 Sam. 18:1–4; 2 Sam. 1:26). The love of a person for his or her neighbor is often dutiful in nature but is commanded by God, who likewise commands us with godlike compassion to love our enemies (Matt. 5:43). Consider, too, a person's love for his or her dog and, even greater perhaps, a dog's love for its master. So, if we look for it, we shall find love everywhere, even in such a fallen world as this—for God is love and God made the world.

But there is no love like His. His love is eternal, for He loves us with an everlasting love (Jer. 31:3), and His love is unconditional (Deut. 7:8). Too, it is incomprehensible (Eph. 3:18–19), for we cannot plumb its depths, nor scale its heights, nor measure its length, nor encompass its breadth. It is the love that drew salvation's plan (John 3:16), the love that took Calvary in its stride (John 15:13), and from which no power on earth—in hell beneath nor in heaven above—can separate us (Rom. 8:31–39).

Above and beyond all that, God's love is that which "the Father hath bestowed upon us that we should be called the sons of God."

The Father! That was practically a new name for God, the way Jesus used it and taught us to use it. The Old Testament saints knew God as Elohim, as Jehovah, and as Adonai. They knew Him as the Most High God (El Elyon) and as El Shaddai. They knew Him as Jehovah Jireh, Jehovah Nissi, Jehovah Shalom, and so on. But it was Jesus who taught us to pray, "Our Father which art in heaven . . ." Now the name *Father* reigns supreme in our thoughts when we think about God.

About a century ago a volume appeared bearing the endorsement of George

MacDonald, the famous Scottish poet and novelist. It was, in fact, an English translation of a Danish work titled *Letters from Hell* and purported to be the correspondence of a lost soul. He told about his sufferings and loss, his thoughts roaming here and there through the terrible world in which he found himself, and through the tragic world of his past.

> "Was there not something in vanished time," he asks, "something that was called the Lord's Prayer, beginning 'Our Father,' a well of blessing to those who opened their hearts to it? Surely I seem to remember, but yet vainly I try to recall, the sacred words. They seem to be hovering about me as though I must need but say *'Our Father'* and all the rest must follow. I set out to say it but never get beyond the *'Our Father.'* I have sometimes repeated these words ten, twenty, fifty times: but it is quite hopeless: they are empty and meaningless. I just remember that there IS a Father, but that He is not MY Father, and I am not His child. Yet I cannot refrain from racking my spirit with the once-blessed words. My soul is thirsting for their comfort; but I can find no drop of water to cool my tongue."[24]

"Our Father!" It is, indeed, the greatest of all names for God, a name that demonstrates that He loves us. More—He loves us enough to make us His children, to put us in His family, and to do all those amazing and wonderful things for us that occupy such a prominent part of Paul's letter to the Ephesians—an epistle that John had doubtless read many times.

That God loves us so much may well be a source of astonishment to the angels, at least to the fallen angels and the legions of demons that haunt our fallen world. No one has caught this idea better than C. S. Lewis in his book *Screwtape Letters.* In this work, imaginary letters, sent by a senior devil named Screwtape to a junior devil named Wormwood, advise him on how to handle his patient, a human being whom Wormwood is responsible to lead safely into hell. In the course of their correspondence, Screwtape lets the cat out of the bag, warning his pupil that his task is made all the more difficult because the "Enemy"—Screwtape's name for God—"has a curious fantasy of making all these disgusting little human vermin into sons."[25] It may, perchance, be a source of astonishment for evil

---

24. Cited by F. W. Boreham, *Life Verses #5 (Temple of Topaz)* (reprint, Grand Rapids: Kregel, 1994), 40.
25. C. S. Lewis, *The Screwtape Letters: Screwtape Proposes a Toast* (New York: Macmillan, 1961), 17.

spirits that God loves us enough to regenerate us and put us in His family. It is a source of wonder and worship for us.

There are three ways that one can get into a family. One can be *born* into the family in the usual way, which might be called *the life principle,* whereby the life of the parent is passed on to the offspring. Or one can be *adopted* into a family, whereby one becomes a member of a family through *the law principle.* Papers are drawn up and legally executed, and the new family member enters into all the rights and privileges enjoyed by a natural born child. Or one can be *married* into a family by means of *the love principle,* whereby one falls in love with a member of the opposite sex, marries that person, and each marriage partner becomes thereafter a member of the other's family.

To make triply sure that we are really and truly placed in His family, God employs all three principles (John 3:5–7; Rom. 7:4; 8:14–15). Our imaginations are overwhelmed at the thought of all that is involved—here and hereafter—in being members of the royal family of heaven. Let us try, however, to picture the grand parade in glory as God reviews, upon His throne, the saints of all the ages as they all come marching in:

Abel, the first martyr of the faith, and Enoch, the first saint to experience rapture; Noah, mighty victor of the Flood and second father to the human race; Melchizedek, priest-king of God most high; Abraham, heralded as "the father of all them that believe" and known in heaven as "the friend of God"; Isaac, the man who became obedient to death and who is highly honored in heaven for being thus so much like Jesus.

We see, too, Jacob, renowned in heaven as "a prince with God";

Joseph, once the Grand Vizier of Egypt and known as Zaphnath-paaneah— "The revealer of secrets . . . the savior of the world";

Job, of whom it was said—and that to Satan himself by God Himself—that there was none like him in all the earth;

Gideon, "a mighty man of valor";

Samuel, last of the judges and first of the prophets;

Moses, who might have been called "the son of Pharaoh's daughter," and might have become Egypt's next Pharaoh and Egypt's god, had he not had an all-victorious vision of Christ;

David, once called "a man after God's own heart";

Daniel, known in heaven as "a man greatly beloved";

John the Baptist, of whom Jesus Himself said that there was not a greater man born of a woman than he.

But wait! It's our turn now. As we come in, the grandstands ring with cheers and all the hosts of heaven stand. The trumpets sound, the flags are dipped on the towers and turrets of the New Jerusalem, and the herald angel announces our fame. "SONS OF GOD" are we; "JOINT HEIRS WITH JESUS CHRIST," destined to be seated with Him in heavenly places far above all the great ones of Israel, and far above angels and archangels, principalities and powers, thrones and dominions, and every name that is named.

"Behold, what manner of love the Father hath bestowed upon us that we should be called THE SONS OF GOD!" This is love beyond all human comprehension. Such is *the love that sought us,* commencing in the heart of God before ever time began. This love that sought us, however, is also *the love that separates us:* "Therefore the world knoweth us not, because it knew him not" (3:1c). We are living in a very knowing world, a highly technical and sophisticated world. My brother and I exchange books that we have written, the difference being that he can understand mine, but I cannot understand his. He's a pathologist and I'm a preacher. Some years ago he sent me a book of his, titled *The Liver: An Atlas and Text of Ultrastructural Pathology.* He began by saying, "The predominant cell in the liver is the hepatocyte which numerically comprises 60% of the total cell population and accounts for 80% of the liver's volume. There are approximately 250 billion hepatocytes in the normal adult liver . . ."[26] That was about as much as I could understand. After that the book became virtually unintelligible to me.

Such books, on thousands of specialized subjects from astronomy to zoology, pour off the presses every day. When it comes to science, modern humans are enlightened, indeed. But when it comes to the things of God, unless we believe the Word of God and are enlightened by the Spirit of God, we are totally blind.

"The world knoweth us not because it knew him not." No one knew that better than John. "[Jesus] came unto his own," he said, "and they received him not" (John 1:11). If such was the blindness of His own people, how blind indeed were all the rest. "The light shineth in the darkness, and the darkness comprehendeth it not," John wrote (John 1:5), the word used for "comprehendeth" being *kata lambanô,* meaning "to overcome." The world was unable to overpower Him, though it certainly tried. As Peter put it on the Day of Pentecost, "Ye men of Israel, hear these words. Jesus of Nazareth, a man approved among you by miracles and wonders and signs which God did by him, in the midst of you, as

---

26. M. James Phillips, Siria Poucell, Jacqueline Patterson, and Pedro Valencia, *The Liver: An Atlas and Text of Ultrastructural Pathology/No. 1765* (New York: Raven Press, 1987).

ye yourselves also know; him, being delivered by the determinate counsel and foreknowledge of God, ye have taken and by wicked hands have crucified and slain" (Acts 2:22–23). Paul likewise accused the Gentiles, pointing out their abysmal ignorance, for all their vaunted knowledge, immortalized by the Greeks: "We speak wisdom among them that are perfect: yet not the wisdom of this world, nor of the princes of this world . . . for had they known it, they would not have crucified the Lord of glory" (1 Cor. 2:6–8).

"The world knoweth us not," says John. Not surprising since they did not know our Lord. Had they known who *John* was, the last surviving member of that inner circle of a dozen men who had known personally and intimately the Lord of glory, they might have beaten a path to his door. As it was, all they saw was an ignorant Galilean peasant. Those who reject the light of the sun (Christ) will have very little use for the light of a candle (the last of the apostles).

(2) Its continuation in the present (3:2a)

"Beloved, *now* are we the sons of God." That is a positive assertion, thus, we need have no doubts about our salvation. The philosophy of some dictates that they will not know until they die whether or not they are saved. What a dismal view of God's "so great salvation." For the most part, the teaching that we can lose our salvation is based on the misinterpretation of isolated texts and of the warning passages of Hebrews. On the other hand, the expression "once saved, always saved" is attacked because of the poor testimony of some whose lives do not adorn their doctrine. How can anyone become unborn once they have been born—whether into a human family or the heavenly family? Misbehavior in the family circle may call for discipline and the withdrawal of fellowship, but a child is still one's child, even if that child's behavior brings his or her testimony into disrepute.

John reminds us that we have a present tense salvation: "Beloved, *now are* we the sons of God." We have a present tense salvation because we have a present tense God. When God arrested Moses beside the burning bush in the backside of the desert, He said, "I am the God of thy father, the God of Abraham, the God of Isaac, and the God of Jacob" (Gen. 3:6). Thus, God declared Himself to be *the God of the past*—the remote past, going back some 150 years to Abraham's call, and to the recent past, to the time when Moses was born just eighty years before.

When Moses argued with God and asked for some authoritative name to use before Pharaoh, God replied with the awesome words, "I AM THAT I AM" (Exod. 3:14), thus declaring Himself to be *the God of the present,* the immediate and abiding present—the God of the *now*. When Moses reluctantly undertook his mission, God foretold the hardening of Pharaoh's heart and the outpouring upon Egypt of great judgments as well as the resulting emancipation of the Hebrews (Exod. 7:1–13). Thus, He is *the God of the future* too.

So, then, God sees time in a different way than do we. So far as our salvation is concerned, it is in three tenses. God sees the past and both forgives and forgets; He sees our prospects and foretells and fulfills them; He sees our present and frames and fills it, for preeminently He lives in the present tense of time, as His name, the I AM, indicates. The latter is true especially of us—the past has gone from us, and we cannot change it; the future has not arrived, and we have little or no control over it. But the present time touches our lives, one fleeting moment at a time. In the present, time becomes real to us, and it is only the present moment that we can shape and form, upon which we can leave a record, and in which we can do a deed, utter a sentence, act or react, for better or for worse.

The present tense for us is made up of swiftly passing moments or fragments of time. We can remember the past and anticipate the future, but only this present moment is ours. As fast as it presents itself to us it is gone. "*Now* is the accepted time" (2 Cor. 6:2), Paul reminds us. But with God all time is "now." The present moment does not flee from Him, and the future lies before Him as an open book. Since the "now" is what we have, and the now is where God dwells, the now is what is important to us. So "now are we the sons of God"—right now, where we can experience it and in it "live and move and have our being," as Paul reminded the scornful Athenians (Acts 17:27–29).

(3) Its consummation in the future (3:2b–d)

Since we are creatures of time we cannot escape either the past or the future. Thus, John now looks at our future—and it is glorious! John anticipates three things, first mentioning a *hidden mystery:* "It doth not yet appear what we shall be." The words "not yet" stand in contrast with the word "now," but what we are *now*, already, as the children of God foreshadows what lies ahead for us. How we could wish that God had written a dozen volumes to tell us all about the wonders He has in store for us. Paul reminds us of our present limitations in this regard: "Eye hath not seen, nor ear heard, neither have entered into the heart of man, the things which God hath prepared for them that love him" (1 Cor. 2:9). The Holy Spirit has, however, given us some indication that great glory awaits us (v. 10), of which our present salvation is a token.

When I was a little boy my father was a businessman in South Wales. From time to time he had occasion to go up to London on business. If he expected to be away for several days, he would say to us children, "If you are good, when I come back I'll bring you something." Of course we wanted to know what it would be, but he had a pat answer for all such questions: "You'll have to wait and see!"

We would so much have liked for God to have written whole volumes about the afterlife, but for the most part, He simply says, "You'll have to wait and see." Still, we can be sure of this—we have a God of omniscient genius, a God of omnipotent power, and He is never going to run out of ideas for making heaven an exciting place to be.

John next anticipates *a holy moment:* "But we know that, when he shall appear, we shall be like him" (3:2c). The great work of the Holy Spirit right now is to conform us, as much as may be, to the image of God's Son, in anticipation of the time when we shall be like Him in body and holiness for all eternity (Rom. 8:28).

We are going to have a body "like unto his glorious body" (Phil. 3:21), and Paul tells us at some length what a wondrous body it will be (1 Cor. 15:35–58). It will be a spiritual body subject to higher laws and with greater powers than these natural bodies we have right now. It will be incorruptible, immortal, invincible, just like the resurrection body of the Lord. Our new body will never grow old, never get sick, never know the touch and taint of temptation and sin.

We shall be like Him, too, in absolute holiness, able to dwell where He dwells, in a light unapproachable, basking in the blazing aurora of the righteousness, holiness, and perfection of God. The sight of Him, in His splendor, was enough to cause John to fall on his face as dead (Rev. 1:17). All that is about to be changed.

The hymn writer, T. Binney, has caught the truth for us:

> Eternal Light! Eternal Light!
> How pure the soul must be,
> When, placed within Thy searching sight,
> It shrinks not, but with calm delight,
> Can live, and look on Thee![27]

---

27. T. Binney, *The Redemption Hymnal* (Eastbourne, England: Kingsway Publications, 1951), no. 60.

Finally, John anticipates *a happy meeting:* "For we shall see him as he is" (3:2d). John had seen Him as He *was* and also "as he *is*" (on the Mount of Transfiguration). John's gospel does not tell us about it, however, because the apostle had doubtless read the gospels of Matthew, Mark, and Luke and knew they had fully described the Transfiguration. But he had been there, had seen the blinding glory. He had seen the face shining as the sun, the very garments aglow with the light of another world. John had seen Him as He is. He had seen Him after His resurrection, seen Him as He is in the Upper Room. John had seen Him step into the sky from Olivet's brow, and he knew that the greatest wonder of the world to come will be that we shall see Him as He is.

We shall climb the star road to glory and go in through the pearly gates of the Celestial City and make our way down streets of gold. We shall see His ministers as flames of fire, and the wonders of the world from whence He came. We shall see, too, the crystal stream and the tree of life in that land where they have no need of the sun and where time is a fast-receding fragment of eternity. We shall see Him on His Father's throne, and we shall see the cherubim and seraphim, the sinless sons of light, by the countless million, as they hang upon His words and rush to do His will. We shall see Him with our very own eyes. We shall see Him as He is.

And, wonder of wonders, we shall be like Him; like Him for all the endless ages yet unborn; like Him in the glory of His appearance and splendor; like Him in thought and word and deed; like Him in character, conduct, and conversation.

Like Him! It is a life beyond all human comparison. Hallelujah—what a Savior!

    b. Our holy conduct as saints (3:3–10)
        (1) As to our standing (3:3–5)
            (a) A purifying hope (3:3)

For John had not only seen the Lord Jesus "as he is" on the Mount of Transfiguration and amid scenes of glory and splendor beyond the sky. He had seen Him as He was living life on human terms down here in a very dirty world. John had seen Him stoop down to lift little children in His arms, reach out and touch a loathsome leper. He had seen Him feed the hungry multitudes, save a wedding feast from disaster, look with eyes full of tears as a rich, young, eager ruler turned his back on Him and walked away. He had seen Him comfort a ruler whose only little one was sick to death, and congratulate a woman who had dared to touch His garment's hem in search of healing. He had seen Him calmly face a demoniac who was driven by a legion host of evil spirits. He had seen Him face His foes with awesome courage and show them glimpses of their own evil hearts. He had seen Him weep with those who wept and rejoice with those who rejoiced.

John had never known Him to tell a lie or shrink from telling the truth, never seen Him exhibit anything but the most overwhelming love. Nor had John ever known Him to have to apologize for anything He said or did. He was pure, unstained, and holy through and through.

And He is coming again, so that we might be like Him while eternal ages roll. In the meantime, this hope we have of His return—the hope that Paul calls a "blessed hope" (Titus 2:13) is to be a purifying hope. The truth of the second coming of Christ, translated to the practical level, is designed to keep us on our toes—"every man that hath this hope in him purifieth himself, even as he is pure" (as John puts it).

One of the aspects of the Lord's coming often overlooked by those interested in prophecy—taken up as they are with signs, seasons, symbols, and the spectacular—is the judgment seat of Christ. The uniform teaching of the New Testament is that all believers will be brought before that throne to give account (Rom. 14:10–11; 1 Cor. 3:9–17; 2 Cor. 5:10). There, our works as Christians will be reviewed. Some comfort themselves with the thought that praise and rewards will be allotted to one and all. And that is certainly true—the Lord found something to praise in almost all the seven churches (Rev. 2–3) Also dispensed, however, will be rebukes as well as rewards, losses as well as gains, tears as well as triumphs. Thus, Paul envisions not a mercy seat but a judgment seat. Surely we cannot expect Demas to receive the same applause as Titus or Timothy, or Ananias and Sapphira to receive the same accolades as Stephen.

This aspect of the second coming of Christ, in and of itself, ought to have a purifying effect upon our lives. Almost the last word of the Lord before closing the New Testament is this: "And behold, I come quickly; and my reward is with me, to give every man according as his work shall be" (Rev. 22:12).

An even higher motivation, however, should be the thought of meeting the Lord Jesus Himself, personally, face-to-face. How terrible to suddenly be ashamed.

Evangelist A. G. Upham told the story of a young man, recently won to Christ, dying as the result of an accident. One of his friends asked him if he was afraid to die. "Oh, no!" he said, "I am not afraid, but I am ashamed. I have not been able to lead even one soul to Christ."

(b) A present hope (3:4–5)

John follows up his thoughts of that "crowning day that's coming by-and-by" with a reminder of how serious a matter sin is in the life of the believer, here and now. He reminds us of *the commandments of the Law:* "Whosoever committeth sin transgresseth also the law: for sin is the transgression of the law" (3:4). It is true that we are "not under law, but under grace," so far as our salvation and service are concerned, that is, grace is the saving and sanctifying principle under which we operate. Love, not law, is the force that motivates us (Rom. 8:1–4; 13:8–10). Nevertheless, the Law still stands. And although we are not under the Law as a *system*—that aspect of the Law applied to the Old Testament people of God—we are under the Law as a *standard.*

The Law exists to define sin, and Paul defends and extols the Law as such even in the midst of his struggle, as a defeated saint, to be emancipated from its power (Rom. 7:1–25). Plenty of people wish to debate the nature of sin, just as the lawyer, seeking to snare Jesus, demanded a definition of the word "neighbor" (Luke 10:25–37). It is amazing how we trifle with sin, justifying our bad behavior, excusing ourselves even as we condemn others, shifting the blame, watering down Bible absolutes, and so on. Modern psychology has provided us with scores of ways to perform such mental gymnastics. God is not impressed. His law still stands, giving us His definitions of sinful behavior; it expresses His standards of right and wrong, and states the punishments He declares our bad behavior deserves.

So our anticipation of the Lord's return needs to make us more alert to His law. For grace does not change God's holiness, although it emphasizes His love. His holiness burns as brightly and as hotly as ever it did.

John, having introduced the Law, moves on at once to higher ground, reminding us of *the character of the Lord:* "And ye know that he was manifested to take away our sins; and in him is no sin" (3:5). What a contrast! What a "great gulf fixed" lies before us in this verse. On the one side we stand with "our sins," and on the other side He stands with "no sin."

Our sins! We could think of the unclean nature of our sins, of the uncountable number of our sins, of the uncompromising nastiness of our sins. Even the holiest of God's saints have wept over their sins and confessed how deceitful and desperately wicked their Adamic nature really is.

When Moses drew near to Mount Sinai at the giving of the Law, "the fire," "the blackness," "the darkness," and "the tempest" struck terror into his heart.

He was face-to-face with the holiness of God. "I exceedingly fear and quake," he said (Heb. 12:19–21).

When Daniel saw that "certain man" who bore all the marks of deity, "a great quaking" fell on his companions, although they, themselves, did not see the vision, and "they fled and hid themselves." As for Daniel, himself, he declared "there remained no more strength in me, for my comeliness was turned in me into corruption, and I retained no strength" (Dan. 10:4–8).

When Isaiah saw the Lord "high and lifted up" and heard the song of the seraphim, he was overwhelmed by a sense of the absolute and appalling (to him) holiness of God. He who had poured out woes on everyone else—well-deserved woes, indeed—now poured out a woe upon himself. "Woe is me," he cried, "for I am undone; because I am a man of unclean lips, and I dwell in the midst of a people of unclean lips: for mine eyes have seen the King, the LORD of hosts" (Isa. 5:18–23; 6:1–5). He confessed himself a leper, indeed, in need of cleansing.

Simon Peter, even before his fall and denial, had a similar experience. It occurred after an episode of doubt and partial obedience followed by a miraculous catch of fish. Overwhelmed with a sense of guilt and of the awesomeness of the Lord, Peter "fell down at Jesus' knees, saying, Depart from me, for I am a sinful man, O Lord" (Luke 5:8). And the Lord had said nothing at all about sin.

John, later, had a similar experience himself, one he would write into his book of Revelation. There loomed up before him such a vision of the greatness and holiness of the Lord Jesus as caused him to lose all grip upon himself. "I fell at his feet as dead," he said (Rev. 1:12–17).

The reason the Lord does not eradicate our sin nature at conversion is, surely, to keep us humble and to stimulate a growing desire for holiness. For the ever-present and, at times, overwhelming sense of the great gulf between us and Him is the experience of all those who are growing in grace and increasing in the knowledge of God. All of a sudden we catch ourselves reacting badly to a situation or falling into one of the many snares of the Devil. We are ashamed and seek cleansing and forgiveness. The older we get, the more we are aware of the dichotomy between what we are, in our Adamic nature, and what He is in His divine-human nature.

No holier man ever lived than George Müller. One who knew him well said,

His habitual attitude toward the Lord was to treat Him as an ever-present, almighty, loving Friend, whose love was far greater to him than he could ever return, and who delighted in having his entire confidence about everything, and was not only ready at hand to listen to his prayers and praises about great and important matters, but nothing was too great to speak to Him about.

So real was this that it was almost impossible to be enjoying the privilege of private, confidential intercourse with him without being conscious that at least to him the Lord was really present, One to whom he turned for counsel, in prayer, or in praise, as freely as most men would speak to a third person present; and again and again most marked answers to prayer have been received in response to petitions thus unitedly presented to the Lord altogether apart from his own special work.[28]

At the same time his biographer says,

One sentence aptly sets forth a striking feature in his Christian character—George Müller, nothing; the Lord Jesus, everything; in himself, worse than nothing; by grace, in Christ, the son of a King.[29]

But further reason that we continue in sin—even after conversion—is to be reminded of He who cleanses us. "We know," John says, "that he was manifested *to take away our sins; and in him there is no sin.*" How well John would remember the day he first learned this truth. At the time, he was a disciple of John the Baptist. John had suddenly pointed his followers to the Lord Jesus, who was heading in their direction. "Behold," he said, "the Lamb of God which taketh away *[airō]* the sin of the world" (John 1:29).

Perhaps the Baptist was thinking of the Day of Atonement, when the high priest solemnly placed both his hands upon the scapegoat and confessed over its head the sins of the people. Having thus symbolically transferred the sins to the substitute, the priest handed the scapegoat over to "a fit man," who took it away into "a land not inhabited" (Lev. 16). What was done in type in the Old Testament was done in truth at Calvary. As the hymn writer J. Denham Smith puts it,

> Rise, my soul! behold 'tis Jesus,
> Jesus fills thy wond'ring eyes;
> See Him now in glory seated,
> Where thy sins no more can rise.

28. A. T. Pierson, *George Müller of Bristol* (New York: Revell, 1899), 412.
29. Ibid., 411–12.

> There, in righteousness transcendent,
> Lo! He doth in heaven appear,
> Shows the blood of His atonement
> As thy title to be there.
>
> All thy sins were laid upon Him,
> Jesus bore them on the tree;
> God, who knew them, laid them on Him,
> And, believing, thou art free.[30]

(2) As to our state (3:6–10)
    (a) Sin's blindness (3:6–7)

Our *standing* before God is perfect because the Lord Jesus has "taken away our sins." Our *state,* however, may well be imperfect. John now challenges us to make our calling and election sure. He would have us examine ourselves to make sure that we are in the faith (2 Cor. 13:5; 2 Peter 1:10). With John, however, there are no shades of gray. As always, John deals in absolutes. It is not always possible to decide whether a wayward one is a backslidden believer or one who has never been saved at all, that is, a person with a false profession of faith. John's absolutes are designed to pull us up short.

He does so, for instance, in the matter of one's *vision of Christ:* "Whosoever abideth in him sinneth not; whosoever sinneth hath not seen him, neither known him" (3:6). In the light of what John has already said about sin in the life of a believer (1:7–2:1), he obviously is not teaching sinless perfection here. The occasional stumble of a believer does not constitute him or her an unbeliever any more than the occasional conformity of an unbeliever to this or that aspect of God's Word constitutes him or her a believer.

The river Nile provides an illustration. The Nile is the longest river on earth (4,160 miles) and is the only river of consequence that flows from south to north. Just north of the fifth cataract, however, the Nile bends to the west. It continues to bend until, some distance from the fourth cataract and on past that cataract, it is actually flowing south. That, however, is only a temporary aberration. Before long the essential northward flow resumes and continues on to the sea.

The same is true of the believer. The flow of a true believer's life is toward obedience

---

30. J. Denham Smith, "Rise, My Soul! Behold 'Tis Jesus," in *Hymns of Worship and Remembrance* (Kansas City, Kans.: Gospel Perpetuating Publishers, 1960), no. 120.

and faith. Occasional lapses may occur, some of them may even be prolonged. But that is not the main trend. The occasional stretches of misdirected behavior represent an interruption of the general trend toward Christlikeness. Backsliders are never truly happy in their wanderings, because the Holy Spirit will not allow them to truly enjoy their worldliness and carnality. With unbelievers the opposite is true. They do not enjoy the things of God and, sooner or later, off they go into the world they love, the flow of their lives being away from God.

Sinning is not something believers enjoy, and it is something they instantly regret, the reason being that their eyes have been opened to what Paul described as "the heavenly vision" (Acts 26:19), the vision of the Lord of glory. John puts it this way: "Whosoever sinneth hath not seen him." For to see Him is to love Him, and to love Him is to want to please Him, and to want to please Him makes sin unattractive and repulsive. Temporary falls only intensify that vision. The Old Testament puts the emphasis on law; the New Testament puts the emphasis on love. The person who can sin without a sense of shame, and even shock, has never seen Him. John has just finished telling us that seeing Him is the very thing that will make us to be like Him forever: "We shall be like him for we shall see him as he is" (3:2).

In the Old Testament there was "life for a look" at the serpent on the pole (see Num. 21:1–9). The glance saves. The gaze sanctifies (2 Cor. 3:18), Paul declares, in a different context.

But not only the vision of Christ is important, so, too, is the *virtue of Christ:* "Little children, let no man deceive you: he that doeth righteousness is righteous, even as he is righteous" (3:7). If we do not have a belief that behaves, we probably do not have a "salvation" that saves.

John has just reminded us that our advocate with the Father is "Jesus Christ the righteous" (2:1). The capacity of the Lord Jesus always to do what was right set Him apart from all other people who have ever lived. A sinner is not a sinner because he or she sins; a person sins because he or she is a sinner. Believers in the Lord Jesus are declared righteous by God (Rom. 4:1–5), because the righteousness of Christ is imparted to them (2 Cor. 5:21). The indwelling Holy Spirit produces righteousness in us as we cooperate with Him (Rom. 8:1–4).

That's what the Christian life is all about. To the aged apostle it was unthinkable, a contradiction in terms, for a genuine believer not to "do righteousness." The false teachers, who lurk in the background of every verse in this epistle, not only condoned sin, they even made it a virtue. When it comes to righteousness, no wonder John leaves no middle ground!

(b) Sin's bondage (3:8)

Behind these false teachers was the very Devil himself: "He that committeth sin is of the devil; for the devil sinneth from the beginning. For this purpose the Son of God was manifested, that he might destroy the works of the devil." Again we have the stark contrast—righteousness on the one hand, sin on the other; Christ on the one side, the Devil on the other. As the Lord Jesus is the source and the force behind every righteous act of one of His own, so the Devil activates and energizes, through the power of fallen human nature and the inspiration and power of countless demon hordes, the sinful acts of saint and sinner alike.

Sin, however, did not begin on earth; it began in heaven, having its source not in Adam or Eve but in the heart of Lucifer, the son of the morning, the anointed cherub. Thus, sin is an exotic import on our planet, introduced to our world by an invader from outer space, an alien intelligence of vast experience, craftiness, and power. That alien is the Devil, and sin is the Devil's graft in the human soul. "He that committeth sin is of the devil." Just the same we get no license to sin from God.

On the contrary, the Lord Jesus came here to "destroy the works of the devil." The word used for "destroy" is *luo,* meaning to "loose, dissolve, demolish," and is used of the breaking up of a vessel when it is shipwrecked (Acts 27:1). How appropriate. Fallen Lucifer came down here and wreaked havoc, but God is going to smash all his works to pieces. And the Lord Jesus has been chosen as the One to do it. Throughout His early ministry, Jesus made bare His arm in mighty miracles that shook Satan's kingdom to its very foundations, and Jesus' death, burial, and resurrection was a mighty triumph over Satan's organized kingdom on earth and in the heavenlies (Col. 2:14–15). In Revelation, John gives detail after detail of the approaching end-time events that will overthrow the last vestiges of Satan's evil works.

So ultimate victory is all a matter of which family we are in and where our loyalties lie.

(c) Sin's birthmark (3:9–10)

And that victory is not only a matter of whose side we are on; it is a matter of whose seed we are. John speaks first of *the divine seed:* "Whosoever is born of God doth not commit sin; for his seed remaineth in him: and he cannot sin, because he is born of God" (3:9). John is emphasizing one side of the issue. John is the great expositor of the new birth (John 3:1–12; 1 John 2:29; 3:9; 4:7; 5:1, 4). Peter mentions it, too, emphasizing the same aspect of the new birth that John highlights here. Peter says that we are "born again, not of corruptible seed, but of incorruptible, by the Word of God which liveth and abideth forever"(1 Peter 1:23).

Paul, however—though not actually mentioning the new birth as such—explains the mechanics of the Christian dichotomy (Rom. 6–8), and he begins by describing *the principles* of our new life in Christ (Rom. 6:11–7:6): Beginning (Rom. 5:21) and ending with (Rom. 6:23; 7:25), "eternal life by Jesus Christ our Lord," Paul links everything to Christ. There is no question here of a believer losing his or her salvation. Rather, the believer possesses eternal life "through Jesus Christ our Lord." Paul turns indignantly upon those who imagine that our eternal security gives us some kind of license to sin. "God forbid!" he exclaims, or "Perish the thought!" as one translator puts it. We are not free *to* sin; we are free *from* sin. Because we who once were dead *in* sin are now dead *to* sin. Paul gives us a *biographical* illustration of the new life (Rom. 6:3–4) as well as a *biological* illustration (Rom. 6:5).

All this is introductory to Paul's getting down to his first great truth. The believer has two natures: one derived from his natural birth, an old, Adamic, fallen nature, a nature that cannot do anything right (Rom. 3:10–20); the other a divine nature, derived from his rebirth, an eternal, sinless, spiritual nature, the very nature of God, a nature that cannot do anything wrong. These two natures are at war with each other.

Because of Calvary, however, the old nature has been thoroughly dealt with by God. Paul gives illustrations, likening the old nature in the believer to *an old man*—now dead (Rom. 6:6–8); to *an old monarch*—now defeated (Rom. 6:9–12); to *an old marriage*—now dissolved (Rom. 7:1–6).

In order to enter into the good of all this—made real to us by our identification with Christ in His death, burial, and resurrection—we need to "know," "reckon," and "yield" (Rom. 6:6, 11, 13). These are the activating verbs that translate this new life from the realm of belief into the realm of behavior. As we "know," "reckon," and "yield," we allow the Holy Spirit to make the new life real in our experience.

Paul then moves on to *the problem* of our new life in Christ (Rom. 7:7–25); Paul thoroughly understood this aspect of the theology of the Cross, but he could not make it work in practical, daily living. He, therefore, set out to dissect and analyze why this was so.

He begins by looking at himself as he was before he was saved—*a doomed sinner, condemned by the Law.* In spite of all his efforts, he found himself unable to produce a standard of behavior that God could accept (7:7–13). Next he looks at himself now that he was saved, *a defeated saint, conquered by lust.* He did things he did not want to do, left undone things he ought to have done. There was "a law of sin in his body warring against the law of God," to which he gave hearty mental assent. As a result he was being torn apart, like a man tied in a horrible embrace to a rotting corpse (7:1–25).

Suddenly, however, the light dawned. He was still *trying* to produce a standard of behavior that God could accept—and failing as badly as when he was still an unsaved man. The light dawned when he thanked God "through Jesus Christ our Lord." How had he obtained eternal life? "Through Jesus Christ our Lord" (6:23). How could he obtain victorious life? "Through Jesus Christ our Lord" (7:25). Achieving a godly life came by trusting, not by trying.

Finally, he turns to *the practice* of our new life in Christ. Again and again through Romans 8, Paul draws attention to the Holy Spirit, who alone can activate the new life as we accept the death of the old life.[31]

The apostle John does not go into all the theology of the victorious life. Paul's epistles were well known by the time John wrote his letters, and John simply endorsed the fact that the believer has a new nature and that it is impossible for that nature to sin. So long as he yields to that nature, he will not sin. The believer is "born of God," which more than compensates being born of Adam.

John now turns to *the Devil's seed:* "In this the children of God are manifest, and the children of the devil: whosoever doeth not righteousness is not of God, neither he that loveth not his brother" (3:10). In other words, "By their fruits ye shall know them" (Matt. 7:20). A person who claims to be a believer but who does not behave like a believer, especially toward his own brother, is self-deceived.

The classic example is the elder brother in the Lord's parable (Luke 15:25–32). His heart was as far from God as was that of the prodigal in his wildest days. The elder brother's attitude came out in his resentful words to his father: "Thou gavest me no kid that I might make merry with my friends," he complained. Music, dancing, a banquet spread, and all for that scapegrace brother of his. It stirred both resentment and envy in the elder brother's pharisaical soul. He had the far country in his own mean-spirited heart but did not have the courage to kick over the traces like his brother. When the father entreated him, he responded

---

31. See Phillips, *Exploring Romans.*

with surly displeasure. "This thy son," was his contemptuous description of the repentant prodigal. "This thy brother," was the father's unavailing reply.

> 2. New love for Christ (3:11–24)
>   a. The truth of that love (3:11–18)
>   (1) The public execration of that love (3:11–13)

John has been expounding *the new life* we have in Christ (3:1–10), and he moves easily to a parallel subject—*our new love* for Christ. John begins with the truth of that love as revealed by the Lord Jesus. First, however, he shows how that love is sometimes execrated by the ungodly. John begins with *the message:* "For this is the message that ye heard from the beginning, that we should love one another" (3:11).

Love! The Greeks had four words to express love. *Eran,* the word that denotes passion and the kind of blind impulse produced by passion, is foreign to the New Testament. It was not necessarily an evil word, however, for Greek writers used it to describe the love of children for their mother.

The word *stergein* refers to natural affection, the kind of love that has its roots in one's own nature. *Stergein* denotes the kind of love that God imparted to Adam at his creation and is the love that survived the Fall. *Stergein* is the kind of love that holds families together, that gives people a love for their own country. It is expressed in acts of generosity, kindness, and forgiveness. The absence of this kind of love is expressed by the word *astorgos* (Rom. 1:31; 2 Tim. 3:3), and people who are devoid of this "milk of human kindness" are cold, hard, and unfeeling. The picture that results is that of a brutal parent, a depraved person, or one who commits savage crimes. The Greeks also used *astorgos* to describe immoral people who, as a result, were incapable of giving their partners in marriage the nobler kind of love that was their due.

A third word for love, *philein,* occurs forty-five times in the New Testament. This love has to do with friendship, and it expresses the ideas of fondness, affection, liking. It responds to something that we find attractive in another person, something we like about that person because it strikes a corresponding chord in our own hearts.

Philein has its bad qualities, however, and can become selfish. The Lord said of the hypocrites that they loved *(philein)* to stand in the synagogues, or on the street corners, where everyone could see them when they prayed (Matt. 6:5). They loved to be seen and applauded of men.

On the other hand, *philein* is used of the Lord's love for Lazarus (John 11:3, 36). And what an interesting and illuminating sidelight that casts on the Son of God. As man, He had the capacity to cultivate close human friendships.

Before leaving the word *philein,* it is worth noting that this word is used on at least one occasion to describe the Father's love for us (John 16:27). He is fond of us—wondrous truth! The reason is that He sees that we hold the same kind of love for His beloved Son that resides in His own heart.

The chief word for love in the New Testament, however, is that expressed by the word *agapan*—the word John uses here in 3:11 and frequently elsewhere in the epistle. *Agapan* was not used much by classical Greek writers but appears in the Septuagint, the Greek version of the Hebrew Scriptures. *Agapan,* in its various forms, occurs about 320 times in the New Testament, where the Holy Spirit endows it with new and higher concepts. Thus, *agapan* is used to describe God's love for us (John 3:16), and Paul eulogized this love in his great poem (1 Cor. 13).

The two words, *philein* and *agapan,* are not used indiscriminately in the New Testament but with absolute precision. And that precision can be depended upon, because the very words of Scripture were—in the original, autographed documents—"God breathed" (1 Cor. 2:13). *Agapan* is never used, for instance, of man's love for God, but in contrast, *philein* and *agapan* are used of God's love for us. When we are told to love our enemies, God uses the word *agapan,* not *philein.* The word *agapan* is never used of an improper love, while *philein* sometimes is. The word used when men are commanded to love their wives (Eph. 5:25) is *agapan.* Wuest points out that the unsaved husband can love his wife in three ways: he can have *eran,* a passionate, sexual love for her; he can have *philein,* a fond affection for her; he can have *stergein,* a natural love for her. His love is controlled by his unregenerate nature, howbeit often in its most refined and disciplined form. The saved husband is controlled by the divine nature and, when fully yielded to the indwelling Holy Spirit, a husband can love his wife with an *agapan* type of love—a love that can purify and sanctify and elevate the lesser forms of love.[32] Nowhere is the contrast between *philein* and *agapan* more evident in the New Testament than in the Lord's exchange with Peter after the Resurrection on the shore of Lake Galilee. There, the Lord was intent upon bringing Peter back to full commitment. Jesus used the word *agapan* twice and *philein* once. Peter, with his recent threefold denial of the Lord on his conscience, could not bring himself to rise to the word *agapan.*

---

32. See Kenneth S. Wuest, "Four Greek Words for Love," *Bibliotheca Sacra* (July 1959): 27.

Rather, he used the lower word *philein* three times (John 21:15–19). How well John would recall the whole incident!

Thus, John tells us we should "love one another." We should love each other with the *agapan* kind of love that God bestows upon us and, as one of the fruits of the Spirit (Gal. 5:22), is produced in us. That's the message.

The second method of execrating love is *the murder:* "Not as Cain, who was of that wicked one, and slew his brother. And wherefore slew he him? Because his own works were evil, and his brother's righteous" (3:12). John takes us back to the beginning, to the first brothers. Most people would not describe Cain's works as evil, for, after all, he was being religious. Indeed, he had just founded a religion—the world's first false religion—based upon good works, self-effort, and human merit, but one that was quite contrary to the revealed truth of God.

And what was Abel doing that constituted him righteous in contrast with his brother? He was living by faith, looking ahead to Calvary, basing salvation upon the shed blood of an atoning sacrifice.

But this is the very reason why the world hates the child of God. Satan, the father of lies (John 8:44), is a genius at inventing false religions, and the great lie at the heart of all the world's false religions is that salvation has to be purchased by penance, pilgrimage, privation, and payment. In other words, the world says that salvation is by works. God says it is through grace, by faith, "not of works lest any man should boast." The truth of God is inimical to the spirit of this world. Cain could not forgive Abel because God readily accepted his offering and rejected Cain's offering out of hand. Just so, the world cannot forgive us for repudiating its religions in order to be accepted by God through Christ.

A great religious lie, inspired by the Evil One and espoused by Cain, was the root cause of Cain's hatred of Abel. He wasted no time in murdering his brother, who thus became the first in a long trail of martyrs. The spirit of the world is activated by lies, for Satan is a liar. The very idiom of his language is the lie. Moreover, he was a murderer from the beginning (John 8:44).

The final way for love to be execrated is *the marvel:* "Marvel not, my brethren, if the world hate you" (3:13). One would have thought that the world would have been thrilled when God sent His only begotten and beloved Son into this world, born of the Virgin Mary, conceived of the Holy Spirit, to become one of us. Surely the world should have delighted in this One who "went about doing good," who healed its sick, cleansed its lepers, fed its hungry multitudes, and even raised its dead. But no. It hated Him because He was good. It hated Him because He told the truth, even when it hurt, because He saw through life's little disguises, exposing its humbug and hypocrisy. The common people heard Him gladly, but the establishment made up its mind, almost from the start, to get rid of Him one way or another. We ought not to marvel at that.

Nor should we marvel that the world hates us too. We ought rather to marvel when it doesn't and search our souls to see if we are compromising with its ways. The popular notion today is to devise a "hearer-friendly" gospel, one that says what the world wants to hear and that avoids plain preaching on sin and death and hell. But the Old Testament prophets preached no such gospel. Nor did the Lord Jesus—denouncing the religious leaders of His day as serpents, as whited sepulchers full of dead men's bones, and as hypocrites (Matt. 23)—attempt to stroke the world's fur the right way. And because the church followed its Founder, for its first three centuries it endured the full, fierce force of this world's hate. Nearly all of John's colleagues in the ministry had been persecuted and martyred.

John himself had tasted persecution. Tertullian is credited with stating that John was in Rome with Peter and was in great peril. One tradition is that John was condemned to death by being boiled in oil but was delivered miraculously. Fourteen years after the Neronic persecution, the emperor Domitian launched a second one, and John was banished to the penal isle of Patmos. There he wrote the book of Revelation. When Domitian was put to death and his cruel edicts annulled by the Senate, John returned to Ephesus, where he remained until the time of the emperor Trajan. Thereafter, he labored at the task of founding churches and died of old age in A.D. 86.

Love. Love incarnate, wrapped around with warm and vibrant life and made flesh, love beyond all thought, indescribable, indestructible, in human form. The love of God in Christ—and it was execrated. Such is the world system under Satan.

(2) The personal experience of that love (3:14–15)

But not execrated by all. Love is, in fact, embraced and experienced by many. John reminds us of *what we know* about love: "We know that we have passed from death unto life, because we love the brethren. He that loveth not his brother abideth in death" (3:14).

How well the aged apostle remembered the heartbeat of the infant Pentecostal church. In those days all that believed were together and had all things in common; and sold their possessions and goods, and parted them to all men, as every man had need (Acts 4:32–35). Barnabas, for example, a Levite from Cyprus, sold his land and put the proceeds at the apostles' feet (Acts 4:36–37). Nor were any who lacked, for "as many as were possessors of lands or houses sold them, and brought the prices of the things that were sold, and laid them at the apostles' feet: and distribution was made unto every man according as he had need" (Acts 4:34–35). In the infant church, their policy was share and share alike, a practical application of the Lord's challenge to the rich young ruler: "If thou wilt be perfect, go and sell that thou hast, and give to the poor, and thou shalt have treasure in heaven: and come and follow me" (Matt. 19:21). That statement was too strong a medicine for him, however, and he "went away sorrowful: for he had great possessions," thus proving that he neither loved his neighbor as himself, as he had claimed, nor loved God above all else. Doubtless, John could still see the look of shock and shame on the young man's face as he turned away from Jesus. And doubtless he remembered the conversation that followed.

Such selfless sharing, which characterized the infant church, could only last so long as the Lord's people loved each other with that highest kind of love. The first crack appeared in the deception practiced by Ananias and Sapphira (Acts 5:1–11), and it was widened in the dispute between Hellenist and Hebrew Jewish believers over the way funds were being shared. That crisis was averted by the spiritual counsel of the apostles (Acts 6:1–6), but the handwriting was on the wall.

Still, the fact remained, one way a person could know that he or she had been born again and was in the family of God was by that person's newfound love for other believers. The fellowship of the church is an extraordinary affair, bringing together rich and poor, master and servant, men and women, old and young, gifted and retarded, strong and weak, Jews and Gentiles. All one in Christ, they blend hearts and voices in the worship of Him who loves each and every one with an everlasting love.

But what about those who, somehow or other, get their names on the church roll but who have no love for the brethren? John is unerring in putting finger on their problem. "He that loveth not his brother abideth in death."

John doubtless had in mind what had happened in the Upper Room on the night of the Lord's betrayal. The Lord had bluntly stated that there was a traitor in their midst. The horrified disciples, knowing the treachery of their own hearts, had chorused out, "Is it I?" Judas had said the same, with the blood money lying in his purse. At last Judas had left, pretending to the end to be one of them. Then the Lord had poured out His heart to the others. John remembered Him saying, "By this shall all men know that you are my disciples, if you have love one for another" (John 13:35). Judas had betrayed himself; he had no love, either for the Master or for the brethren.

John reminds us further of *what we show* in regard to love: "Whosoever hateth his brother is a murderer: and ye know that no murderer hath eternal life abiding in him" (3:15). That's very strong language, indeed. In the Sermon on the Mount the Lord warns that a murderer is not only the person who actually kills another; the person who is angry with his brother is a murderer (Matt. 5:22). John follows the same line of reasoning here—the end result of hatred is murder. An act of murder demonstrates that the murderer is devoid of eternal life. And by the same token, hatred—which is the root of the sin of murder—likewise proves that the person who entertains this murderous spirit is devoid of eternal life. Both the fruit and the root reveal the unregenerate nature of such a person.

Paul had dealings with just such a man, and he warned his young friend Timothy about him. The man's name was Alexander, a coppersmith by trade, who, along with a man named Hymenaeus, became an active apostate. Hymenaeus had a busy tongue, claiming that the resurrection of the saints had already occurred, and he had succeeded in overthrowing the faith of some. Paul handed the pair of them over to Satan that they might learn not to blaspheme.

If the Alexander of 1 Timothy 1:20 is the same as the Alexander of 2 Timothy 4:14, which seems likely, then he became a virtual murderer, for when Paul was on trial for his life before Nero, this man spoke up against Paul. Paul warns Timothy, "Alexander the coppersmith did me much evil: the Lord reward him according to his works. Of whom be thou ware also; for he hath greatly with-stood our words." Not long afterward, Paul was murdered by Nero. The man Alexander was an apostate, having once professed the faith but had thrown it over. The heart of Alexander thus stands exposed by his attitude to Paul, an attitude of hatred. As an active enemy of Paul at his trial, Alexander contributed to Paul's martyrdom, and he has Paul's blood on his hands in a lost eternity.

(3) The perfect example of that love (3:16)

John comes back to the positive. He draws his readers' thoughts back to basics, speaking first of *the love of the Christ:* "Hereby perceive we the love of God, because he laid down his life for us" (3:16a); and then he speaks of *the love of the Christian:* "and we ought to lay down our lives for the brethren" (3:16b).

John remembered the Lord's words: "Greater love hath no man than this, that a man lay down his life for his friends" (John 15:13). Jack London, in his famous book *White Fang,* tells about the lengths to which a wild animal will go in protecting and providing for its young:

> The famine broke. The she-wolf brought home meat. It was strange meat, different from any she had ever brought before. It was a lynx kitten, partly grown, like the cub, but not so large. And it was all for him. His mother had satisfied her hunger elsewhere, though he did not know that it was the rest of the lynx litter that had gone to satisfy her. Nor did he know the desperateness of her deed. He knew only that the velvet-furred kitten was meat, and he ate and waxed happier with every mouthful.
>
> A full stomach conduces to inaction, and the cub lay in the cave, sleeping against his mother's side. He was aroused by her snarling. Never had he heard her snarl so terribly. Possibly in her whole life it was the most terrible snarl she ever gave. There was reason for it, and none knew it better than she. A lynx's lair is not despoiled with impunity. In the full glare of the afternoon light, crouching in the entrance of the cave, the cub saw the lynx-mother. The hair rippled up along his back at the sight. Here was fear, and it did not require his instinct to tell him of it. And if sight alone were not sufficient, the cry of rage the intruder gave, beginning with a snarl and rushing abruptly upward into a hoarse screech, was convincing enough in itself. The cub felt the prod of the life that was in him, and stood up and snarled valiantly by his mother's side. But she thrust him ignominiously away and behind her. Because of the low-roofed entrance the lynx could not leap in, and when she made a crawling rush of it the she-wolf sprang upon her and pinned her down. The cub saw little of the battle. There was a tremendous snarling and spitting and screeching. The two animals thrashed about, the lynx ripping and tearing with her claws and using her teeth as well, while the she-wolf used her teeth alone.
>
> Once the cub sprang in and sank his teeth into the hind leg of the lynx. He clung on, growling savagely. Though he did not know it, by the weight of his body he clogged the action of the leg and thereby saved his mother much damage. A change in the battle crushed him under both their bodies and wrenched loose his hold. The next moment the two mothers separated, and before they rushed together again the lynx lashed out at the cub with a huge forepaw that ripped his shoulder open to the bone and sent him hurtling sidewise against the wall. Then was added to

the uproar the cub's shrill yelp of pain and fright. But the fight lasted so long that he had time to cry himself out and to experience a second burst of courage; and the end of the battle found him again clinging to a hind leg and furiously growling between his teeth.

The lynx was dead. But the she-wolf was very weak and sick. At first she caressed the cub and licked his wounded shoulder; but the blood she had lost had taken with it her strength, and for all of a day and a night she lay by her dead foe's side, without movement, scarcely breathing. For a week she never left the cave, except for water, and then her movements were slow and painful. At the end of that time the lynx was devoured, while the she-wolf's wounds had healed sufficiently to permit her to take the meat-trail again.[33]

But the acts of the she-wolf demonstrates only instinctive, *creature* love. What can we say of *Calvary* love?—which will not let us go and is stronger than death? What can we say of the love that drew salvation's plan and of the grace that brought it down to man? What can we say of that love, which, before time ever began, reached out to lost sinners in all the ages of time? What can we say of that love, which is described thus: "While we were yet sinners, Christ died for us" (Rom. 5:8)? When we think of who He is and of what we are, we are simply overwhelmed.

But God's love goes far beyond that. Paul reminded the Ephesians—among whom the aged apostle John now lived—that God "who is rich in mercy, for his great love wherewith he loved us, even when we were dead in sins" has quickened us and raised us up and actually seated us together in the heavenlies in Christ—so that "in the ages to come he might shew the exceeding riches of his grace in his kindness toward us through Christ Jesus" (Eph. 2:4–7). In other words, we are to be an everlasting exhibit to all the universe of how magnificent and magnanimous is God's love. Creation was stage enough for Him to demonstrate God's wisdom and His power. Calvary demonstrates His love.

John's application—if Christ loved us enough to die for us, we ought to love His people, our brothers and sisters in Christ, enough to lay down our lives for them. As we are to be exhibits in eternity of God's great love to us and of Christ's great work for us, so there ought to be some in heaven, in a coming day, who will be exhibits of our Christlike love for His own. It is not given to everyone to

---

33. Jack London, *White Fang,* ed. G. F. Maine (reprint, London: Collins, 1960).

demonstrate his or her love by dying on another's behalf, but it is given to us all to demonstrate our love by living for others. We may not be called upon to give our lives in sacrifice; we are certainly called upon to give our lives in service.

I have two friends, Don and Eddy, who are brothers in Christ as well as being natural brothers. Eddy was an optometrist, and for years, when we lived in the same city, he took care of my vision and also the needs of my whole family. He did so as a labor of love, refusing any remuneration, and he did the same for many others of the Lord's people.

But he was a sick man, suffering from a kidney disease, which became progressively worse. In the end he had to spend considerable periods of time on a dialysis machine. As he grew older before our eyes, it was evident that, without a kidney transplant, he would not live long.

Don was a former missionary, a much loved and greatly gifted Bible teacher, and a radio pastor to a large listening audience. Tests showed that Don's kidneys were compatible with his brother's, but would he be willing to donate one of his kidneys so that Eddy could have a new lease on life? There were risks involved, but Don hesitated not a moment. Of course he would give one of his kidneys!

The operation was performed, and within weeks Eddy was a new man. He went back to work, put on weight, and felt as though he'd come back from the grave. The donor took very much longer to recover. The operation was much harder on him than on his brother. But, in the end, he too was restored to active life and to a renewed ministry.

In "lay[ing] down our lives for the brethren," John has this kind of sacrificial love in mind. For love, after all, is a very practical thing. It is the greatest thing in the world.

(4) The practical expression of that love (3:17–18)
(a) The callous man (3:17)

John moves backward and forward, from the negative to the positive, and back again. He does so for emphasis. As a jeweler displays his diamonds against a black background, so John explains love by means of contrast. "But whoso hath this world's good and seeth his brother have need and shutteth up his bowels of compassion from him, how dwelleth the love of God in him?"

John remembered the story Jesus told about the rich man and Lazarus. The rich man had everything—a magnificent house, garments fit for a king, and he "fared sumptuously every day." The word used for "sumptuous" suggests that he ate in splendor, or gorgeously. But he had five brothers about whose welfare he had some concern.

One thing irritated the rich man—the presence of a wretched beggar, Lazarus, at his gate. The text says that Lazarus was "laid" there. He did not hope for much, just for a few scraps from the rich man's table, the kind of picked-over leavings one would throw to the dog. Moreover, Lazarus was "full of sores," the Greek word for "sores" being *helkos,* which suggests ulcers and comes from a word meaning "a wound." Altogether this man was in desperate need.

The rich man's dilemma was how to get rid of this eyesore. It would be bad for the rich man's image to drive him off his precincts with a whip. But here was a surer way—let him starve. The beggar had one consuming hope—"Desiring to be fed" is the way Jesus put it, and the Greek word means "eagerly desiring." It reminds us of the prodigal son in the far country at the end of his resources, when he "would fain have filled" his empty stomach with the slops he gave to the pigs (Luke 15:16). "No man gave unto him," Jesus said. Likewise the rich man, seemingly, gave nothing to the beggar at his gate, either. He let him sit there until he starved to death.

About the same time the beggar died, the rich man died. He woke up in a lost eternity, his hell being made all the hotter by the sight of Lazarus in glory (Luke 16:19–31).

"How dwelleth the love of God in the rich man?" John would have asked. It didn't. Nor does it dwell in the heart of a professing Christian who has "bread enough and to spare" but who steels his heart against the desperate needs of the poor. And those needs are everywhere. We see them in the slums of our own big cities, and multiplied a thousand times in the appalling ghettos of the Third World.

Recently a preacher visited one of the Caribbean Islands. There, the pastor of the church where he was preaching told him that he was trying to help evangelize some Haitian refugees on an adjoining island. Some of these destitute people had come to know Christ, and with help from the outside they had cleared a piece of vacant land and built a humble meeting place. The neighbors, however, were annoyed at the sight of those vagabonds who congregated, so to speak, in their backyard. They wanted needy people to be around because they would do the most menial and miserable tasks for starvation wages. But the employers expected the hirelings to keep out of sight and live in clapboard shacks. The sight of that humble meeting place near to his property was too much for one of the neighbors, so he rented a tractor and demolished it. The pastor drove the visiting preacher around so that he could see for himself the want and poverty in which these people lived. They had no rights, illegal aliens liable to be deported at any time. Those among them who had a hen or two were considered rich.

Here the visiting preacher was, comparatively, "rich and increased with goods"; there were they, "wretched and poor and miserable." The church in which the visiting preacher was ministering was generous to its guests. But this one declined the money. "No," he said, "give it to those poor Haitians. They need it a thousand times more than I do." We are to be touched to the heart by such needs all about us and then give liberally when our heart is moved.

(b) The compassionate man (3:18)

"My little children, let us not love in word, neither in tongue; but in deed and in truth." For here is another trap. It's easy, when the heart has been moved, to settle for talking about the need instead of doing something about it. We describe some people as being "all talk," and we say, "talk is cheap." The early Christians, however, were nothing if not practical.

William Carey certainly thought that mere talk was not enough. On May 31, 1872, the Nottingham cobbler preached his famous sermon. The text was plain enough, practical enough: "Lengthen thy cords, and strengthen thy stakes; for thou shalt break forth on the right hand and on the left; and thy seed shall inherit the Gentiles, and make the desolate cities to be inhabited" (Isa. 54:2–3).

For some time, God had been preparing Carey's heart. In his workshop he kept a homemade map of the world on which he noted the population, religion, and other appropriate information about the various countries. But he was up against hyper-Calvinism. He broached the question, Is the Lord's command to go into all the world and preach the gospel to all nations still binding? One minister told him to sit down. "When God pleases to convert the heathen," he was bluntly told, "He'll do it without consulting you or me."

Later came his famous sermon: "Expect great things from God!" he cried in conclusion, "Attempt great things for God." The people, however, did not weep in response to the plight of the pagan. They did not even wait. They just stood up as usual and prepared to go. Carey grasped the arm of his friend Andrew Fuller. "Aren't we going to *do* anything?" he cried. "Oh, Fuller, call them back! Call them back!"

All the world knows now how, then and there, the first modern missionary society was formed, how Carey went to Calcutta and how mightily he *did* something about the spiritual darkness of those in heathen lands.

If we love people as Jesus loved people, we will want to *do* something for them. The first question that fell from the lips of the suddenly regenerated Saul of Tarsus, there on the Damascus road, concerned *doing*. He had been blinded by the heavenly vision, yet the vision of the Lord from glory filled his soul. "Lord," he said, "what wilt thou have me to *do?*" (Acts 9:6, emphasis added).

In a coming day, when the remnant of the nations is arraigned in the Valley of Jehoshaphat, they will not be condemned for the terrible things they have done. They will stand convicted for the things they had not done. The record reads thus: "Then shall he say also unto them on the left hand, depart from me, ye cursed, into everlasting fire, prepared for the devil and his angels: for I was an hungered, and ye gave me no meat: I was thirsty and ye gave me no drink. I was a stranger, and ye took me not in: naked, and ye clothed me not; sick and in prison and ye visited me not. Then shall they also answer him saying, Lord, when saw we thee an hungered, or athirst, or a stranger, or naked, sick, or in prison, and did not minister unto thee? Then shall he answer them saying, Verily I say unto you, inasmuch as ye did it not to one of the least of these, ye did it not to me" (Matt. 25:41–45).

Consider the words of Abner to the men of Israel. Abner had made his peace with David and he appealed to the hesitating tribes to make a like move. He said, "Ye sought for David in times past to be king over you: now then, do it" (2 Sam. 3:17). They did, and it was the turning point in the history of those times. That's what John says to us: "Now then, do it!" "Let us not love in word . . . but in deed and in truth." For to say we are moved by a need and to do nothing about meeting that need is to be self-deceived.

b. The tenderness of that love (3:19–22)
   (1) A quiet heart (3:19–21)

John now invites us to take a threefold look at the condition of our hearts. One condition is the *confirming heart:* "And hereby we know that we are of the truth, and shall assure our hearts before him" (3:19). God has various means of giving us assurance of our salvation. Generally speaking, that assurance is founded on the Word of God, the work of Christ, and the witness of the Spirit. Here, John adds the assurance that comes from translating pious affirmations into positive action. Good works are not the ground of our conversion, they are the result of it. And, as such, they help confirm, deep in the heart, that our faith is not in vain, that the root faith is indeed in us.

Second is the *condemning heart:* "For if our heart condemn us, God is greater than our heart, and knoweth all things" (3:20). At times our own hearts make us feel guilty, so John here lifts us above subjective feelings to solid facts—God is infinitely greater than our hearts. On occasion, we let ourselves down, that is, we do not come up to even our own expectations, let alone God's. We discover afresh and with sorrow and shame that the human heart is, indeed, "deceitful above all things," as God declares, and "desperately wicked" (Jer. 17:9). We find our hearts full of pride, anger, bitterness, resentment, lust, and we are tempted at times to wonder if we are saved at all. At such times it is comforting to know that God is greater than our hearts and that our salvation does not depend upon how we feel but upon God. The order in which we experience salvation is fact, faith, feeling. The unalterable facts of history are that God has provided salvation—full, free, and forever—in Christ. Faith then appropriates those facts, making them no longer merely abstract statements of truth but integrating them as part and parcel of our lives. The feelings follow, and we enter into the joy of our salvation. The sevenfold fruit of the Spirit, after all, begins with love, joy, and peace. So, even when we have a condemning heart, God is greater. His salvation takes care of all our sins, including those temporary and regrettable lapses from that higher and holier life to which we have been called.

The third condition is the *confident heart:* "Beloved, if our heart condemn us not, then have we confidence toward God" (3:21). How precious are those moments when we are so at peace with ourselves and with God that we can approach Him with confidence.

In the Old Testament, God taught truth by means of types and symbols. At one end of the tabernacle, for instance, God sat enthroned in all His holiness upon the mercy seat, upon the ark, between the cherubim, behind the veil, in solitary and terrifying splendor. At the other end of the tabernacle stood the sinner in all his guilt and shame. Between them was blood (the brazen altar) and water (the brazen laver). The great question was how could that guilty sinner approach that holy God?

He takes a step or two toward God and comes to the brazen altar and learns that blood had to be shed, that an innocent victim must die. The sinner learns that—because sin is so radical a condition, needing a radical cure—he needs a *radical* cleansing from sin.

Having learned the lesson of the brazen altar, the cleansed sinner proceeds toward God and comes at once to the brazen laver. It was made from the mirrors of the women, so it reveals to him that he has again become defiled, just in taking those few steps. Thankfully his defilement is not only revealed, it can be removed, for there is water in the laver, with which he can remove the defilement he has picked up on even that shortest of walks. He learns now that he needs a *recurrent* cleansing. Thus, as we move toward God, we must be cleansed both by the blood of Christ and by the Spirit-applied "washing of water by the word" (Eph. 5:26).

On the annual Day of Atonement, the process of approaching a thrice-holy God was consummated. On that day, provision was made for the high priest, as representative of all Israel, to enter through the veil into the Holy of Holies itself, observing the most elaborate ritual precautions. With a burning censer in one hand—blotting him out, as it were, by the fragrant, ascending incense cloud—and with a basin of blood in the other hand, he was allowed to approach God. He came to the mercy seat, where God sat enthroned in the glory cloud between the golden cherubim, and with trembling hand the priest sprinkled the blood before and on that throne.

This must have been a terrifying experience. The mysterious Shechinah glory cloud was there upon the mercy seat, the visible token of God's presence. But the priest need have no fear; he could approach with confidence because he had availed himself of the appropriate sacrifice and had brought the blood of the atonement with him. His heart had no occasion to condemn him, and he had confidence toward God. He came in, he performed the required sprinkling, and he came back out. He had seen God—and lived.

All this symbolism is lifted to a higher level in the New Testament. Our Great High Priest has gone into the Holiest in heaven and presented His own most precious blood to God. Consequently, we are "accepted in the Beloved" (Eph. 1:6). The veil has been torn aside, and the Holy Spirit tells us to have "boldness to enter into the holiest by the blood of Jesus, by a new and living way which he hath consecrated for us, through the veil, that is to say, his flesh." We have "an High Priest over the house of God," so we are to "draw near with a true heart, in full assurance of faith, having our hearts sprinkled from an evil conscience, and our bodies washed with pure water" (Heb. 10:19–22).

So, then, "we have confidence toward God." Not because we have done something meritorious but because Calvary takes care of our sin.

(2) A quickened hope (3:22)

We come into the presence of God to worship and to present our petitions: "And whatsoever we ask, we receive of him, because we keep his commandments, and do those things that are pleasing in his sight." That is the secret of getting answers to prayer—asking and doing. God never does for us what we can do for ourselves. "What is that in thine hand?" He asked Moses, when preparing to send him as His ambassador to the court of Pharaoh (Exod. 4:2). "What hast thou in the house?" Elisha asked the widow whose two sons were about to be sold into bondage as payment of her debts (2 Kings 4:2). John himself remembered that, at the raising of Lazarus, the Lord told the others to "take away the stone" from the sepulcher and, later, to "loose him" from his grave clothes (John 11:39, 44). Prayer is no substitute for whatever action we, ourselves, can generate.

George Burns was the founder of the famous Cunard Line, father of the modern ocean liner, pioneer of an enormous oceanic traffic. Burns was knighted by Queen Victoria when he was ninety-four (the oldest baronet ever created) in recognition of his enterprise and success. But it was not wealth, honor, and success he prized the most, rather the church, the Lord's Day, and the family altar.

When other steamship companies saw the success of the Cunard Line they, too, plunged into the profitable business of racing people around the world in luxury. The competition for passengers grew fierce, and soon some of Sir George's rivals were building ships that were faster than his. But he refused to be discouraged. While he considered the importance of speed, with each order that he sent to the shipyards he always considered safety first. Several of his competitors lost ships at sea with fearful loss of life, but the Cunard ships continued to hold the record for safety. Two of his competitors went bankrupt, while the fortunes of the Cunard Line continued to rise. Some spoke of the company's wonderful run of luck. Sir George did not.

"I believe in the power of prayer," he would say, "but I also believe in doing work well, and subordinating profit and speed and public opinion to safety, comfort, and efficiency." He made it his rule not to pray for his ships unless he had done everything that skill, engineering, and ingenuity could suggest in making sure they were safely constructed.[34]

The apostle John believed in the same thing: "Whatsoever we ask we receive of him, because we keep his commandments."

Dr. Adam Clarke, the famous Methodist preacher, theologian, and commentator, wrote an eight-volume commentary on the Bible, the work of forty-five years of writing and publishing. He also wrote a six-volume biographical dictionary. He was, however, a notoriously slow worker, producing his books by long,

---

34. Edwin Hodder, *Life of Sir George Burns* (n.p., n.d.).

laborious toil. A young preacher once asked him how he managed to produce so much material. "Do you pray about it?" he asked. "No," the doctor replied, "I get up!" John would have approved of that.

It is little use praying if we are lazy, careless, and lax in our personal discipline. We cannot expect God to answer our prayers unless we "do those things that are pleasing in his sight."

      c. The triumph of that love (3:23–24)
         (1) The commandment of the Son (3:23)

"And this is the commandment, that we should believe on the name of his Son Jesus Christ, and love one another, as he gave us commandment."

God makes no bones about it. He commands people to believe on the name of His Son, the name that is above every name, the name before which every knee will bow and which every tongue will one day confess (Phil. 2:10–11). God commands all men everywhere to pay homage to that name.

This commandment was given in the Upper Room, and John was there when it was given. As the Lord passed on to His disciples the great truths He had received from His Father (John 14:13–15; 15:12–16; 17:14), so John now passes them on in his turn.

God is very jealous of the name of His Son. That name is honored in heaven but too often is dishonored on earth. The name of Jesus is the last of a series of names whereby God, in days gone by, revealed Himself to men. The greatest name for God in the Old Testament was Jehovah, and it is lamentable that this name finds its way into the King James Version only four times (Exod. 6:3; Ps. 83:18; Isa. 12:2; 26:4).

The Jews stood in exaggerated awe of the third commandment: "Thou shalt not take the name of the LORD *[Jehovah]* thy God in vain; for the LORD *[Jehovah]* will not hold him guiltless that taketh his name in vain" (Exod. 20:7). Thus, they refused to pronounce the name, even when reading the Scriptures, and they actually changed the name in the text to *Adonai* (Lord). That name found its way into the Septuagint, using the word "Lord" instead of "Jehovah." The translators of the King James Version, however, arranged for the divine title "Lord" *(Jehovah)* to be printed in capital letters—LORD. The word LORD, then, in our English Bible, indicates that the original word is *Jehovah*.

The name *Jehovah* itself is a compound word made up of the three tenses of the Hebrew verb "to be." It occurs about seven thousand times in the Hebrew text, occurring first in connection with Elohim (Gen. 2:4) and alone for the first time in Genesis 4:1, 3. The name signifies that He always was, always is, and ever is to come. We have it thus translated and interpreted in Revelation 1:4.

Jehovah is a combination of the three tenses of time, and periods of existence, in one word. First *Yehi* (He will be, long tense), second *Hove* (being, participle), third *Hahyah* (He was, short tense used in the past). Taking the first letters of YEHi (YEH), the two middle letters of hOVe (V), and the two last letters of hahyAH (AH), we have YEHOVAH (Jehovah) in full.[35]

God is both the ever living One and the ever loving One and, as John reminds us here in our text, He reaches out to us. Our salvation was planned in a past eternity, is being worked out in an ever unfolding present, and has its perfect goal in an eternal future. *Jehovah* being God's covenant name, it reminds us that God is immutable. His promises and His purposes are as changeless as He. He is "the same yesterday, and today, and for ever" (Heb. 13:8), loving us with an everlasting love (Jer. 13:3).

John joins the name and the love together. "This is the commandment, that we should believe on the name of his Son, Jesus Christ, and love one another, as he gave commandment."

Dr. A. T. Pierson says, "Were this great name always reproduced in the English, and especially in the New Testament quotations from the Old, it would prove that our Lord Jesus Christ is absolutely equal and identical with the Father; for passages which in the New Testament contain the name 'Jehovah' are so quoted and applied to Him in the New Testament, as to demonstrate Him to be JEHOVAH-JESUS, one with the God of the eternal past, Himself God manifested in the flesh in the present, and the coming God of the future."[36]

In other words, the Jehovah of the Old Testament is the Jesus of the New. John points out that if we believe in His name, we will behave with His nature. The name is *the power that enables,* love is *the proof that ennobles,* and taken together, they sum up the Christian life.

(2) The confirmation of the Spirit (3:24)

The mystical relationship between Christ and the Christian is maintained by the various, supernatural ministries of the Holy Spirit. Here, John summarizes

---

35. Thomas Newberry, *The Newberry Bible* (London: Hodder & Stoughton, 1893), xxii.
36. A. T. Pierson, *Knowing the Scriptures* (Grand Rapids: Zondervan, 1910), 70.

that mystical relationship, telling us of *the saint abiding in the Son:* "And he that keepeth his commandments dwelleth in him, and he in them" (3:24a); and we are told of *the Spirit abiding in the saint:* "And hereby we know that he abideth in us, by the Spirit which he hath given us" (3:24b). Here again, John is drawing upon the Upper Room ministry of the Lord Jesus, His last, long teaching session with His disciples before He went to Calvary. He prayed, "That they all may be one; as thou, Father, art in me, and I in thee; that they also may be one in us" (John 17:21).

There existed a mystical relationship between the Lord Jesus, as man here on earth, and His Father in heaven, and an unfathomable blending of deity and humanity. The Lord Jesus never ceased to be God, yet we see Him on earth acting constantly as man. As God, He was coeternal, coequal, and coexistent with the Father. As man, He knew what it was to be hungry, thirsty, and tired, and as man He wept and prayed, bled and died. Jesus, as God, had the right and power to do all His marvelous works on His own, yet He chose to do them in subjection to His Father. We cannot probe into this mystery, that Jesus was truly God and truly man. Every single moment of every single day He was both God and man, the God-man. And, from the womb to the tomb, the Holy Spirit was involved in the process (Luke 1:35; Rom. 1:4; Heb. 9:14).

This mystical relationship is now carried over to the believer. Moment by moment, day after day, and situation by situation, believers are to make themselves available to the Lord Jesus. And in response, the Lord Jesus makes Himself correspondingly available to believers. And, from the moment of regeneration until the final redemption of the body in resurrection, the Holy Spirit is involved in the whole process (John 3:5; Rom. 8:23).

The relationship goes even deeper—we dwell in Him; He dwells in us. How do we know that? "By the Spirit," John says, "which he hath given us."

God's Little Children— Longing for Home While in the Sphere Where the Father Is Loathed

1 John 4:1–5:21

A. A serious warning (4:1–6)
1. The wicked spirit (4:1–4)
a. The sobering word (4:1)

We are not home yet. We are still in the world, and the world is in the hands of the Enemy. No sooner does John introduce the Holy Spirit (3:24) than he thinks of the evil spirit in whose lap the whole world lies and who is its prince and its god (John 12:31; 14:30; 2 Cor. 4:4; 1 John 5:19).

In a day when so-called "charismatics" avidly seek extrabiblical revelations by means of "tongues," utterances, and spirit-instigated "prophecies," Satan is all too willing to oblige. Thus, John's warning in this passage is potent. Satan's domains are cosmic and extraterrestrial. He has at his command the high but fallen dignities described by Paul as "principalities and powers, the rulers of this world's darkness," fallen angels of great power, intelligence, and ability. Satan also has "wicked spirits" in high places (Eph. 6:12), which likely include the countless demon hordes that infest our planet and outer space. Such are beings of diabolical wickedness and unspeakable impurity, who, moreover, have a craving to inhabit, possess, and control the bodies of men. All these angelic and demonic hosts are allied under Satan to lie, cheat, and deceive the human race.

In the year 1665, the Great Plague broke out in London. In just one week, twelve thousand people were dead. The mortality rate rose so high that it was not at all uncommon for an inheritance to pass to three or four successive heirs in a single day. Grave diggers, usually dead drunk, could not keep pace with the rising tide of corpses they had to bury. In the end, they simply stacked up the corpses outside the stricken houses like so much cordwood.

The dead began to outnumber the living, but nobody knew how to cure people inflicted with the plague. People fled into the countryside and carried the dread disease with them. Farmers and country folk prepared to shoot down refugees who came their way. And still the terrible pestilence spread.

The College of Physicians announced that fresh air was the culprit. They advised people to retreat inside their homes, seal up their houses, choke their chimneys, and burn stinking messes on their hearths, breathing in deeply the foul stench of smoldering filth!

Suppose someone were to have announced that the doctors were absurdly wrong, that the disease was carried by infected fleas and that it was spread by rats that hosted the fleas. Suppose someone, far in advance of his day and age, were to have informed the college that the plague was caused by bacteria, one-celled organisms, minute particles of life so small that thousands of them could find an ample ocean in a single drop of water. Suppose, further, that this person prophesied that in a coming day men would invent instruments, high-powered microscopes, that would actually enable them to see these deadly organisms, and that men would link them to a host of diseases—to anthrax and diphtheria, to syphilis and to gonorrhea, to leprosy, pneumonia, tetanus, tuberculosis, typhoid, whooping cough, and food poisoning. Such a person would have been considered mad.

Similarly, the modern secular humanist discounts as absurd the fact that our planet has been invaded from outer space and that it is held in thrall by an organized, invisible empire of evil spirits, some of them creatures of vast intelligence and power. Our colleges scoff at such information. Man is evolving, we are told, and there is no law of sin. The world of the occult is a world of the weird, the phony, and the deluded, and modern psychology and sociology can solve people's behavior problems. And as for belief in Satan, evil spirits, demons, and the like, well, such notions belong to the Dark Ages. Nevertheless, the Bible is right and the humanists are wrong.

New Agers sense that something is out there in the twilight zone of time and space. They don't realize, however, that they are in danger of becoming the victims and dupes of those man-detesting, God-hating, Bible-contradicting, Christ-rejecting demonic hordes.

But John knew. He had seen the Lord cast out hosts of evil spirits, had cast them out himself. The occult world was real, and serious spiritual perils were to be faced and fought. Even Christians were in danger, especially when they craved the sensational, the supernatural, and the extrabiblical. So he warns of the wicked spirit, one he calls "the spirit of antichrist."

He begins with a sobering word, setting before us, first, *the requirement:* "Beloved, believe not every spirit, but try the spirits whether they be of God" (4:1a). And he gives us *the reason:* "because many false prophets are gone out into the world" (4:1b), false prophets energized by wicked spirits.

We must beware of the incredible gullibility of those who speak in tongues or who listen avidly to those who claim to have the gift of prophecy and who accept without question and as gospel truth the communications they receive. It is bad enough when otherwise intelligent but worldly people attend séances, play with ouija boards, put faith in horoscopes, visit palm readers, and drink in the words of psychics—all such communications being forbidden in the Bible. A great deal of fraud is connected with these practices, as well as the danger of becoming obsessed and even possessed by evil spirits. It is worse when professing Christians dabble in the occult. The modern charismatic movement exposes people to the occult, only it is done in the name of Christianity and of the Holy Spirit. The Holy Spirit here, through the pen of the apostle, warns us not to be taken in. Just because something is tinged with the supernatural does not validate it. We are bluntly warned, as those beloved of God, to be skeptical of all extrabiblical communications and to be wary of accepting them as valid. In this advanced age of Christianity in which we live, the so-called "charismatic" gifts—transitional at most—have long since been withdrawn by the Holy Spirit Himself (1 Cor. 12:14).[1]

The plain, Holy Spirit requirement is "Believe not every spirit." John gives us the reason—"many false prophets have gone out into the world." John remembered the Lord's parable of the wheat and the tares, about the man who sowed the good seed being followed by the enemy, who sowed the tares. "The field is the world," the Lord explained, "the good seed are the children of the kingdom; but the tares are the children of the wicked one; the enemy that sowed them is the devil" (Matt. 13:24–30, 36–43).

The whole purpose of the Enemy is to deceive the human race. The word for "deceive" is found nineteen times in the New Testament and it always has to do with the Devil and his works. The Devil does not destroy God's wheat, because he cannot do so (Luke 10:19). So he imitates it. Wheat and tares look very much alike in the early stages of their growth, but tares are not only worthless, they are poisonous. God sows His children into the world, and Satan sows his counterfeit agents into the same world. Not all unbelievers are children of the Devil, the vast majority are simply unregenerate children of Adam. The "sons of the devil" are those people Satan has taught, inspired, energized, and sent forth as his emissaries. Historically, every time God sends His anointed servants into the harvest field, Satan sows a crop of his own deceivers behind them.

No sooner did God sow the apostles into the world than Satan sowed a crop of Judaizers, legalizers, and Gnostics, along with a bevy of false messiahs—the Jews never had a false messiah until they rejected the true messiah. Then they had a whole rash of them.

No sooner did God sow Martin Luther into the world (1483–1546) than Satan sowed Ignatius Loyola (1491–1556), the Jesuits, and the Countereformation.

No sooner did God sow John Wesley into the world (1703–1791) than Satan

---

1. See John Phillips, *Exploring 1 Corinthians* (reprint, Grand Rapids: Kregel, 2002); idem, *Exploring the Book of Jude* (Grand Rapids: Kregel, forthcoming); idem, *Exploring the Future* (reprint, Grand Rapids: Kregel, 2003).

sowed Deism—Voltaire (1694–1778), with his agnosticism and sneering hatred of revealed religion and biting ridicule; and the deist Thomas Paine (1737–1809), with his praise of the French Revolution and his appeal to England to throw off their monarchy. Both launched an uncompromising, ignorant, and daring attack on the Bible, and both were Satan's tares.

No sooner did God sow C. H. Spurgeon (1834–1892) and D. L. Moody (1837–1899) into the world than Satan sowed another crop of tares—Robert Ingersoll with his oratory and his bitter hatred of Christianity; Joseph Smith (1805–1844) and the even more formidable Brigham Young (1801–1877) and the Mormon cult; Charles Taze Russell (1852–1916) and the Jehovah's Witnesses; Mary Baker Eddy (1821–1910) and so-called Christian Science.

No sooner did God plow up the field and sow into the world the modern missionary movement—pioneered by men like William Carey (1761–1834), often called the father of modern missions; Adoniram Judson (1788–1850) of Burma fame; David Livingstone (1813–1905); Hudson Taylor (1832–1905)—than Satan sowed another crop of false apostles into the world—Karl Marx (1818–1883), whose teaching spawned Soviet and Chinese communism, which has kept millions in atheistic darkness for two or three generations; Sigmund Freud (1856–1939), motivated by a bitter hatred of Christianity, calling religion "the neurosis of humanity," an extension of "the father ideal" as a refuge from fear; Bertrand Russell (1872–1970), a pacifist with radical views on religion and morals; H. G. Wells (1866–1946), whose vitriolic hatred of God and Christianity was coupled with great ability and success as an author; Sir Arthur Conan Doyle, who became spiritualism's greatest spokesman.

God sows good seed. Satan sows tares. God sowed Billy Graham into the world, giving him audiences beyond all those of history, along with the ears of kings and world leaders. At once a counterreligious movement arose, one infatuated with the Holy Spirit, careless of, if not avowedly hostile to, sound doctrine, and marked by outrageous forms of excess. An example of such is manifested by television evangelists and exemplified by the so-called "Toronto blessing," where people under the influence of either mass hysteria or evil spirits gave vent to demonical laughter and barked like dogs—in the name of the Spirit of God.

The enemy moves from one target to another. At one time he attacks the Word of God. Consider the so-called "higher criticism" of a past generation, and that is taught as truth in many seminaries. Consider, too, in our day the bewildering assortment of new Bible versions, so many it's almost impossible for those who use them to determine the true Word of God.

At one time he attacks the person of Christ, denying now His deity and now His humanity. At another time he attacks the Spirit of God, contradicting His plain teaching about Himself in the Bible, or counterfeiting apostolic-age Holy Spirit signs. John, in his day, was battling an assault on the Son of God and on the Spirit of God. His warning was brief and blunt: "Beloved, believe not every spirit, but try the spirits, whether they be of God; because many false prophets are gone out into the world."

>   b. The soundest wisdom (4:2–3)
>   (1) What is demanded by way of confession (4:2)

"Hereby know ye the Spirit of God: every spirit that confesseth that Jesus Christ is come in the flesh is of God." That is the test, and the Holy Spirit demands that we apply it to all utterances of a supposed supernatural nature. "What think ye of Christ?" (Matt. 22:42). That is the acid test.

John was facing the Docetic heresy, a denial of the incarnation of the Son of God. Evidently this false teaching was being propagated not only by false prophets but also by spirit utterances, that is, by "tongues" and ecstatic declamation by those who claimed to have the gift of prophecy. The use of signs was about over in John's old age, for he was the last of the apostles and prophets, and with his writings the New Testament canon would close. The Jewish nation in the Promised Land, for whom the sign gifts were particularly given (1 Cor. 1:22), was now no longer in existence. The unbelieving Jews themselves were scattered far and wide, seeking spiritual consolation in the growing Talmud and becoming increasingly hardened in their rejection of Christ. Thus the need for sign gifts was almost over. With the completion of the canon, the Holy Spirit would point people exclusively to His Word. In John's day, cultists were still claiming to speak in tongues and prophecies by inspiration of the Holy Spirit. Thus, John warns people to be on their guard.

One test of a "tongue," an "interpretation," or a "prophecy" was simply this—what was being taught concerning the person of Christ, particularly concerning His Incarnation? This test was especially important to a church facing the Docetic heresy.

The word *docetism* comes from a Greek word *dokeo,* meaning "to seem," and it occurs a number of times in the New Testament. Docetism was the doctrine that the Lord Jesus Christ did not actually become flesh, but He merely seemed to be a human being. This was one of the first doctrinal heresies to appear in the history of the church. The first known champion of this heresy was Corinthus (about A.D. 85), who is generally believed to have been an Alexandrian disciple of the Jewish philosopher Philo. He taught that Jesus differed from other people only insofar as He was better and wiser than they, and that the divine "Christ" descended upon Jesus at the Jordan and left Him at the Cross. The net result of this pernicious teaching was to make the Incarnation a lie. John, who had known Jesus nearly all His life (as His cousin), and who had become the Virgin Mary's guardian from the time of Calvary, knew such teaching to be a lie. John was energized by the Holy Spirit to expose this false teaching, and he bluntly declares that such teaching came from a lying spirit, the very spirit of antichrist. The essence of this heresy seems to have influenced Muhammad and lives on in some Islamic doctrines concerning Jesus. It has its modern counterpart in various cults, such as Christian Science, which considers matter to be essentially evil.

John demands of everyone—of every believer, of every teacher or prophet, of every tongues speaker, and of every spirit—the unequivocal confession that Jesus Christ is come in the flesh. The Incarnation is as essential to Christianity and the truth as is the crucifixion, the resurrection, and the ascension of Christ.

(2) What will be disclosed by way of confession (4:3)
   (a) What the deceiving spirit is not (4:3a)

"And every spirit that confesseth not that Jesus Christ is come in the flesh is not of God." When a person speaks in tongues or by supposed revelation of the Spirit, the spirit speaking through the medium must always be challenged to make this confession. No lying spirit can make it. God the Holy Spirit sees to that. Lying spirits are very crafty, however, as genuine believers have discovered.

The forerunner to the present-day "charismatic" movement and modern Pentecostalism was Irvingism, founded by Edward Irving (1792–1834), who was deposed as a heretic from the Presbyterian ministry in 1832. Irving and his associates were deeply interested in the gifts of the Spirit, especially tongues, prophecy, healing, and raising the dead. D. M. Panton, author of a number of books and periodicals, including the *Dawn* magazine, attended some of the tongues-speaking meetings of the Irvingites in order to test spirits making utterances. He and his colleagues applied the test demanded here by John and discovered for themselves how subtle, evasive, and deceptive the spirits (naively believed to be the Holy Spirit) turned out to be.

They discovered, for example, that when the spirit who speaking through the medium (often a genuine believer) was challenged to make the confession, it ignored the challenge. That, in itself, was sufficient to prove the presence of a lying spirit, since the Holy Spirit has pledged Himself to make the appropriate answer. When the questioner persisted, "Spirit, do you confess that Jesus Christ is come in the flesh?" the reply was evasive. The spirit would say something complimentary about the Lord, something essentially true, but it would not answer the question itself—again, evidence of the presence of a lying spirit. But the deception went even further. The alerted interrogator would continue to challenge the spirit for a direct answer to the question. When thus driven to the wall, the lying spirit would release the medium and allow the human instrument to answer the question in the affirmative—so that it was not the spirit but its victim giving the appropriate response.

No wonder John tells us what the deceiving spirit is *not*—it is "not of God." It is a lying agent of the Evil One, doing what he does best—deceiving even the very elect. How gullible must they be who attend such services and blithely accept tongues utterances as being of God. Nor does the presence of an "interpreter" prove anything, as the interpreter can be equally deceived. Cases have been reported of people speaking blasphemies and obscenities in "tongues" and of "interpretations" being phony. Truly we need to beware. A so-called "charismatic" experience is no substitute for sound doctrine.

(b) Why the deceiving spirit is named (4:3b–c)

John now names the deceiving spirit by one of the numerous names by which he is identified in the New Testament. The driving intelligence behind all deception is Satan, who has some forty names and titles in the Bible, one of which John gives us here. Indeed, John has named him already in this letter (2:18). He is "the *spirit* of antichrist." John here draws attention to two facts. First, the spirit of antichrist has been predicted: "This is that *spirit* of antichrist, whereof ye have heard that it should come" (4:3b).

The Antichrist will be a person, and he, too, has various names and titles. Daniel identified him as "the little horn," the ruler of the revived Roman Empire in the last days (Dan. 7:7–28)—and as "the king" (Dan. 11:36–45). Paul identified him as "that man of sin" and as "the son of perdition," as well as "that wicked one" (2 Thess. 2:2–10). In the book of Revelation, John calls him "the beast" (out of the sea), and "the beast that was, and is not, and yet is," he who is "the eighth and is of the seven, and goeth into perdition" (13:1–10; 17:8–11). He is also called the beast out of the bottomless pit (11:7; 17:8). A considerable eschatology appears in both testaments about this incarnation of all wickedness in the end times. This Antichrist, a real person, Satan's false Christ, has a coming that has been predicted.

Second, the spirit of antichrist is now *present:* "even now already is it in the world" (4:3c). For behind this monster—who is diabolical, clever, daring, and wicked—is Satan himself. He is "that spirit of antichrist," the one who energizes and indwells the Antichrist, the one who raises him from the dead, inspires him to speak all manner of blasphemies, empowers him to perform soul-destroying, man-deceiving miracles, and guides his career until he controls the whole world.

Throughout history, as far back as Nimrod and the tower of Babel, Satan has been preparing the world for the coming of this one. Time and again he has almost succeeded but each time failed because of the restraining ministry of the Holy Spirit (2 Thess. 2:7). God allows wickedness to rise and then sends a revival, and Satan's schemes are set back for a generation or so. Nimrod, Antiochus Epiphanes (the "little horn" of Dan. 7), Napoleon, Mussolini, Nero, Hitler, Stalin, and others were *types* of the Antichrist. And the same spirit has energized all of them.

Paul could say in his day, too, that "the mystery of iniquity doth already work" (2 Thess. 2:7), that the spirit of antichrist was "even now already" in the world. Only the hindering work of the Holy Spirit has prevented end-time judgments from bursting into full power and fruit in John's day. The restraining ministry has operated on this planet now for two thousand years. Thus, God in His mercy has lengthened out the day of grace. But now, once again, the stage is being set for the coming of the personal Antichrist. However long his coming may be yet delayed, his spirit is already here. End-time deceptions are overshadowing the world once more, possibly for the last time. We can see that the "falling away first," of which Paul writes, is all about us. This time, however, instead of sending revival, God may send rapture, followed by a rapid fulfillment of all end-time prophetic events (2 Thess. 2:3). "Now the Spirit speaketh expressly, that in the latter times some shall depart from the faith, giving heed to seducing spirits, and doctrines of devils" (1 Tim. 4:1). Paul adds that the time will come when "they will not endure sound doctrine . . . and they shall turn away their ears from the truth, and shall be turned unto fables" (2 Tim. 4:3–4).

Those days were already casting their shadows on the closing years of the first century when John wrote; the shadows are much darker and heavier now. Large numbers of professing believers prefer the dubious phenomena generated by the charismatic movement than sound doctrine based on proper hermeneutical principles and sound exegesis.

c. The spiritual war (4:4)

For the end-time war has already begun. Indeed, it had already begun in John's day. John wants us to know two things about this agelong, end-time struggle. First, we are *invincible in this struggle:* "Ye are of God, little children, and have overcome them" (4:4a). The Enemy might be able still to muster his men and put on a fair showing, but the real battle is already over. "We . . . have overcome!" was John's exultant shout. Not even "the gates of hell" can triumph over God's "little children"—what Jesus called His "little flock" (Luke 12:32) in this world (Matt. 16:18).

John also wants us to know: we are *indwelled by the Spirit:* "Because greater is he that is in you, than he that is in the world" (4:4b). In other words, the Devil is no match for the Holy Spirit.

Satan is a creature of great power and skill and of vast experience. Before he introduced the mystery of iniquity into the universe, he was the highest of all created intelligence. He was "the anointed cherub," Lucifer, "son of the morning," the choirmaster of glory, full of wisdom, perfect in beauty, ablaze with gems, with his place on the holy mountain of God, able to walk in the midst of the stones of fire (Isa. 14:9–14; Ezek. 28:12–15). So great was his influence that a third of the heavenly host followed him and now own his power and do his will (Rev. 12:1–5). Though he has become a warped, twisted, and bent one, clothed with titles of infamy, he retains much of his former wisdom and power. Now, however, those attributes are dedicated to wrath, malice, and craftiness. He hates the human race with a passion that beggars description. He wishes us nothing but ill, and he summons all the resources of his being to keep this world in thrall. What he lacks in omnipotence, omniscience, and omnipresence he seeks to overcome by the strategic employment of that countless horde of evil, spiritual beings who own him lord, "prince of the power of the air," and prince and god of this world. He has his unseen agents everywhere, able to assign six thousand of them, in the days of our Lord's sojourn on this planet, to hold captive just one poor human soul (Mark 5:1–13).

John had seen something of Satan's power. The days of our Lord's earthly sojourn had been marked by unprecedented demon activity, as though Satan had mobilized all his infernal resources to oppose and defeat the incarnate Son of God. It was all in vain. Satan was defeated every time, not once, in thought or word, did he win the ghost of a victory over the Lord Jesus. He met the Evil One in the wilderness and overcame him by the power of the Word, demons fled from Him, and when they confessed Him, He silenced them with an authority that has lasted to this day. Disease and death, fruits of the Devil, were powerless before Him. The Lord Jesus, indeed, had come to "destroy the works of the devil" (3:8).

Now the Spirit of God lives in us. He, too, is God, and Satan is as powerless before the unleashed might of the Spirit of God as he was before the exerted might of the Son of God. We have the same weapon that Jesus had—"the sword of the Spirit which is the Word of God" (Eph. 6:17). And although Satan may not be afraid of us, he is desperately afraid of God's Word, God's Son, and God's Holy Spirit. "Greater is he that is in you than he that is in the world."

> 2. The worldly spirit (4:5–6)
>   a. The great divide (4:5–6a)

A great divide exists between those with secular interests and those with spiritual interests. John mentions, first, *those with secular interests:* "They are of the world: therefore speak they of the world, and the world heareth them" (4:5). The world is Satan's sphere of operation. Many are actually lying in his lap (5:19). In the days of the early church a sharp line was drawn between the world and the church. So long as the world turned a scowling face upon those who loved the Lord, it was not hard to visualize the world as a foe. When, however, the world began to turn a smiling face toward the church, it was not so easily recognizable as a foe. For the first three hundred years of its history, *the church was in the world* and faced its fury in wave after wave of persecution. Then as a result of the work of Emperor Constantine, thereafter, *the world was in the church.* And as a result, the church's influence on the world was practically annulled, as was its spiritual power and influence for God. The margin between the world and the church has become blurred today. But in John's day the line was sharply drawn. Thus, John writes in terms of "they" and "we."

"They are of the world," says John, "they" being those who were following the cultists. The christ they preached—a watered down christ, a mere man—suited the world. The world has always been ready to make room for a christ like that, because such a christ poses no threat to this world's policies, pleasures, philosophies, or pursuits. The world has no trouble accepting an emasculated christ such as the one preached by the Jehovah's Witnesses, or a carnal christ as proclaimed by the Mormons, or a metaphysical christ advocated by Christian Science, or a de-supernaturalized christ as presented by the liberals, or a ghost christ as recognized by the spiritists. People who proclaim all such false christs "are of the world: therefore speak they of the world, and the world heareth them." They can thus gather large followings, build massive empires, and appear very successful. But the apostle Paul exposes them: "They that are such serve not *our* Lord Jesus Christ," he says (Rom. 16:18, emphasis added).

On the other side of that great divide are *those with spiritual interests:* "We are of God: he that knoweth God heareth us" (4:6a). Only the person who knows God hears and heeds the apostolic message. Many a person would listen to the aged apostle speaking about the Lord Jesus Christ—the One he had known so well and served so long—and then listen to Cerinthus and his phony philosophical views about Christ. The two Christs were incompatible, so that person would then have to make a decision—take sides. We must still take sides today. That's one reason why God allows cults to arise, to weed out those who are not of God. Those who are of God recognize the truth of God. Those who are not of God sooner or later wander off into open unbelief or into some false teaching.

b. The great disclosure (4:6b)

"Hereby know we the spirit of truth, and the spirit of error." The "spirit of truth" is one of a dozen titles in the Bible for the Spirit of God. The spirit of truth inspired the writing of the sacred Scriptures. But behind all the false cults and religions is "the spirit of error." We do not have to read all the many hurtful and foolish books published by those who advocate error. On the contrary, all we need do is hold fast to the truth.

An anxious passenger approached the captain of the ship on which she was voyaging. The ship was approaching a headland, and the breakers were dashing themselves to foam on hidden reefs on every hand. The passenger asked, "Captain, are you sure you know where all the rocks are?" "No, madam," the captain replied, "I do not know where all the rocks are, but I know where the deep water is!" That's all that is required of us. If we stay with the Spirit of truth, we shall not have to spend much time studying the subtleties and absurdities of the cults.

Recently a flood of near perfect, counterfeit U.S. hundred dollar bills poured into banks from forgers in Iran. The plates for these forged bills appear to have been etched in Germany. The currency of the United States is a favorite target of forgers. Interpol is said to have identified no less than eighteen thousand varieties of counterfeits, a large number of them one-hundred-dollar notes. Most are crude enough, run off on photocopy machines, on inferior paper with poor ink, easy enough to detect. But the Iranian forgeries were in a class by themselves, detectable only by microscopic examination and comparison with genuine hundred dollar bills. The paper used was almost identical to that used by the U.S. Bureau of Engraving and Printing. The printing presses, too, which had unique features to ensure that the bills produced had the right "feel," were of the same kind used by the bureau—said to cost ten million dollars each. As a result, the Iranian forgeries were so like the real thing that most people would not know they were being duped. The situation called for the strongest measures by the United States to protect itself, including a more sophisticated currency and unmistakable warnings to Iran and its colleagues. The Iranian plot was unveiled when an alert teller in the Hong Kong branch of the Republican National Bank spotted something wrong with a batch of one-hundred-dollar bills he was processing. He inspected the currency under a microscope, and sure enough, careful comparison with genuine bills revealed a flaw scarcely visible to the naked eye.

Satan is the master counterfeiter of the ages. It is in the Bible, and the Bible alone, that the genuine currency of the kingdom is found. "Hereby know we the spirit of truth, and the spirit of error," says John. Apostolic truth is to be the touchstone of all teaching in this age, just as "the law and the testimony" were to be the touchstone of all Old Testament teaching (Isa. 8:20). Our task is to know the genuine, so that Satan's forgeries, however sophisticated, may be instantly exposed.

    B.   A spiritual walk (4:7–5:5)
        1. Divine love (4:7–10)
           a. The overflow of God's love (4:7–8)

All true faith is built on the gold standard of love, and that's the standard to which John ever returns. The section of this epistle now opening up before us (4:7–5:5) is John's hymn of love, comparable to Paul's (1 Cor. 13). John begins with divine love—where else could he begin?—telling us of the overflow of that love in our own hearts and lives. More specifically, he tells us *who we should love:*

"Beloved, let us love one another: for love is of God; and every one that loveth is born of God, and knoweth God" (4:7).

That it should even be necessary to tell us so says something about our natural degeneracy. It ought to be obvious and instinctive that we love those who love the Lord. Not just those who are nice to us, or who are useful to us, or with whom we have a natural compatibility—but all those who love the Lord.

Loving others is the one great lesson I learned from my wife. She loved people—all kinds of people—rich and poor, old and young, clever people and not so clever. It made no difference to her—she loved people. I often marveled at her love for people. She would sit for hours with her outsize prayer book on her knees, conscientiously praying over the endless stream of requests that came by almost every mail. Our list of people to whom we sent Christmas cards grew and grew. "We can't drop this one," she would say. "We must send a card to that one." Some of the people on our Christmas card list we hadn't seen for years. She was as keenly interested in their great-grandchildren as she had been in them for years. When she came with me on a speaking tour, she was soon talking to everyone, adding new people to the list of her friends. She gathered information about this one and that one: "Oh, that's Grace Crumplittle. She has bad arthritis." "That's Dr. McSnipp. He teaches surgery in the hospital. His son was killed in a car accident. His wife runs the nursery." And so it went. I wish I were more like her. She was a constant reminder to me that we should love one another, for love is of God; and everyone that loves is born of God, and knows God. When she was dying, she showed her love for me in many ways. For instance, she told me who I should marry when she was gone. In due time I did as she wished—and, lo and behold, her choice was flawless. My second wife is as full of love and good works as was my first one.

John also tells us *why we should love:* "He that loveth not knoweth not God; for God is love" (4:8). There it is at last, the ultimate revelation about God—"God is love." The truth has been there all the time, woven into the tapestry of Scripture from Genesis to Revelation. The Mosaic Law, for all its great principles, precepts, and terrible penalties, is quite unable to hide the benevolence of God. Throughout the Psalms and prophecies, the dark skies of judgment are not able to conceal the rainbow of His love. It was manifest in the flesh in everything Jesus was and did and said, shining out in the Epistles in many a pragmatic demand that we love the Lord and love the lost and love the Lord's own people. Now John writes it down without quibble or qualification—"God is love."

How thankful we can be that the gods of Greece and Rome are dead, that

Mount Olympus has been forsaken of its proud, quarrelsome, lustful, capricious, and vengeful gods. Who could ever feel at home with Jupiter, father of the gods and men, who himself was a creature born? His father was Saturn, described as a monster who devoured his children. Thunder was Jupiter's weapon, and his son Mars gloried in war. Another son, Vulcan, was favored by Jupiter because he forged the thunderbolts that Jupiter hurled. But Jupiter was born lame, an offense that so displeased his mother, Juno, that she flung him out of heaven. And these are but the beginning of sorrows when one thinks of God as the Greeks and Romans thought of god.

Until Jesus came. Now those venal and vengeful gods are gone, banished into a well-earned oblivion by a God who is love. Gone, too, is the Egyptian pantheon of cows, cockroaches, and crocodiles. The fierce, frivolous, and foul gods of the Hindus linger on as an example to the world of the abysmal follies of idolatry. But even these gods stand no chance when their devotees realize that God is not like that at all. God is love.

He suffers long and is kind; He never loses patience, ever seeks ways to help. He knows no envy, is not possessive, does not seek to impress us with His wisdom or His power. He is never unseemly, never controlled by His own interests, never selfish. He is never touchy, nor does He keep score of our faults and failings, nor does He gloat over human wickedness. On the contrary, He rejoices when truth triumphs. He knows no end to His endurance, no end to His trust, no end to His ability to hope, as it were, for the best. He is confident of the certain triumph of His wise and wondrous purposes. Although everything else and everyone else fails, He never fails. He is love. That love has become incarnate in the Lord Jesus. But from all past eternity, and on through the fleeting years of time to eternities not yet born, that is what God is, always has been, and always will be—love!

That is why we should love, because God is love. And His supreme purpose in grace is to make us like Himself. We are to be caught up in the overflow of God's love.

> b. The object of God's love (4:9–10)
>> (1) The expression of that love (4:9)

"In this was manifested the love of God toward us, because that God sent his only begotten Son into the world, that we might live through him." God was not taken by surprise by Adam's fall and the consequent ruin of the human race. That was foreknown before the foundation of the world, before ever the rustle of an angel's wing disturbed the silence of eternity. God knew full well that the human race would need a Savior, and, way back then, the eternal Son of the living God became the great champion of our poor, lost cause. So, "when the fullness of time was come, God sent forth his Son, made of a woman, made under the law, to redeem" (Gal. 4:4–5). Well might we sing,

> Oh, the love that drew salvation's plan,
> Oh, the grace that brought it down to man,
> Oh, the mighty gulf that God did span
> At Calvary![2]

These basic facts of our faith are either the most awesome truths ever revealed or else they are the most outrageous pack of lies ever foisted on a gullible race.

At Bethlehem, One was born who transcended time, One who is eternal, uncreated, and self-existent. He is the second person of the Godhead, the Creator of the universe, and the center of angelic worship. This One had a human mother but no human father. He was the Child born and the Son given of Isaiah 9:6, and in Him was perfectly blended both deity and humanity.

He lived on this planet for thirty-three and a half years, living a life free from any taint of sin. At the age of thirty He began to preach to a chosen people, in a chosen place, and for a chosen period. He went about doing good, performing all manner of miracles and proclaiming truth in a particularly pungent and penetrating form. Above all, He was love itself. He loved everybody, even those who hated Him. He could say, "If you want to know what God is like, just look at Me" (see John 14:8–10). "What He is, I am; what He does, I do; what He says, I say."

The establishment turned against Him almost at once. An attempt was made to murder Him at His birth, and plots were hatched against Him throughout His years of ministry. At last His enemies were successful, hiring false witnesses, bullying the Roman governor, inciting the mob. This glorious person was scourged to the bone, crowned with thorns, mocked, and spit upon. Then He was taken to a place of execution, nailed hand and foot to a wooden cross, and hung up to die one of the cruelest and most agonizing deaths ever devised. Not content with that, His enemies derided Him as He hung, in seeming helplessness, on that Roman tree.

---

2. William R. Newell (1868–1956), "At Calvary," in *Hymns of Truth and Praise* (Ft. Dodge, Iowa: Gospel Perpetuating Publishers, 1971), 322.

The very elements of nature united to protest what was being done on that skull-shaped hill. The earth shook. The rocks rent. Darkness blanketed the land.

Then, God heaped the sin of the world upon Him and, during three hours of supernatural darkness, He became our substitute, bearing our sins in His own body on the tree. Twelve legions of angels poised to put a full and final end to the human race, awaiting only a word. That word never came.

At the end of it all, He sovereignly dismissed His spirit and died. But death had no power over Him. For three days His body lay in a rich man's tomb, untouched by the natural process of corruption and decay. Then He bodily arose! For forty days He showed Himself alive "by many infallible proofs" (Acts 1:3), preparing His small band of followers for a monumental change in dispensations. Then He ascended bodily into heaven, before scores of credible witnesses. He is now "seated at the right hand of the majesty on high" (Heb. 1:3), anticipating a return to this planet in glory and power, watching as the Holy Spirit completes the work He Himself began, and functioning in the meantime as the Great High Priest of all who put their trust in Him.

"In this was manifested the love of God toward us," John says, "because he sent his only begotten Son into the world, that we might live through him." To which we say, "Hallelujah—what a Savior!"

(2) The expectation of that love (4:10)

"Herein is love, not that we loved God, but that he loved us, and sent his Son to be the propitiation for our sins." What did God expect from us? Nothing! Paul says, "For when we were yet without strength, in due time Christ died for the ungodly. For scarcely for a righteous man will one die; yet peradventure for a good man some would even dare to die. But God commendeth his love toward us, in that, while we were yet sinners, Christ died for us" (Rom. 5:6–8). More—it was while "we were by nature the children of wrath . . ." that God "who is rich in mercy, for his great love wherewith he loved us, even when we were dead in sins . . . quickened us together in Christ" (Eph. 2:3–5). When we were yet "alienated and enemies" (Col. 1:21) God set in motion the whole process of reconciliation and propitiation. The entire plan was driven by the force of His love. There was nothing in us to prompt God to love us. God's love is spontaneous and finds its sole and adequate source in Him.

The idea of propitiation is often misunderstood because of the influence of pagan ideas upon our thoughts. The Greeks spoke of propitiating the gods, necessary because the gods had no natural goodwill toward the human race. Goodwill had to be earned, and the gods appeased. Such a notion is entirely foreign to the Word of God, although it is common to many false religions.

Nothing that man can do or say can bring God to adopt a favorable attitude or kindly disposition toward us. God is propitiated because His holy and righteous character has been vindicated by means of the vicarious and expiatory sacrifice of Christ. He has removed our guilt and sin so completely that He can show mercy to believing sinners like us. Love found the way.

Similarly, God is never said to be reconciled to us. All the enmity exists on our side, not His. We need to be reconciled with God, not He with us. He has always been ready to embrace us, and God is immutable, changeless, always the same. He can *act* differently toward those who approach Him, but such action is based solely upon the ground of the propitiatory work of Christ at Calvary, not because He has changed. He can act differently toward the believer because Calvary, having removed our sin and guilt, makes it possible for Him to do so. He always acts in keeping with His changeless righteousness as well as in keeping with His boundless love.

"Herein is love" indeed! Well might we sing—with Isaac Watts as we, with him, survey "that wondrous cross on which the Prince of Glory died"—the words that ought to be our instinctive response to Calvary:

> Were the whole realm of nature mine,
> That were an offering far too small;
> Love so amazing, so divine,
> Demands my heart, my life, my all.[3]

We did not love Him. He loved us. But we love Him now and will go on loving Him, with an ever-deepening warmth and appreciation throughout the endless ages of eternity.

2. Duplicated love (4:11–21)
   a. Its cause (4:11–13)
      (1) God's love perpetuated by us (4:11)

"Beloved, if God so loved us, we ought also to love one another." Of course we should! On the Damascus road, Saul of Tarsus fell in love with Jesus. He saw the

---

3. Isaac Watts (1674–1748), "When I Survey the Wondrous Cross."

print of nails in His hands. He heard the tender tone of His voice. He gave his heart, mind, and will to that glorious "Lord from heaven," as he was mindful to recall Him (1 Cor. 15:47). Paul was willing to speak with the tongue of men and angels to tell the story of redeeming love; was willing to employ the gift of prophecy, to explore all mysteries, and master all knowledge to persuade men; willing to develop such faith as would move mountains. Paul was eager to bestow all his goods to feed the poor, was willing and more than willing to give his body to be burned. Because he was a man possessed and prompted by love.

That love took him from Damascus to Arabia and on to Sinai. There, for three years, he thought through the Old Testament Scriptures in the light of Calvary, and in the process he became the foremost scholar and theologian of the church, one captivated by the love of God.

His newfound love took him back to Cilicia, the scenes of his boyhood days, to preach Christ. That love brought him to Antioch in Syria to help build the church with total disregard for the old Jewish prejudice against Gentiles.

That some love drove him forth on the first great missionary crusade of the infant church, up into the wild Taurus mountains, and on through the Cicilian Gates to Galatia, there to win souls, plant churches, suffer persecution, and face stoning. And it was love that drew him back to establish proper leadership in the infant churches he had just founded, before heading back to Antioch.

It was love that sent him to Jerusalem to fight for the freedom of Gentile Christians from the shackles of Judaism, from circumcision, Sabbath-keeping, and Jewish dietary rules.

It was love that sent him forth again to take Europe by storm, singing when scourged, rejoicing when thrown out of synagogues, and praising God when hounded from city to city. It was love that drove him forth yet once more to strengthen churches planted on previous missions, love that took him to pagan Ephesus to preach and teach the love of Christ, and then move on.

It was love that moved him to collect a great financial gift for the poor saints in Jerusalem, and it was love for the Jews, for Jerusalem, and the Jewish church that brought him back again and again to the religious capital of the world.

It was love for his narrow-minded Jewish fellow believers that took him, against all the warnings and tears of his friends, into the temple courts, in a show of solidarity with those who ran the Jewish church. It was love that bore him through his captivities, that inspired his pen, that won him converts to Christ from the ranks of the Roman guards.

It was love that caused him to witness a good confession before Nero, and an overwhelming love for the Lord Jesus that enabled him to face the headsman's axe with a final shout, "Absent from the body, present with the Lord!"

"If God so loved us," says John, "we ought also to love one another." Paul lived his life according to the logic of that rule. Love for Jesus, love for lost people, love for God's blood-washed saints shone in all his ways. Nothing could stop him—set him free and he turned the world upside down; incarcerate him and he won his jailers to Christ and wrote deathless books filled with soul-saving, life-transforming, mind-dazzling, heartwarming truth. Kill him and you fling wide for him the gates of glory and speed him on his way to the goal and object of his life—Jesus!

Locked in the stocks of the darkest, deepest corner of a Philippian prison, Paul sang and shouted for joy until the prison was shaken to its foundations, and the jailer, shaking in his shoes, was brought into a saving knowledge of Christ. The Jews hated and hounded him, dogged his steps, subverted his converts and plotted again and again against his life, and he said, "My heart's desire and prayer to God for Israel is, that they might be saved" (Rom. 10:1). He faced storm and shipwreck, beatings and scourging, perils on lonely mountain passes, on crowded city streets; he faced imprisonment, injustice, persecution, and death, and what did he say? "I am persuaded that neither death, nor life, nor angels, nor principalities, nor powers, nor things present, nor things to come, nor height, nor depth, nor any other creature shall be able to separate us from the love of God which is in Christ Jesus our Lord" (Rom. 8:37–39).

(2) God's love perfected in us (4:12–13)

First, John sets before us the principle: "No man hath seen God at any time. If we love one another, God dwelleth in us, and his love is perfected in us" (4:12). In other words, just as God was incarnate in Christ, and everyone could see and sense the presence of the invisible God in the character, conduct, and conversation of the Lord Jesus, even so God is now indwelling us. Therefore, people ought to see Him in us by the way we display what He is—love!

God's love is supernatural, not of this world at all. Yet, as C. H. Dodd reminds us, it has planted its feet solidly in this world, and that for two reasons: because real love cannot help but express itself in practical conduct; and the crowning demonstration of love actually took place "one April day about A.D. 30, at a supper table in Jerusalem, in a garden across the Kidron valley, in the headquarters of Pontius Pilate, and on a Roman cross at Golgotha."[4]

---

4. C. H. Dodd, *The Interpretation of the Fourth Gospel* (London: Cambridge, 1953), 199.

That love now dwells in every believer's heart, awaiting its awakening in our submission to the Holy Spirit within. That love will once again be demonstrated in history, and we shall be the agents of it when that happens.

"No man," says John, "has seen God at any time." The word he uses here for "seen" is *theaomi*. It means "to view attentively," differing from the word *theōreō*, which means to be a spectator. Our English word *theater* comes from the same root, and it is used, therefore, of bodily sight. The word *theōreō* puts the emphasis on the object being gazed upon, while the word *theaomi* puts the emphasis on the one doing the gazing, implying the earnest contemplation of the one beholding. We cannot see God that way because He is invisible. But we can see the results of His presence as did Moses (Exod. 33:18–23) and Elijah (1 Kings 19:9–13). To explain to Nicodemus His being unseen yet seen, the Lord used the illustration of wind (John 3:7–9). We cannot actually see the wind, but we can certainly feel it and see its effects.

God has been made visible in Christ—in the theophanies of the Old Testament and the incarnation of Christ in the New Testament. People can see the effects of God's presence whenever God's people show love one to another, and those effects are something that they can feel and behold and contemplate.

Now John sets before us *the process:* "Hereby know we that we dwell in him, and he in us, because he hath given us of his Spirit" (4:13). It is patently obvious that we do not have what it takes to produce *agapē* love, because we cannot live as Jesus lived. Everything that has to do with the Christian life, as defined and demonstrated in the New Testament, is supernatural. Thus, we have been given the Holy Spirit, the third member of the Godhead, to indwell us and reproduce the Christ life in us.

The essayist E. W. Boreham wrote a five-volume set of minibiographies under the general title of *Texts That Made History,* now reprinted under the general title of *Life Verses.*[5] Boreham delved into the lives of dozens of great Christians, found out what biblical passage formed their lives and inspired their faith, and reduced it all to a series of fascinating biographical sketches. David Livingstone's text was "Lo, I am with you always, even to the end of the world." Martin Luther's was "Now abideth faith, hope, love, these three; and the greatest of these is love."

Adoniram Judson's is a fascinating story. To begin with, Judson was an out-and-out skeptic, and a brilliant one at that, an admirer of Thomas Paine in an age when the French and English atheists were in vogue. Young Judson was shaken, however, by the terrible death of a much admired, skeptical college friend. The

---

5. E. W. Boreham, *Life Verses,* 5 vols. (reprint, Grand Rapids: Kregel, 1994).

young man died in soul agony and mortal terror of eternity, and Judson happened to be in the next room. Judson didn't know the dying man next door was his admired agnostic friend—he just heard his screams and cries of terror, and his appalling fear of death. The next morning Judson was shaken to discover the identity of the wretched man next door. Soon after, Judson was saved and his life transformed.

He went to Burma with his bride and arrived in Rangoon in July 1813. The couple lived in a primitive hut on a swamp just outside the town. It was a dreadful spot—the haunt of wild beasts, a place where the city's filth was dumped, and where the dead were buried.

They were not wanted, and their gospel was not wanted. They suffered appalling privation and persecutions. On one occasion, Judson, reduced to a skeleton, was driven across the desert, his back bleeding from the lash, his feet burned and blistered by the scorching sand. On another occasion he was imprisoned, and for two long years he was locked in a foul cell and tormented by every cruelty that could suggest itself to his brutal guards. In the meantime, his wife was left destitute and the house stripped of all its furniture. His oldest girl came down with smallpox and his youngest child was threatened with starvation.

Then a sentence of death was passed upon the missionary. The date was set; the hour drew near. But then Judson was smuggled away, and his wife, now completely abandoned, had no idea where he was or if he was still alive. She herself was scarred and maimed, a living skeleton, shorn of her hair and dressed in rags. Eventually, Judson buried his wife and all his children in that heathen land.

But souls were saved. Judson lived long enough to greet his first convert, establish a church, see it grow to a hundred members, and to translate the whole Bible into Burmese. Then, after thirty years, he took his first furlough.

What, then, was Adoniram Judson's text? What was it that took him to Burma and kept him there? It was this: "To know the love of Christ, which passeth knowledge" (Eph. 3:19). The phrase "the love of Christ" was often on his lips, and it showed ever and always in his letters. "Think much on the love of Christ," he urged his converts. He died with the words on his lips.

But how? How does one think on the love of Christ through such dreadful hardships? By His Spirit! John, the apostle of love, crystallizes the lesson to that. Indeed, were it not for the Holy Spirit, actually called "the Spirit of love" (2 Tim. 1:7), the Christian life would have to be written off as impossible.

>   b. Its confession (4:14–16)
>   (1) The truth of that confession (4:14)

"And we have seen and do testify that the Father sent the Son to be the Saviour of the world." That's another way of telling us that God loves us (John 3:16).

God has, in justice, at times sent His Son into this world to condemn the world (John 3:17)—sending Him into the world, for example, to pour out His wrath upon Sodom (Gen. 18:1–3, 17). The two accompanying angels were sent on ahead to Sodom while the Lord Himself remained behind to hear Abraham's intercessory prayer. Moreover, the angels saw to it that Lot's family was given an opportunity to be saved.

But the Lord Jesus, at His birth, did not come into this world to condemn the world but to purchase salvation for the lost. As they nailed Him to the tree, the Lord Jesus proved He had come to be the Savior of the world by praying for the very ones who did the dreadful deed of nailing Him to the cross (Luke 23:34), thus holding back the ministers of vengeance—twelve angelic legions already poised to obliterate this planet.

The Savior of the world! That is said to be the meaning of the name Pharaoh gave to Joseph. Everything about Joseph reminds us of Jesus. He was the father's well-beloved son, "went about doing good," could say, "I do always those things that please the Father." He was, however, "despised and rejected of men." His kinsmen according to the flesh, the children of Israel, hated him. They hated him for the life that he lived and for the truth that he taught and the future he foretold. They conspired against him and sold him for the price of a slave.

Rejected by his own and handed over to the Gentiles, he was falsely accused and made to suffer for sins not his own. They put him in the place of death, but that prison house could not hold him. He was brought out of that place and exalted to the right hand of the majesty on high. Then he was given that name above all other names before which every knee was made to bow—Zaphneth-paaneah (Gen. 41:45)! That name has been variously interpreted—to the Hebrews, meaning "the revealer of secrets," and to the Egyptians meaning, "the savior of the world." Others say it means "abundance of life," again a foreshadowing of the Lord Jesus, who says to those living under the shadow of death, "I am come that ye might have life, and have it more abundantly."

The exalted Joseph was then given a Gentile bride—a bride, such as others in the Old Testament, who picture Christ and His church. In time, Joseph set about the task of saving the children of Israel. He overruled in their affairs, worked

upon their consciences, dealt with their love of money. He awoke their consciences until, still blind to who he really was, they confessed one to another the
terrible wrong they had done to him so many years before. "We are verily guilty
concerning our brother," they said. Then he revealed himself to them, and they
were overwhelmed. He settled them under the shadow of his wing and spoke of
them to him who sat upon the throne. The years of tribulation having come to
an end, and the children of Israel reconciled at last to him, Joseph turned to the
Gentiles. "All nations came to Joseph," we read. He became, indeed, the savior of
the world.

All of which makes Joseph a magnificent type of Christ. He is the real Savior
of the world, and right now He is enthroned on high, and the Holy Spirit remains down here bringing the word of salvation to all men. He has servants
everywhere, millions coming and finding that Jesus indeed saves from the
"guttermost" to the uttermost. Countless will be the stories told in the ages to
come on that bright and blessed shore.

He has yet to deal with His "kinsmen according to the flesh"—the nation of
Israel. The Great Tribulation lies ahead for them, "the time of Jacob's trouble"
(Isa. 30:7; Matt. 24:15–22), along with the Battle of Armageddon. But He is
coming back to be once more, in a political as well as a spiritual sense, "the Savior
of the world." Israel, purged and cleansed, will dwell beneath the shadow of His
wing, as he reigns "from the river to the ends of the earth" (Ps. 72:8), and all
nations will rise up and call Him blessed. John had heard Him talk about these
things.

(2) The terms of that confession (4:15)

"Whosoever shall confess that Jesus is the Son of God, God dwelleth in him,
and he in God." "Jesus is the Son of God." John keeps stressing this great truth.
"God sent *his Son* into the world, that we might live through him" (4:9). "The
Father sent *the Son* to be the Savior of the world" (4:14). "[H]e sent *his Son* to be
the propitiation for our sins" (4:9, 10, 14). "He that hath *the Son* hath life"
(5:12). And here, "Whosoever shall confess that Jesus is *the Son* of God, God
dwelleth in him, and he in God." We must confess, unequivocally and without
reservation, that Jesus is the Son of God.

Yet one influential pastor-teacher takes the position that "Eternally He is God,
but only from His incarnation has He been the Son; Christ was not Son until His
incarnation." The teaching, known as "incarnational Sonship," has been around

for a long time, and it sounds plausible. The only problem is that it simply is not true.

(3) The tone of that confession (4:16)

It must *ring through our belief:* "And we have known and believed the love that God hath to us" (4:16a); and it must *resound in our behavior:* "God is love; and he that dwelleth in love dwelleth in God, and God in him" (4:16b). God loves us. God is love. We love. God dwells in us. John never gets tired of ringing the changes on this great theme.

For love is what Christianity is all about, winning its battles by wielding the weapon of love, not logic. Although, of course, Christianity is strictly logical. It alone can explain the greatest mysteries of the universe—the problems of sin, sorrow, suffering, and death. It alone has a flawless explanation to such questions as "Where did I come from? Why am I here? Where am I going?" Pagan religions do not have the answer. Philosophy, psychology, and science are soon all out of their depth in these waters. God's Word speaks with authority and with flawless logic.

Still, logic is not that upon which Christianity takes its stand. Lord Beaconsfield (Benjamin Disraeli, one of Britain's greatest statesmen) declared in his book *Coningsby,* "How limited is the force of human reason! We are not indebted to the *reason* of man for any of the great achievements which are the landmarks of human progress. It was not *reason* that besieged Troy: it was not *reason* that sent forth the Saracen from the desert to conquer the world: it was not *reason* that inspired the Crusades and instituted the Monastic orders: it was not *reason* that created the French Revolution. Man is only truly great when he acts from the passions, never irresistible but when he appeals to the imagination."[6]

Christianity goes beyond reason, beyond passion, it goes to the very heart. It takes its stand on love alone—on God's love for us, on the fact that we have now moved into a new home, more fashionable than any mansion on the river of life, near Rainbow Square, on Beulah Boulevard, in Glory. We now live in love, and that means we live in God.

c. Its consequences (4:17–19)
(1) Our boldness (4:17)

---

6. Lord Beaconsfield (Benjamin Disraeli), *Coningsby* (n.p., n.d.).

Now comes one of the greatest statements in the New Testament—a book full of great statements: "Herein is our love made perfect, that we may have boldness in the day of judgment: because as he is, so are we in this world."

"Boldness in the day of judgment!" That in itself is a revolutionary concept, in view of what we are and who is the Judge. Regarding the Great White Throne judgment, the end-time, last-day judgment of sinners, it can confidently be said that not a single person will be bold there. Shakespeare says that "conscience doth make cowards of us all." The wicked dead will no longer boldly utter their former blasphemies and unbelief. They will tremble and cry to the rocks and hills to hide them from the wrath of the Lamb.

But at the judgment seat of Christ, to be convened to deal with saints, some, indeed, will have cause for tears, cause enough to tremble. But some will have boldness. The apostle Paul will be one. He, on the eve of his execution, could say, "I am now ready to be offered, and the time of my departure is at hand. I have fought a good fight, I have finished my course, I have kept the faith: henceforth there is laid up for me a crown of righteousness, which the Lord, the righteous judge, shall give me at that day" (2 Tim. 4:6–8).

And now, as to that outstanding statement, "As he is, so are we in this world," what an astonishing collection of monosyllables! Nine one-syllable words, six of them with only two letters! What could be simpler than that? Or more sublime?

Think first of *the plan:* "As he is . . ." That's what God had in mind all along—that we should be "as he is." As Jesus is.

The life that the Lord Jesus lives today is different from the life that He lived before His incarnation. Back then, He was the eternal, uncreated, self-existing, second person of the Godhead, God the Son. He was omnipotent, omniscient, and omnipresent. He was holy, undefiled, and of purer eyes than to behold iniquity—God over all, blessed forevermore.

John does not say: "As he *was,* so are we." There's a difference between what He was (even in the days that He lived on earth) and what He now *is.* We read that He "learned obedience," for instance, going back to Nazareth with Mary and Joseph and being "subject unto them," (Luke 2:51). He is certainly not subject to them now, although the Roman Church would like to think He is. That is what He *was,* not what He now *is.*

It is recorded of Him that He was "made perfect through sufferings" (Heb. 2:10). Before His Incarnation, nobody ever punched Him, or scourged Him, or mocked Him, or nailed Him to a tree. The idea is unthinkable. But through these astounding things that happened to Him when He lived down here as a man among men, He has now become "a merciful and faithful High Priest" (4:17–18).

It is recorded of Him that He was "tempted of Satan" (Mark 1:12–13). That was then. Never again! Satan fears Him now with a terror that defies description and would doubtless like to put billions of galaxies between himself and that sinless One.

Peter said that Jesus was "a man approved of God among you by miracles and wonders and signs" (Acts 2:22). That is what He was. He was a miracle worker. He healed the sick, raised the dead, cleansed the lepers, cast out evil spirits, and fed the hungry multitudes. The age of such miracles "on demand," as it were, has gone.

John passes over all that, although he knew the whole story so well, because it all related to what Jesus *was* when He lived down here. "As he *is*, . . ." John says. In the first place, He is battle scarred. The hymn writer well reminds us of those "rich wounds, still visible above, in beauty glorified." But all that is behind Him now. Calvary belongs to the past. He has conquered the cross and the tomb forever, but the scars remain.

He is God the Son—uniquely and in three dimensions. He is God's *infinite* Son, the One who ever was, ever is, and ever is to be coequal, coeternal, coexistent with the Father, as God the Son, and so named in Psalm 2:12 and in Isaiah 9:6. He is God's *incarnate* Son, the One who entered into time, "born of the Virgin Mary" but "conceived by the Holy Ghost," of whom the angel said to the mother-to-be, "that holy thing, which shall be born of thee, shall be called the Son of God" (Luke 1:35). He is God's *invincible* Son, the One of whom it is written, "concerning his Son Jesus Christ our Lord, which was made of the seed of David, according to the flesh, and declared to be the Son of God with power, according to the Spirit of holiness, by the resurrection from the dead" (Rom. 1:3–4).

He is also man, man as God always intended man to be—man inhabited by God. He is "crowned with glory and honor" (Heb. 2:6–9), is our "advocate with the Father" (1 John 2:1), and has "sat down on the right hand of God; from henceforth expecting till his enemies be made his footstool" (Heb. 10:12–13). He is welcoming into the family those who respond to the gospel message, taking the keenest interest in the work of the Holy Spirit, down here, who is "calling out a people for his name" (Acts 15:14). Seeing the travail of His soul, He is satisfied (Isa. 53:11).

John, then, is thrilled to see Him "as he is," seated on His Father's throne, a man in a glorified human body, God over all, blessed forevermore. John had yet to see Him as he saw Him later, in the book of Revelation. His immediate reaction to that vision was to fall at His feet as dead (Rev. 1:12–18).

Now comes the astounding part: "*As* he is, *so* are we . . ." Mark the words "as" . . . "so." It is an often used formula of the New Testament. Jesus said to Nicodemus, "*As* Moses lifted up the serpent . . . *so* must the son of man be lifted up" (John 3:14). He reminded His disciples: "*As* the days of Noah were . . . *so* shall also the coming of the son of man be" (Matt. 24:37). Peter wrote to the church, "*As* he which hath called you is holy, *so* be ye holy . . ." (1 Peter 1:15). John says, "*As* he is . . . *so* are we."

For that is the great goal toward which the whole wondrous plan of salvation is moving. We are to be like Jesus.

As noted, the kind of life Jesus lives now is different from the kind of life He lived before His incarnation, inasmuch as He has added a human dimension to His mode of being. Similarly, the kind of life we are now living is not the same kind of life as we lived before we met Christ. All has been changed. God now indwells us by His Holy Spirit. The Lord Jesus who once gave His life *for* us now gives His life *to* us (Rom. 1:2–4). Salvation is not a matter of forgiveness alone. It is a new life altogether, a new life in Christ. The Son of God has become the Son of man so that the sons and daughters of men might become the sons and daughters of God. Now we can be people as God intended people to be—people inhabited by God. As Christ is our advocate, so we too can become intercessors for others. As He has sat down in heaven, so we too are seated with Him in the heavenlies (Eph. 2:6). As He is now confidently expecting the hour of His return, so we too anticipate eagerly that coming day. "As he is, so are we."

But now comes something else that is truly amazing. John does not say: "As he is, *so shall we be,* in *that* world," a statement that, of course, contains elements of truth. He has already said, "When he shall appear, we shall be like him; for we shall see him as he is" (3:2). But John goes beyond that, using the present tense and pointing to the present time: "As he is, *so are we, in this world.*" This calls to mind Paul's magnificent statement: "Whom he did foreknow, he also did predestinate to be conformed to the image of his Son, that he might be the firstborn among many brethren. Moreover whom he did predestinate, them he also called: and whom he called, them also he justified: and whom he justified, them he also glorified" (Rom. 8:29–30), in which all the verbs are in the past tense, signifying that, so far as God is concerned, even our glorification is an accomplished fact.

"As he is, so are we in this world" has to do with our position and with our standing, with how God sees us, not just in the "then and there" but in the "here and now" as well. Sad to say, our state does not always come up to our standing down here. That's why the apostle, perhaps, introduces this astounding statement with a reference to having boldness in the day of judgment (at the judgment seat of Christ, that is). That, too, is why we have been given the Holy Spirit to baptize us and indwell us and fill us and anoint us and do all the marvelous things for us that He is able and willing to do in order to make us like God's Son. It is the Holy Spirit's work to make this statement as true regarding our state as it is regarding our standing—"as he is, so are we in this world."

An illustration of this statement appears in the Old Testament. Elisha had asked the prophet Elijah to give him a double portion of his spirit. Elijah made a promise to Elisha that this blessing would be his so long as he saw Elijah at the moment of his departure to glory. Thereafter, we can be sure, Elisha did not take his eyes off his master nor wander from his side.

In due time Elisha saw the chariot of fire and saw Elijah caught up into glory. Elisha picked up Elijah's mantle and advanced on the Jordan to perform his first Elijah-like miracle and to cross over, dry-shod. Soon others recognized that the spirit and power of Elijah now rested on Elisha. He, indeed, wore Elijah's mantle. Thereafter, as Major Ian Thomas has put it, there was a man in heaven and a man on earth. The man on earth lived the life of the man in heaven, and the man in heaven had once been on earth, treading the path of obedience. The man on earth had observed that life, and now he, too, lived it.

"As he is, so are we in this world." That's the Christian life summed up in nine words. We are to be like Jesus. As the little chorus puts it,

> Earthly pleasures vainly call me,
> I would be like Jesus;
> Nothing worldly shall enthrall me,
> I would be like Jesus.
>
> Be like Jesus, this my song,
> In the home, and in the throng;
> Be like Jesus, all day long,
> I would be like Jesus.[7]

---

7. B. D. Ackley, "I Would Be Like Jesus!" in *Alexander's Hymns No. 3,* ed. Charles M. Alexander (London: Marshall, Morgan & Scott, n.d.), 434.

Some years ago a wealthy Christian woman saw a little ragged, homeless boy gazing into the window of a shoe store. She asked him what he was doing. "I was praying, ma'am," he said, "that God would give me some shoes." The lady took the little boy into the store, summoned a bowl of water, washed the little fellow's feet. She then bought for him a pair of warm socks and put them on him, and then bought him a pair of strong, comfortable boots. The boy, amazed at what had been done, looked at the kind woman's face and said, "Please, ma'am, are you Christ's wife?" That's how to "have boldness in the day of judgment."

(2) Our bliss (4:18)

"There is no fear in love; but perfect love casteth out fear: because fear hath torment. He that feareth is not made perfect in love." John, it would seem, still has the Day of Judgment in mind. Many years before, Moses, in his memoirs, in his last great song before he stepped into glory, pointed Israel to the eagle. "As an eagle," he said, "stirreth up her nest, fluttereth over her young, spreadeth abroad her wings, taketh them up, beareth them on his wings, so did the Lord lead (Jacob)" (Deut. 32:11). Rotherham, in *The Emphasized Bible,* uses the masculine not the feminine. It is the male bird that acts with such astonishing tenderness. What a picture the eagle presents to us of strength in beak and claw. He is majestic and terrible, first seeing life from a nest that is perched higher than other birds fly. Everything about him is awesome—keenness of vision, vast sweep and span of mighty wings, power of rapid, soaring flight. But the *terribleness* of the eagle had not impressed Moses, rather its *tenderness.* He had often seen that monarch of the sky occupy itself with its brood. The little fledgling in the nest would look up at its father's approach, and the fierce beak, the bright, all-seeing eye had no terror for the eaglet. For him, this terrible eagle, with power to rend and rip its prey to shreds, had nothing but love. The eagle presents us with a picture of terrible might combined with tender, brooding love.

Moses used the illustration to magnify God's gracious dealings with wandering Jacob and, by extension, with the wayward tribes of Israel. Jacob knew what it was to be afraid. He had done enough things to make him afraid. He was afraid of his Uncle Laban, pressing hard on his trail, determined to do him harm. And he was afraid of his brother Esau, not far ahead of him, coming to meet him with four hundred armed men. Well, God was able to deal with both Jacob's foes and Jacob's fears. And so He did.

It was a new Jacob who left the Jabbok to meet his brother Esau. The last word he had from Esau was a threat to kill him. But Jacob had now become Israel, a prince with God, and love conquered all. This new, humble Jacob won even Esau's wild heart (Gen. 33:4).

"Fear hath torment," said John. And so it does. Archbishop Cranmer proved the truth of that. He was Henry VIII's archbishop and lived in fear of his terrible king, becoming almost fanatical in his obedience. When Henry wanted to marry Anne of Cleves, Cranmer ruled the marriage would be lawful. Six months later, when Henry wanted to divorce her, he ruled that the marriage had been unlawful. No wonder Henry liked his archbishop! When Cranmer was installed as Archbishop of Canterbury, he took the oath to be subject to the pope. The day before, however, he signed a statement making him subject to Henry. Cranmer spoke against Henry's "Six Articles," which were thoroughly Romish, but as soon as they were signed into law he capitulated.

True, Cranmer had his moments of greatness. His *Book of Common Prayer,* the liturgy of the Anglican Church, was a masterpiece, and his *Forty-two Articles* helped the Anglican Church toward the Reformation. But Cranmer was afraid of Henry VIII, with good reason. Henry is said to have murdered more than seventy thousand people in his long and violent reign. Cranmer was even more fearful of Mary, Henry's Roman Catholic heir to the throne, also with good cause. Mary executed nearly three hundred Protestants, including Cranmer, whom she hated.

While in prison Cranmer, charged with treason and heresy, vacillated back and forth, driven by fear. He was forced to witness the martyrdom of Latimer and Ridley, and Ridley had taken a long time to die. The fallen archbishop's trial was long, and his imprisonment was lonely and severe. He recanted of his Protestant faith five times, the final one being a total capitulation to Rome. No recantation, however, was going to satisfy Mary, who was determined to have him burned at the stake.

His last night came. Before him lay the speech he was to give at the stake, in which he confirmed his renunciation of the truth and exalted the pope. Before him also was another speech in which he renounced the papacy and all it stood for. All that night the battle raged. Which would triumph? His fear of man or his love for the Lord?

In the end, perfect love cast out fear. He determined to remain true to the Lord who had bought him. Fear was slain, and he would be "more than conqueror," as Paul puts it in his great discourse on love (Rom. 8).

Cranmer arrived at the place of execution, still troubled in his soul about the nearly half dozen recantations he had signed when fear had ruled his heart. His now ascending love for Christ, however, taught him what to do. When he was given leave to speak, he first disarmed his foes with his opening words, which voiced the sentiments of his foes. Then he boldly denounced his own former weakness in signing things contrary to that which was in his heart.

He raised his voice, and his words rang out. "Forasmuch," he said, "as my hand offended in writing contrary to my heart, therefore my hand shall first be punished. It shall be the first burned in the fire." Perfect love had cast out fear. Thus, he died, with the flames leaping up around him, and his offending right hand held resolutely in the hottest part of the fire.

(3) Our blessedness (4:19)

John cannot say it often enough. "We love him, because he first loved us." He has loved us with a causeless love. Moses reminded the children of Israel that God loved them simply because He loved them (Deut. 7:7–8). There was no other explanation. Centuries later Jeremiah reminded the Hebrews that God loved them with a timeless love: "Yea, I have loved you with an everlasting love; therefore with lovingkindness have I drawn thee" (Jer. 31:3). When it comes, then, to love and to "the love that drew salvation's plan," obviously, all the initiative was and is with God. God is love! That is the driving force behind the whole divine scheme to provide redemption for the fallen ones of Adam's ruined race. As John has put it elsewhere, "God so loved the world, that he gave his only begotten Son, that whosoever believeth in him should not perish, but have everlasting life" (John 3:16).

Love, however, by its very nature is reciprocal. Nothing, in fact, is more tragic than unrequited love. Surely the most tragic person in the Old Testament was the prophet Hosea. When he was still a young man, God called him to preach to His apostate people Israel. He preached for a long time, possibly between sixty or seventy years.

Soon the young prophet felt his need for a wife, and God confirmed him in this desire. No doubt Hosea had in mind for himself someone like Sarah or Jochabed or Hannah. But then he met Gomer. Her name means "completion," and that seemed to settle it for him. She would be Eve to his Adam.

God told him to marry her, "a wife of whoredoms," indeed. We cannot be sure whether Hosea knew what kind of a woman she was, but he soon found out. In any case, God knew. If Hosea had any prior intimation as to what kind of a woman Gomer was, perhaps he assured himself she would become another Rahab and a true mother in Israel.

But the marriage soon turned sour. When his boy was born, Hosea was told to call him Jezreel, a name weighted down with judgment. Gomer could not have been too enthusiastic about that. In any case, she was getting tired of being married to a preacher. By the time the second child was born, Hosea suspected his wife was leading a double life, and he had strong doubts as to who the father was. By the time the third child arrived, he knew for sure the little boy was not his.

After this, Gomer abandoned all pretense. She left home and took to the streets. Hosea's love, however, remained the same—undaunted. From time to time he caught a glimpse of her as she lived her wild and wicked life, and he noted that she had added a new vice to her lusts. She had become a drunkard. Still Hosea's love held true.

He watched and waited. Then the day came when the wretched woman touched bottom, and she sold herself as a slave. Hosea sought out the man who owned her, he bought her, and took the reeking wreck of womanhood back home. She now belonged to him by right of purchase. He cleaned her up and put her under restraint. Taking the two unfortunate younger children of the marriage, he enfolded them in the embrace of his love. We are not told whether or not Gomer ever responded to the extraordinary love of Hosea. All was a parable of God's love—and the longing of that love for love in return. The tragedy in Hosea's home life became a parable, ordained of God, of the tragedy in Hosea's homeland. The book ends with God saying of the Hebrew people, "I will heal their backsliding, I will love them freely" (Hos. 14:4), and with the added assurance, "Ephraim shall say, What have I to do any more with idols? I have heard him, and observed him" (Hos. 14:8).

So God first loved us. The response of the redeemed heart is best expressed, perhaps, by the little chorus:

> Oh, the love that sought me,
> Oh, the blood that bought me,
> Oh, the grace that brought me to the fold;
> Wondrous grace that brought me to the fold.[8]

---

8. W. Spenser Walton, "Oh the Love That Sought Me," in *Sacred Songs and Solos,* comp. Ira D. Sankey, rev. and enlarged (London: Marshall, Morgan & Scott, n.d.), 59.

(d) Its counterfeit (4:20–21)

John now turns to *the logic of love:* "If a man say, I love God, and hateth his brother, he is a liar: for he that loveth not his brother whom he hath seen, how can he love God whom he hath not seen?" Very blunt! Love and hate are opposites. Love for God ought to expel all hate, even toward the most cantankerous, critical, and contradictory of the Lord's people. No one ever loved God like Jesus. "He went about doing good," was Peter's one-line summary of the Lord's attitude toward people (Acts 10:38). The Lord had His enemies, but He loved them. At times He had to expose and condemn them (Matt. 23:13–39), but He never stopped loving them. He loved poor, lost, pagan Pilate just as much as He loved beloved, blundering Peter. He died just as truly for crafty, unscrupulous Caiaphas as for generous, open-minded Cornelius. He had as big a heart of love for Barabbas as He had for Bartholemew. He wept as brokenly for Jerusalem—which killed the prophets and stoned them who were sent to her—as He did for bereaved and beloved Martha and Mary. He was as eager to save Saul—who "breath[ed] out threatenings and slaughter"—as He was to save the earnestly seeking Ethiopian. We cannot imagine Jesus hating anyone, still less one who belonged to, however unworthily, the family of God.

With John, our feelings toward others are either love or hate. We try to put shades of gray between the two emotions, but John sees love driving out hate and everything in between. The acid test of belief is behavior; the acid test of life is love. I cannot dislike a brother and claim to be in love with the Lord. We want to blur the lines, move to an in-between zone where we can prevaricate and find excuses for our attitudes that are all too often less than Christlike. John refuses to accommodate us. He makes no room for relative morality, for half love. He deals in unyielding absolutes. I can't say I love God while harboring resentment.

This pragmatic response to God's love has become the driving force, down through the centuries, of Christian missions. Paul saw himself a debtor to all mankind (Rom. 1:14). "Have come to pay my debt," said Benjamin Cobbe, a white, fragile-looking new arrival at the Lualuba crossing, deep in the interior of Africa. Already fever had laid its hand upon him, failing, however, to kill his glad smile.

Dan Crawford—a spiritual giant of a man himself and one of Africa's early pioneers, following hard on the steps of David Livingstone—was awed by Cobbe, this new arrival. But Cobbe didn't live long. The African proverb, "The straightest trees are the first felled" proved true in his case. His motto was, "To grow up, you must grow down." Here's how Crawford described Cobbe:

Watch the sequel. This holy man, if you please, had drunk so deeply of God's wine of joy—the new wine that came to him last in life—that it kept him going at high pressure right on to the end. The new wine, in fact, was busily at work breaking up his old bottle of a body, for when these two meet in Africa then one of the two must be lost, but that one thing will never be the new wine—that is hid with Christ in God. So the fragrant saint died at his post, the "old skin bottle" broken in a ferment of fever. Africa got the holy dust, and God received him into glory. [Cobbe] foresaw it all—saw certain death ahead, yet resolved to pay his debt to the heathen.

Now, far from this being a *de mortuis nil nisi bonum* panegyric, here we come to the curious sequent. I have called his a fragrant life; but as the years passed it began to dawn on us that the perfume of Mr. Cobbe's piety had stolen far out beyond our sphere. That gleam of the life eternal so often seen to shoot out of his hazel eyes was far more eloquent than long-winded speech. And, traveling one day in Lubaland, I was appalled to find out that a negro, whom I met, had promoted Mr. Cobbe to the literal rank of a "god." After a few exploring remarks, I ferreted out from the sealed sanctuary of his black breast a little private scheme of salvation he had concocted for his own particular benefit.

And thus, even thus, did the uncanny thing run.

Yes, he had known Mr. Cobbe in the old days—fragrant and holy in word and deed. The memory of the heavenly things he saw in this saint never left that negro, and away he went back to Lubaland with "the living epistle" graven on his mind. "Look up, for we are going up—and oh, so soon!" was a fond phrase of Cobbe's, so this negro thought much and long, and knew that the saint had really gone to God. *That* thing he had actually seen in him could not be killed by fever. *He* had only died into glory as the stars die at sunrise. Hence the daring idea of this poor benighted soul to evolve a private religion of his own with Mr. Cobbe as central "saviour." "Ah," said the negro, "when I am in a fix in life this is what I do, I just send up a prayer to Bwana Cobbe as mediator, and he will arrange it, for he has a big say with God." "He will pass it along to God; he will have a big say with God!" Of course, I righted his wrong theology. Of course, I deplored and implored that this was the unkindest cut of all—that this was stabbing him, not kissing him. But oh! the bitter-sweet reflection notwithstanding—this that a mere dust-to-dust man should be chosen as a daysman between God and his soul: "a living epistle"—a walking and talking Bible. They saw—may I dare the phrase?—the gleam of the life eternal shooting out of his honest hazel eyes; they *saw*, I say, and they believed in a man of God. How much more will they believe in the Man in the Glory, the Man who is Jehovah's Fellow?[9]

John will let us get away with nothing less than *agapē* love. He turns from the logic of love to *the law of love:* "And this commandment have we from him, that he who loveth God love his brother also" (4:21). This is not a suggestion; it is a command. Love, in the Bible, is not so much emotional as volitional. The Lord Jesus summed up the entire Old Testament in two commandments and, in so doing, reduced all of life's obligations to the twofold law of love. We are to love God with all our hearts, minds, souls, and strength, and we are to love the other fellow as much as we love ourselves (Matt. 22:36–40).

General Booth, founder of the Salvation Army, says, "I pushed into the midst of it [hell] in the East End of London. For days I stood in those seething streets, muddy with men and women, drinking it all in and loving it all. Yes, I loved it because of the souls I saw. One night I went home and said to my wife, 'Darling, I have given myself, I have given you and our children to the service of these sick souls.' She smiled and took my hand, and we knelt down together. That was the first meeting of the Salvation Army."

> 3. Dutiful love (5:1–5)
>   a. Our attitude toward God's children (5:1–2)

John now expands the truth he has just been discussing, proffering two propositions. First, he tells us *how we know we love God personally—we love God's people:* "Whosoever believeth that Jesus is the Christ is born of God: and every one that loveth him that begat loveth him also that is begotten of him" (5:1). Then, he tells us *how we know we love God's people—we love God personally:* "By this we know that we love the children of God, when we love God, and keep his commandments" (5:2). The two statements are interlocking. More yet, they are like the revolving doors in large buildings. Once you get into one of them, it's sometimes hard to get out, especially if the place is busy and each of the compartments

---

9. D. C. Crawford, *Thinking Black* (New York: George H. Doran Co., 1912), 102–3.

in the contraption is full and everybody is in a hurry, and everyone is pushing on the part of the door in front of him. It's possible to go round and round, locked in by the motion.

The two statements are like those "envelope" psalms, ending with the same words with which they begin—Psalm 103, for instance. The psalm begins with the words "Bless the LORD, O my soul." It ends with the words "Bless the LORD, O my soul." Thus, the last verse takes us back to the first verse and we go down through the psalm again. Once more the last verse becomes the first verse—and so on ad infinitum. Once we get in we are locked in.

That seems to be John's idea here. He wants to get us locked into the endless round of loving God and loving man, loving man and loving God. Round and round we go in a cycle, which will continue throughout the endless ages of eternity.

The cycle begins with the new birth: "Whosoever believeth that Jesus is the Christ is born of God." Belief puts us into the family, and once we are in the family the wondrous, endless cycle begins, a cycle in which love is all in all.

> b. Our attitude toward God's challenge (5:3–5)
>   (1) To obey the Word (5:3)

"For this is the love of God, that we keep his commandments: and his commandments are not grievous." God does not ask us to do things that are unreasonable or to strive after goals unobtainable.

Nobody knew that better than Paul. What a catalog of seemingly terrible things he was called upon to face. He summed up some of them for his friends at Corinth, but the list is by no means complete. At least one more shipwreck and two terms of imprisonment lay ahead, along with a growing certainty of martyrdom. Hard work, prison sentences, more beatings than we can count, facing death time and time again—this was just his opening summary. More specifically, he remembered five beatings at the hands of the Jews and three thrashings at the hands of the Gentiles. He had been stoned once, shipwrecked three times, and had drifted in the open sea on one occasion for twenty-four hours. As for dangers, he had faced them all—dangers from rivers and floods, from bandits, from pagans, and from his own countrymen; dangers in city streets and in the desert; dangers on the high seas and dangers from false brethren. As for his other hardships, those seemed almost normal—exhaustion, pain, long lonely vigils, hunger, thirst, cold, lack of clothing, and the burden and responsibility of all the churches he had founded. His prayer book bulged with names of people and places that demanded an interest in his prayers. Luke, in the book of Acts, tells us only a tiny part of the story.

Paul faced all these things in the line of duty—and facing them was Paul's way of keeping God's commandments. John says that those commandments are not "grievous." The word he uses is *barus,* meaning "burdensome." Paul uses the word himself in describing the "grievous wolves," the oppressive enemies of the gospel who would invade Ephesus after he was gone (Acts 20:29), the very wolves John was now battling right there in that same city. The Lord used *barus* Himself to describe the heavy, legalistic burdens the Pharisees laid on the Jewish people (Matt. 23:4).

Well, Paul? What do you say? Are God's commandments grievous? Is His will too onerous, His demands too great? Not a bit of it! All he had done was put to the proof that God's will is "good, and acceptable, and perfect" (Rom. 12:2).

(2) To overcome the world (5:4–5)

First, victory is *expected:* "For whatsoever is born of God overcometh the world" (5:4a). The unsaved person feels at home in the world. Unbelievers were born into it, and it's all that they know. It appeals to their fallen natures, offering them the kinds of things they like. The world can mask its satanic nature behind a smiling face, offering pleasure, prosperity, and power. Too, it is a total system, offering culture, religion, philosophy, art, science, organization, variety. And it can threaten, punish, persecute, oppress, and kill. It can be noble, inspiring, and attractive; or it can be base, disgusting, and cruel. But it is the world, and it is all the unsaved person has.

Those "born of God" belong to another world, for their citizenship is in heaven. They are children of God, in this world but not of this world, here as ambassadors for Christ. This world is not their home. Like the patriarch Abraham, they have caught the vision of "a city which hath foundations, whose builder and maker is God" (Heb. 11:10) and have become "pilgrims and strangers" on the earth (1 Peter 2:11). God will not allow us the luxury of dual citizenship. This world murdered His Son, and God calls upon us to overcome the world regardless of whether it turns toward us a smiling face or a scowling face. We are to recognize the world for what it is—an enemy, a system energized by Satan and gratifying to the flesh.

Victory over the world is not only expected of us, it is *explained* to us: "And this is the victory that overcometh the world, even our faith. Who is he that overcometh the world, but he that believeth that Jesus is the Son of God" (5:4b–5). Faith. That is the key, faith focused on none other than the Son of God, who so gloriously overcame the world.

Hebrews 11 is the great New Testament chapter on faith that overcomes. It begins with Abel, who overcame the *pride* of this world. His altar stands in sharp contrast with Cain's, on which was lavished all that hard work and love of beauty could devise. Abel's altar, by contrast, reeked with the blood of the slain lamb. Abel poured contempt on all his pride and looked away to Calvary.

Enoch overcame the *progress* of this world. Stricken Cain, far from daunted by the brand on his brow, founded a glamorous civilization with a strong emphasis on science, art, and commerce. Enoch, by contrast, walked with God, resolutely turning his back on the advancements of a glittering society and a dynamic civilization. Thus, Enoch's daily quiet times with the Son of God made him one who overcomes and a candidate for rapture.

Noah, by faith, overcame the *pollution* of this world. He lived in a pornographic society in which "every imagination of men's hearts was only evil continually." Noah, by contrast, was counted righteous by God—something that happens only when the righteousness of the Son of God is imputed to one. Moreover, he built an ark "to the saving of his house."

By faith Abraham overcame the *prospects* of this world. And brilliant they were. Abraham was a wealthy citizen of an up-and-coming city. He caught the vision of another world, however, and set out to find a heavenly city. Not surprisingly, he met Melchizedek, sat at the Lord's table with the bread and wine before him, symbols of the broken body and poured-out blood of the Son of God, and was able to turn down with utter contempt the clumsy offer of the king of Sodom to make him rich. Moreover, he was obedient to the heavenly vision to the point of taking his only begotten son to the place called Mount Moriah. He was willing there to offer him up as a burnt offering, even though all the promises of God for the coming into the world of His Son were centered in Isaac. He even caught a glimpse, not only of Calvary but also of the resurrection of Christ.

By faith Sarah overcame the *paralysis* of this world. Although ninety years of age and although her womb was dead, she received strength to conceive. Thus, she brought Isaac into the world, one who would, himself, be a direct ancestor of the Son of God.

Isaac, too, became one who overcomes. He overcame the *passions* of this world. He almost missed it, however, in his lust for Esau's savory meat. For a dish of venison he was almost persuaded to give the patriarchal blessing to favored Esau, a man wholly unspiritual and unfit for any such blessing. Circumstances intervened, however, and he unwittingly gave the blessing to Jacob, to whom it rightfully belonged. And with that blessing went the right to be a human progenitor of the Son of God. Isaac, in a sudden upsurge of spiritual perception and power, trod his passions beneath his feet and, now very much alive to the fact that God had overruled, spoke out with the voice of faith, "Yea, and he [Jacob] shall be blessed." Nor could Esau's exceeding great and bitter cry make Isaac change his mind.

Jacob overcame the *perspective* of this world. It took a long time to bring the perspective of the world to nothing in Jacob's life and to replace it with the prospect of glory. Right from the start, however, we see a man hungry for the believer's birthright and for the blessing of God. The focus became sharper at Bethel when he saw the ladder that reached to heaven—a symbolic vision of the Son of God (John 1:47–51). Things came further still into focus when he wrestled at the Jabbok with One who was none other than the Son of God. The focus was perfected on his deathbed when he blessed his boys, bringing the Son of God before them in one utterance after another.

The parents of Moses overcame by faith the *prince* of this world. How boldly they defied the murderous order of Pharaoh that would have given Moses to the river and the crocodiles. They were "not afraid," the Holy Spirit declares.

Moses, too, was one who believed and overcame, overcoming the *power* of this world by refusing to be called the son of Pharaoh's daughter. The implication is that he was actually offered Egypt's throne and a seat in Egypt's pantheon as the son of the sun. He chose rather to suffer affliction with the people of God, esteeming the reproach of *Christ* greater riches than the treasures of Egypt. His vision of the Son of God gave him the grace and power to overcome the world.

Last, Rahab overcame the *punishment* of this world. Before long the trumpet would sound and Jericho's walls would come tumbling down. She believed what she had heard about God's redeeming His people from Egypt, and now they were on their way to Canaan, and not all of Jericho's walls and warriors could stop the approaching doom. By faith she hung that scarlet line in her window, thus signifying her trust in the Son of God—a human ancestress of whom, indeed, she actually became.

"Who is he that overcometh the world, but he that believeth that Jesus is the Son of God?" (5:5). Once that great truth is enthroned in our hearts, our attitude toward this world changes. We see the world as He saw it and the world sees us as it saw Him, and a great gulf is fixed.

C. A sufficient witness (5:6–13)
  1. The witness of the Spirit to the Son (5:6)

The great work of the Holy Spirit in this world is to bear witness. He bears witness to the Savior (John 15:26) and He bears witness to the saint (Rom. 8:16; Heb. 10:14–15), as Abel discovered (Heb. 11:4). John now deals with this twofold witness of the Spirit, beginning with the Holy Spirit's witness to the Son. That witness is twofold also. The Spirit bears witness to *how He lived out His life:* "This is he that came by water and blood, even Jesus Christ" (5:6a). The water takes us at once to the Jordan and to that awesome moment when Jesus was publicly acclaimed from heaven to be God's Son. By this time, John the Baptist knew exactly who Jesus was, and he demurred at the thought of baptizing Him. For John's baptism was a baptism of repentance, and there was nothing in the immaculate Christ of God that called for repentance. The Lord's baptism, however, was His means by which He identified Himself with the ruined race, which He had entered by birth and with which He was to be forever linked. No sooner had He taken this act of submission than heaven opened, the Holy Spirit descended in form as a dove and rested upon Him, and the Father proclaimed Jesus to be His Son, the One in whom He was well pleased (Matt. 3:13–17).

The "water," then, which we associate with the Lord's baptism, highlights the Lord's manner of life—obedience. He did always those things that pleased the Father. His life—from His birth to His baptism, all those hidden years—had been lived under the approving eye of His Father in heaven. The same was true of His open, public life and ministry. God again voiced His approval on the Mount of Transfiguration, where He again declared Jesus to be His Son (Matt. 17:5). Then, as the shadows of Calvary began to loom, God bore witness one more time to His Beloved (John 12:27–33).

The Holy Spirit bears witness, too, to *how He laid down His life:* "Not by water only, but by water and blood. And it is the Spirit that beareth witness, because the Spirit is truth" (5:6b). Doubtless John has in mind here the lies being circulated about the Lord Jesus by Cerinthus and his followers. John, with that heresy in mind, emphasizes the fact of the Lord's genuine humanity. More, he emphasizes that the Holy Spirit Himself endorses the genuine humanity of Christ. More, still, the Spirit of God is the Spirit of truth.

By blood. The Lord Jesus was a true man. Blood flowed in His veins. But what blood! Not a drop of Joseph's blood flowed in Jesus' veins, for Joseph was only

His foster father, and Jesus was in his family only by adoption. There was no drop of Mary's blood in His veins either; the blood that flows through the veins and arteries of a babe still in its mother's womb is not its mother's blood. It is the baby's own blood. Only after the embryo has been impregnated does the baby's blood—like any other cell in the body—begin to develop. Not one drop of blood passes from the mother to the child. Indeed, such a transfusion would be dangerous if the mother had a different blood type from that of the developing child. But the blood type of the Lord Jesus was like no other blood type. It was the blood of an absolutely unique, completely sinless person, blood rare beyond all imagining. The Holy Spirit calls it "precious blood" (1 Peter 1:18–19).

The blood of the Lord Jesus was shed for us in the suffering that began in the Garden of Gethsemane and that ended on the cross of Calvary. According to the book of Hebrews (chap. 9)—and in keeping with the mathematical exactness of Old Testament typology and its New Testament fulfillment—the Lord Jesus took His blood to heaven, there to be placed on the mercy seat in the heavenly Holy of Holies.

> 2. The witness of the Spirit to the saint (5:7–10a)
>   a. The character of the witness (5:7–8)
>   (1) The witness in the heavenly realm (5:7)

This is a complex paragraph, made all the more difficult by those who think that two or three lines ought to be removed altogether from the text. Indeed, so confident are some commentators, they simply eradicate the disputed statements without so much as a comment or explanation. The general position is that everything between the words "in heaven" (in 5:7) and "in earth" (in 5:8) should be crossed out of the Scripture text. The reason given for such drastic surgery is that these words are not found in any Greek manuscript before the sixteenth century, and that they first appeared in the margin of some Latin copies, from whence they, supposedly, had crept into the text. Still, the words are found in the King James text and will be dealt with here accordingly. Certainly the structural analysis on which this commentary is built can accommodate the disputed phrases. They appear to fit in, so why cross them out?

John is still dealing with the witness of the Spirit, showing how He witnesses to the *Son* of God. Now John shows how He witnesses to the *saints* of God (5:7–10a), demonstrating the *character* of this witness (5:7–8) and the *credibility* of this witness (5:9–10a). The character of that witness is revealed by the very thoroughness of the witness. It is in two realms—the *heavenly* (5:7) and the *human* (5:8). An exact parallelism exists between the two—the heavenly and the human—as can be seen by the structural outline of the passage.

Beginning with the *heavenly* realm (5:7), *three voices* give *separate* testimony (5:7a–c): "For there are three that bear record in heaven, the Father, the Word, and the Holy Ghost"—in other words, the three members of the Godhead. No wonder Paul could exclaim, "If God be for us, who can be against us? He that spared not his own Son, but delivered him up for us all, how shall he not with him also freely give us all things? Who shall lay any thing to the charge of God's elect? It is God that justifieth. Who is he that condemneth? It is Christ that died, yea rather, that is risen again, who is even at the right hand of God, who also maketh intercession for us" (Rom. 8:31–34).

Throughout the Scripture, the Father is seen as the great adversary of the world, the Holy Spirit is depicted as being the great enemy of the flesh, and the Son as being the foe of Satan. So let the world, the flesh, or the Devil raise a voice against us, and singly or all together they do not stand a chance. Each member of the triune Godhead is ready to take up our cause.

There's more. *These voices* give *supporting* testimony: "And these three are one" (5:7d), united, they speak on our behalf. John later affirms, from personal experience, that the voice of the Lord Jesus alone is "as the sound of many waters" (Rev. 1:15). Many a time I have stood at Niagara Falls and watched the endless flow of water pouring over the precipice and down into the yawning gulf below. Every minute, thirty-five million gallons of water fall with a thunderous roar 180 feet into the gorge, sending up voluminous clouds of spray. On the Canadian side of the falls, it is possible to descend a shaft and then proceed along a tunnel to a ledge behind the falls. All around the water thunders down, so it's no place to make a speech or conduct a conversation. The Indians who inhabited Niagara long before the advent of the white man actually called it the Place of Thundering Waters. Niagara, then, can be likened to God's answer to all our foes—let them try to make themselves heard in the face of the united thundering voices of the Father, Son, and Holy Spirit.

(2) The witness in the *human* realm (5:8)

Again, *three voices* give *separate* testimony: "and there are three that bear witness in earth, the spirit, and the water, and the blood" (5:8a–c). The Holy Spirit bears witness *in* us, confirming quietly in our hearts that we have been born again, baptized into the mystical body of Christ, indwelled by God. Satan may try to silence that inner witness, sin temporarily causing us to doubt our salvation. But back it comes—that still, small voice of God bringing its assurance that all is well. Sometimes He uses His Word to speak peace to our troubled hearts, sometimes assurance comes from a kindly word from a fellow believer, at other times it's just an inner assurance as He bears witness with our spirit that we are the children of God (Rom. 8:16).

The water bears witness *by* us. The water, here, surely corresponds with the water in verse 6. There, it refers to the water of Jordan and the baptism of the Lord Jesus. Here, the reference is to the water of our baptism, whereby we give witness to the world that we have passed from death to life. The Bible knows nothing, however, about the baptism of infants and still less about baptismal regeneration. New Testament baptism is "the answer of a good conscience towards God" (1 Peter 3:21), and the mode of baptism is by immersion (Acts 8:35–39). By means of baptism the Lord Jesus identified Himself with us, and by means of baptism we proclaim our identification with Him. The outward expression of an inward experience, by baptism we take our stand in the water—an element that spells death to the natural man. We are put beneath that water in a graphic symbol of burial, then we are raised by the power of another's arm, emerging from that watery grave to walk in newness of life. Thus, in an act of obedience to the Lord's command, we bear witness to a lost world—the essential fact of the gospel—when He died, we died; when He was buried, we were buried; when He was raised, we were raised.

The blood bears witness *for* us. It is there, on the mercy seat in heaven, to testify for all eternity that our salvation has been purchased, once and for all, at infinite cost, to the total satisfaction of a thrice-holy God. That blood "speaketh better things than that of Abel" (Heb. 12:24), for Abel's blood cried aloud for vengeance, but the Lord's blood assures us that our debt is fully paid.

Moreover, *these voices* give *supporting* testimony: "And these three agree in one" (5:8d). Many centuries before, in the Mosaic Law, God had established the principle: "In the mouth of two or three witnesses shall every word be established" (Deut. 17:6; 19:15; 2 Cor. 13:1). For, as Solomon said, "A three-fold cord is not easily broken" (Eccl. 4:12). So, here, we have a unanimous threefold witness. That is enough.

b. The credibility of the witness (5:9–10a)

Great and wonderful and manifold and varied is the witness of God to the efficacy of the work wrought on our behalf by His Son. John points out now that this witness *carries its own commendation:* "If we receive the witness of men, the witness of God is greater: for this is the witness of God which he hath testified of his Son" (5:9).

Most of the things that we know, we have been told or we have read. Most of the information thus received comes from human sources, meaning that in almost every case we accept "the witness of men." Nearly all the facts of history and science we have imbibed in this way, seldom exercising our critical faculty. The information passed along to us goes down into our memory bank as part of our general knowledge. Much of that information, however, is more or less useless. What difference does it make to us, for example, that Lindbergh flew the Atlantic alone in May 1927, or that men landed on the moon on July 20, 1969? What difference does it make that the diameter of Aldebaran (Alpha Tauri), the "bull's eye of Taurus," is about eight hundred times larger than the sun or that the interstellar dust in our galaxy alone is equal to sixty-five trillion earths? The *Encyclopedia Britannica* is full of knowledge, much of which is totally useless to most of us.

But if that information is, for the most part, useless, it at least is usually correct. Many of the things that people "know," however, are wrong. For over a century the academic world has been obsessed by the theory of evolution, the scientific elite bombarding us day and night with propaganda designed to convert us to their evolution religion. Many people accept the theory, ignorant of the fact that it is totally unproved and that it is promoted with such zeal simply because it provides a working hypothesis for atheism.

Similarly, millions of people embrace the teaching of false religions, some of which have been around for a long time. Others find pleasure in filling their minds with human philosophy and are careless of the fact that human reasoning, however clever and convincing, cannot provide the answer to life's ultimate questions—Why am I here? Where did I come from? If there is a God, why is He silent? Why is there so much injustice and wickedness in the world? What happens to us when we die?

It is against this background of our receiving the witness of humans that John introduces his telling argument: "The witness of God is greater." The Word of God must take precedence over the word of people— because people make mistakes; they are finite and are often wrong. God is omniscient and makes no mistakes. He speaks with authority. The Bible is true—and it is absolutely incumbent upon us that we believe the Lord Jesus Christ and accept God's Word at its face value.

In other words, we must believe God's witness and especially His witness concerning His Son. God's Word is the absolute, inerrant, and infallible truth, and when its teachings conflict with the teachings of men, we must believe God.

The greatest insult we can offer to anyone is to say, "I don't believe you," or "I cannot trust you." Yet millions daily offer that insult to God, accepting the witness of men and repudiating the witness of God. An unbeliever once said to D. L. Moody, "But, Mr. Moody, I can't believe." "Young man," said Mr. Moody, *"Whom* can't you believe?" To tell God you don't believe what He says betrays a desperate state of soul.

Thus, John lays out the credibility of the witness. We are not being asked to believe the unreasonable; we are, however, confronted with the greatest information ever presented to the human race. And it is true! The witness *carries its own commendation*—divine revelation is as far above human reasoning as the heavens are high above the earth (Isa. 55:8–9).

Moreover, the witness *carries its own conviction:* "He that believeth on the Son of God hath the witness in himself" (5:10a). God sees to that. When, in Bunyan's work *Pilgrim's Progress*, Christian and Hopeful, on their way to the Celestial City, attempted a shortcut through By-path Meadow, they soon found themselves doubting their very salvation. Indeed, they became the prisoners of Giant Despair. Bunyan tells the tale:

> Now there was, not far from the place where they lay, a castle, the owner whereof was Giant Despair, and it was in his grounds they now were sleeping; wherefore he, getting up in the morning early, and walking up and down in his fields, caught Christian and Hopeful asleep in his grounds. Then, with a grim and surly voice, he bid them awake, and asked them whence they were, and what they did in his grounds. They told him they were pilgrims, and that they had lost their way. Then said the giant, "You have this night trespassed on me by trampling in and lying on my grounds, and therefore you must go along with me." So they were forced to go, because he was stronger than they. They had also but little to say, for they knew themselves in fault. The giant, therefore, drove them before him, and put them into his castle, into a very dark dungeon, nasty and stinking to the spirits of these two men. Here, then, they lay from Wednesday morning till Saturday night, without one bit of bread or drop of drink, or light, or any to ask how they did; they were, therefore, here in evil case, and

were far from friends and acquaintance. Now, in this place Christian had double sorrow, because it was through his unadvised haste that they were brought into this distress.

Now Giant Despair had a wife, and her name was Diffidence. So, when he was gone to bed, he told his wife what he had done; to wit, that he had taken a couple of prisoners and cast them into his dungeon for trespassing on his grounds. Then he asked her also what he had best to do further to them. So she asked him what they were, whence they came, and whither they were bound; and he told her. Then she counseled him, that when he arose in the morning, he should beat them without any mercy. So, when he arose, he getteth him a grievous crab-tree cudgel, and goes down into the dungeon with them, and there first fell to rating of them as if they were dogs, although they never gave him a word of distaste. Then he falls upon them, and beats them fearfully, in such sort that they were not able to help themselves, or to turn them upon the floor. This done, he withdraws and leaves them there to condole their misery and to mourn under their distress. So all that day they spent their time in nothing but sighs and bitter lamentations.

The next night she, talking with her husband about them further, and understanding that they were yet alive, did advise him to counsel them to make away with themselves. So, when morning was come, he goes to them in a surly manner, as before, and, perceiving them to be very sore with the stripes that he had given them the day before, he told them that, since they were never like to come out of that place, their only way would be to forthwith to make an end of themselves, either with knife, halter or poison: "For why," said he, "should you choose life, seeing it is attended with so much bitterness?"[10]

Indeed, so overwhelmed were the pilgrims with their doubts and despair they did consider suicide as a way out of their distress. The dreadful days and nights dragged on. But the end was in sight. Bunyan continues his tale:

Well, on Saturday about midnight, they began to pray, and continued in prayer till almost break of day.

Now, a little before it was day, good Christian, as one half amazed, brake out into this passionate speech: "What a fool," quoth he, "am I to

---

10. John Bunyan, *Pilgrim's Progress.*

lie in a stinking dungeon, when I may as well walk at liberty! I have a key in my bosom called Promise, that will, I am persuaded, open any lock in Doubting Castle." Then said Hopeful, "That is good news, good brother: pluck it out of thy bosom, and try."

Then Christian pulled it out of his bosom, and began to try at the dungeon door, whose bolt, as he turned the key, gave back, and the door flew open with ease, and Christian and Hopeful both came out. Then he went to the outward door that leads into the castle yard, and with his key opened that door also. After, he went to the iron gate, for that must be opened, too; but that lock went damnable hard, yet the key did open it. Then they thrust open the gate to make their escape with speed; but that gate, as it opened, made such a creaking, that it waked Giant Despair, who, hastily rising to pursue his prisoners, felt his limbs to fail; for his fits took him again, so that he could by no means go after them. Then they went on, and came to the King's highway again, and so were safe because they were out of his jurisdiction.[11]

Many a believer has been imprisoned in Doubting Castle and fallen foul of Giant Despair. But the key is at hand. Assurance of our salvation lies as near as the promises of God. "Hath the witness in himself," says John. Paul affirms the same: "Say not in thine heart, who shall ascend into heaven? (that is, to bring Christ down from above:) or, who shall descend into the deep? (that is, to bring up Christ again from the dead.) But what saith it? The word is nigh thee, even in thy mouth, and in thy heart: that is, the word of faith, which we preach" (Rom. 10:6–8). In other words, assurance of our salvation is ours for the taking. The Incarnation has brought Christ down from above; the Resurrection has brought Him up from the deep. Now He lives in each believer's heart and all is well. We can banish Giant Despair and demolish Doubting Castle at will.

  3. The witness of the Spirit to the Scripture (5:10b–13)
     a. What John wrote (5:10b–12)

But what if the record is *refused?* John deals with that: "He that believeth not God hath made him a liar; because he believeth not the record that God gave of his Son" (5:10b). That record is found not only in the Old Testament Scriptures but in the four Gospels, the book of Acts, the Epistles, and the book of Revela-

---

11. Ibid.

tion. God is a great believer in writing things down. Both Judaism and Christianity are based on a Book, which records historical events, things that took place in a space-time context. The great laws, teachings, prophecies, and events are all on record.

Above all, God has given us the record of His Son. We will do well, when interpreting the Scriptures, to keep a sharp eye open for details that speak of Christ. We see Him in Genesis as the Creator, as the seed of the woman, as the star that will rise out of Jacob, as the lion of Judah. We see Him in the story of Abel's lamb, in the ark of Noah, in what happened at Mount Moriah, in the story of Joseph. We see Him in Exodus in the Passover lamb, in every part of the tabernacle, in the Shechinah glory cloud, in the manna, and in the riven rock. We see Him in Leviticus in the offerings and as the Great High Priest, in the ritual for cleansing the leper, in the goats of the Day of Atonement, in all the annual feasts. We see Him in Numbers in the red heifer, in the serpent on the pole, in the parables of Balaam, in the cities of refuge.

In Deuteronomy He is the prophet like to Moses; in Joshua, the captain of our salvation. In Judges, He is the deliverer of His own; in Ruth, the kinsman-redeemer. In Samuel, He is the ark and the rejected king brought at last to the throne. In Kings and Chronicles He reigns as Solomon in splendor and glory. In Ezra, He is the ready scribe; in Nehemiah, He is seen in every city gate. In Esther, He is the One who provided the salvation.

He is to be seen in almost all the Psalms. He is the blessed man of Psalm 1, the Son in Psalm 2, the shepherd in Psalm 23, the suffering Savior in Psalm 22 and Psalm 69. He is the King of Glory in Psalm 24, the perfect man of Psalm 8, and the mighty God of Psalm 45. Almost every one of the Psalms has a prophetic overtone, many of them plainly messianic. In Proverbs, He is wisdom incarnate; in Ecclesiastes, that sad book of worldly wisdom, He is the forgotten wise man who saved the city. In the Song of Solomon, He is the shepherd who won the Shulamite's heart and who triumphs over all the blandishments of the world.

In Isaiah, He is the Lamb, led to the slaughter in chapter 53 and the One who treads the winepress in chapter 63, the glorious Messiah of a hundred hopes and longings in stanza after stanza of the book. In Jeremiah, He is the great sufferer and the Lord our righteousness; in Lamentations, the One acquainted with grief. In Ezekiel, He sits on the throne; in Daniel, He is the One cut off and the stone cut without hands.

In Hosea, He is the forgiving, long-suffering husband and David's far greater king. In Joel, He pours out His Spirit on all flesh. In Amos, He stands on the altar, sifts the house of Israel, and brings in millennial blessing at last. In Obadiah, He ushers in the dreaded "day of the Lord" and stands on Mount Zion. In Jonah, He is prefigured in His death, burial, and resurrection; in Micah, He is seen as the One to be born at Bethlehem and as the One who will bring millennial blessing to all humankind; also He is the great shepherd and the One who pardons iniquity. In Nahum, He is the great avenger, before whom the mountains quake but a stronghold and a refuge to His own. In Habakkuk, He is the holy one of Israel and His people's strength and song. In Zephaniah, He brings in kingdom blessing; in Haggai, He builds again the temple of the Lord, shakes the nations, and is the chosen of the Lord. In Zechariah, He brings in the Apocalypse, is the Great High Priest, pours out the Spirit of the Lord upon men, is the headstone of the corner, the great judge. He rides into Jerusalem on a colt, is sold for the price of a slave, opens a fountain for uncleanness in Jerusalem, is the branch and the coming King of Kings. In Malachi, His coming is heralded by a forerunner, and He is the sun of righteousness.

In Matthew, He is the King of the Jews; in Mark, the servant of Jehovah; in Luke, the Son of Man; and in John, He is the Son of God. In Acts, He is the ascended head of the church; in Romans, our righteousness; in Corinthians, the firstfruits from the dead. In Galatians, He is the end of the Law, and in Ephesians, He is all in all to His church—foundation for the building, head of the body, Bridegroom of our hearts. In Philippians, He is in the form of God and the One who supplies all our needs. In Colossians, He is the Creator, sustainer, and owner of the universe, preeminent overall. In 1 Thessalonians, He comes again for His church; in 2 Thessalonians, He comes to judge the world. In 1 Timothy, He is the one mediator between God and man, and in 2 Timothy, He is the judge of the living and the dead.

In Hebrews, He is the great antitype of all the types: son, priest, sacrifice, and heir. He is greater than Aaron or Melchizedec, greater than Moses or Joshua, greater than the angels. He is both Son of God and Son of Man. In James, He is the Lord of Sabbath and the One who heals. In 1 Peter, He is our inheritance and the shepherd of our souls; in 2 Peter, He is the One from the excellent glory. In 1 John, He is the incarnate Word; in 2 John, the One who prospers our souls, and in 3 John, the One for whose name's sake the gospel goes forth. In Jude, He is the preserver, the only Lord God, the only wise God, our Savior, glorious in majesty. In Revelation, He is the Lamb and the lion; the King, who is soon to come, who even now upholds all things by the power of His Word. He is the One who stands astride all the factors and forces of space and time, and who bends all things to His sovereign will.

To become acquainted with the record and to refuse it is a serious matter, tantamount to calling the living God a liar. More guilty still are those who, under the cloak of Christianity and in the guise of "scholarship," arrogate to themselves the title of "higher critics," rending and tearing the Bible to shreds.

John turns from that crime of crimes—rejecting the record and calling God a liar—to tell us what happens when the record is *received* (5:11–12). Two things happen. First, there occurs a *revelation to us:* "And this is the record, that God has given to us eternal life, and this life is in His Son." Those who accept the record that God has given to us of His Son open their hearts to Him and become partakers of that eternal life that is in His Son.

The great longing of the human heart is to live forever in a state of blessedness and bliss. We hate and fear death, knowing it instinctively as an intruder and an enemy who has terrible power. We have it written in our innermost consciousness that we were engineered for eternity, that it is outrageous that our days on earth should be so fleeting and so few.

That was Solomon's complaint throughout the book of Ecclesiastes. He wrote the book in his old age, haunted by the thought of death. "Why shouldest thou die before thy time?" he says (7:17). "There is no man that hath power over the spirit to retain the spirit, neither hath he power in the day of death," he complains (8:8). "There is one event unto all," he groans, "they go to the dead" (9:3). "A living dog is better than a dead lion," he grumbles. And in a classic statement of untruth he declares "the dead know not anything" (9:5), a statement belied by the experiences of the rich man and Lazarus (Luke 16:19–31). "Whatsoever thy hand findeth to do, do it with all thy might," he counsels, "for there is no work, nor device, nor knowledge in the grave whither thou goest" (9:10). We have heard of "the fly in the ointment," an idiom that comes straight out of the book of Ecclesiastes. And, of course, it is a dead fly. For such is the fly in the ointment of life—we are going to die. The last chapter in the book is a poetic description of old age. Solomon must have known he did not have long to live, yet he wanted to live forever. "He hath set the world [eternity] in their heart," he cries (3:11).

So much for the wise man of old. "God has given to us eternal life, and this life is in his Son," John says. "Jesus Christ," says Paul, "hath abolished death and hath brought life and immortality to light through the gospel!" (2 Tim. 1:10). Hallelujah—what a Savior!

The second thing that happens when the record is received is a *revolution in us:* "He that hath the Son hath life; and he that hath not the Son of God hath not life" (5:12). The unregenerate person has a body and a soul. That person likewise has a human spirit, but it is empty and without God. Consequently, the unregenerate person, no matter how brilliant, loving, or decisive that person may be, is spiritually dead. He or she "hath not life." By contrast, the human spirit of a regenerated person is indwelled by the Holy Spirit of God and by the Son of God. Therefore, that person "hath life."

A person, then, is either indwelled by Christ—or not. There is no middle ground, for God does not mince matters.

b. Why John wrote (5:13)

It was John's privilege to write the last five books of the Bible—his gospel, his three epistles, and Revelation. Here he tells us why he wrote: "These things have I written unto you that believe on the name of the Son of God; that ye may know that ye have eternal life, and that ye may believe on the name of the Son of God."

Some in John's day were hailing the name of Cerinthus, a name guaranteed to take them to a lost eternity, the name of one of John's "antichrists." Many think that the name of Mary is the all-important name. Not so. It is the name of a woman who confessed herself in need of a Savior (Luke 1:47). There is only one name good for salvation in heaven, and that is the name of Jesus, the Son of God.

John remembered the day he and his friend Peter had been hauled before the Sanhedrin for healing a lame beggar in the name of Jesus. He would never forget the scene. A galaxy of great ones of the nation assembled—rulers and elders and scribes—"Annas, the high priest, and Caiaphas, and John and Alexander, and as many as were of the kindred of the high priest" (Acts 4:5–6). Here were Peter and John, a couple of Galilean fishermen, accompanied by a beggar. But there was no question who had the authority and the power—it was Peter and John. They spoke boldly: "Be it known unto you all, and to all the people of Israel, that by the name of Jesus Christ of Nazareth, whom ye crucified, whom God raised from the dead, even by him doth this man stand here before you whole. This is the stone which was set at nought of you builders, which is become the head of the corner. Neither is there salvation in any other: for there is none other name under heaven given among men, whereby we must be saved" (Acts 4:10–12).

Well did John know the power of the name of the Lord. He uses the name *Son of God,* giving the Lord Jesus Christ His highest title. Woe to those who dared to downgrade the person of God's beloved Son. By denying the incarnation of the Son of God, the heretics proved themselves to be unbelievers. John knew Jesus to be the Son of God; Peter, as the spokesman for the others, had so confessed Him (Matt. 16:15–17). Only an omnipotent, omniscient, and omnipresent One could provide and administer a salvation of eternal dimensions, to be offered to all mankind, throughout the ages of time. Only such a One could overcome all obstacles, hold in perfect balance and poise all the facts of each individual case, satisfy all the claims and demands of God's throne, provide adequate payment for all the enormous indebtedness of the race, and carry out God's purposes in grace throughout all the unborn ages of eternities yet to be.

That, then, is why John wrote—"that you may know that ye have eternal life, and that ye may believe on the name of the Son of God."

Now John comes to his last paragraph. He picks up, one more time, some of his favorite words and expressions. He picks them up, puts them down, passes them on. He is reminded yet again that this world is a wicked world, but he will soon be done with it. Others will have to battle it. How wicked is it? Wicked enough to kill the Son of God and persecute those who believe in Him.

> D. A sinful world (5:14–21)
>   1. This world's limits (5:14–15)

It is a wicked world. It is Satan's world just now. But we need not fear, for *God hears us:* "And this is the confidence that we have in him, that, if we ask any thing according to his will, he heareth us" (5:14). That is a plain statement of his omniscience.

I sometimes gather with a group of God's people who, when they meet for prayer, all pray out loud at the same time. There is a sudden uprush of sound, and one voice, the voice of the leader, rises authoritatively above the others. All around, however, men are pouring out their prayers and petitions to God, each as earnest and sincere and as concentrated on his praying as though he were the only one in the room. Not being accustomed to that form of united prayer, I usually stop after the first few sentences. Not so the others. They pray on with abandonment and zeal. Occasionally, I try to sort out the prayers of this one, that one, and the other one. All in vain. I catch a word or two here, a half sentence there, a snatch of a petition over yonder. And that's only one small prayer meeting. Only God can sort out all the petitions pouring into His throne room, moment by moment, day and night, in a thousand tongues and dialects from a million voices, along with all the unspoken requests voiced in groaning that cannot be uttered.

Says John, referring to the Son of God, "And this is the confidence that we have in him that if we ask anything according to his will, he heareth us." What a Savior He is.

Moreover, *God heeds us:* "And if we know that he hear us whatsoever we ask, we know that we have the petitions that we desire of him" (5:15). That is an equally plain statement of His omnipotence.

The key, of course, to receiving what we pray for is "if we know that he hear us," which, in turn, hinges on the statement, "if we ask any thing according to his will, he heareth us" (5:14). John had been there in Gethsemane when the Lord had prayed "with strong crying and tears." Jesus prayed with tears and blood that the dark and dreadful cup, now being offered to Him, be allowed to pass from Him. But He conditioned that plea: "Nevertheless, not my will but thine be done" (Matt. 26:39). Thus, when we pray along the line of God's will, we can with confidence expect to receive that for which we pray.

The story of George Müller abounds with such instances of praying in accordance with God's will. George Müller built and ran the orphanages in Bristol, England, on the principle of faith in God and of telling God, and God alone, his financial needs. During the many years he did this, he not only established a powerful testimony for God but he learned many valuable lessons about prayer and faith. His biographer records his spiritual progress:

> Frequent were the instances of the habit of translating promises into prayers, immediately applying the truth thus unveiled to him. For example, after prolonged meditation over the first verse of Psalm lxv, *"O Thou that hearest prayer,"* he at once asked and recorded certain definite petitions. This writing down specific requests for permanent reference has a blessed influence upon the prayer habit. It assures practical and exact form for our supplications, impresses the mind and memory with what is thus asked of God, and leads naturally to the record of the answers when given, so that we accumulate evidences in our own experience that God is to us personally a prayer-hearing God, whereby unbelief is rebuked and importunity encouraged.
>
> On this occasion eight specific requests are put on record, together with the solemn conviction that, having asked in conformity with the word and will of God, and in the name of Jesus, he has confidence in

Him that He heareth and that he has the petitions thus asked of Him. He writes:

"I believe *He has heard me.* I believe He will make it *manifest* in His own good time *that He has heard me;* and I have recorded these my petitions this fourteenth day of January, 1838, that when God has answered them He may get, through this, glory to His name." . . .

It was in this devout reading on his knees that his whole soul was first deeply moved by that phrase, "A father of the fatherless." (Psalm lxviii.5.)

He saw this to be one of those "names" of Jehovah which He reveals to His people to lead them to trust in Him, as it is written in Psalm ix.10:

> They that know Thy name,
> Will put their trust in Thee.

These five words from the sixty-eighth Psalm became another of his life-texts, one of the foundation stones of all his work for the fatherless. These are his own words:

"By the help of God, this shall be my argument before Him, respecting the orphans, in the hour of need. He is their father, and therefore has pledged Himself, as it were, to provide for them; and I have only to remind Him of the need of these poor children in order to have it supplied."

This is translating the promises of God's Word, not only into praying, but into living, doing, serving. Blessed was the hour when Mr. Müller learned that one of God's chosen names is "the Father of the fatherless."

This method of *holy argument*—ordering our cause before God, as an advocate would plead before a judge—is not only almost a lost art, but to many it actually seems almost puerile. And yet it is abundantly taught and exemplified in Scripture. Abraham in his plea for Sodom is the first great example of it.

George Müller stored up reasons for God's intervention.

These were *His* orphans, for had He not declared Himself the Father of the fatherless? This was *His* work, for had He not called His servant to do His bidding, and what was that servant but an instrument that could neither fit itself nor use itself? Can the rod lift itself, or the saw move itself, or the hammer deal its own blow, or the sword make its own thrust? And if this were God's work, was He not bound to care for His own work? And was not all this deliberately planned and carried on for His own glory? And would He suffer His own glory to be dimmed? Had not His own word been given and confirmed by His oath, and could God allow His promise, thus sworn to, to be dishonoured even in the least particular? Were not the half-believing church and the unbelieving world looking on, to see how the Living God would stand by His own unchanging assurance, and would He supply an argument for the skeptic and the scoffer? Would He not, must He not, rather put new proofs of His faithfulness in the mouth of His saints, and furnish increasing arguments wherewith to silence the caviling tongue and put to shame the hesitating disciple?

In some such fashion as this did this lowly-minded saint in Bristol plead with God for more than threescore years, *and prevail.*[12]

God hears us and God heeds us. What can the world do against such triumphant faith? How limited, after all, are the world's resources, how small its intellect, how puny its power when weighed in against a George Müller, a Hudson Taylor, or a "Praying Hyde." Truly,

> The devil trembles when he sees
> The weakest saint upon his knees.

For down through history, in answer to His people's prayers, God draws the line in the sand and hurls back Satan's fiercest waves. This world has its limits.

2. This world's lusts (5:16–17)

Still, Satan has his victories. So John gives a final warning, reminding us of *the seriousness of sin:* "If any man see his brother sin a sin which is not unto death, he shall ask, and he shall give him life for them that sin not unto death. There is a sin unto death: I do not say that he shall pray for it" (5:16). If ancient history is to be believed, John evidently thought that Cerinthus was in such a case. The story comes from Polycarp and is related by Irenaeus, a legend that the apostle John left the public baths at Ephesus in great haste when he heard that Cerinthus had

---

12. A. T. Pierson, *George Müller of Bristol* (New York: Revell, 1899), 143–53.

entered. "Let us flee," he said, "lest the baths fall in while Cerinthus the enemy of truth is within."[13]

Having just laid down the golden rule of prayer, John now encourages prayer for a brother in spiritual need. He thus endorses another principle of prayer, namely, that it should be free from selfishness. The Lord is pleased when we are concerned in prayer about the spiritual needs of others.

The phrase "sin a sin" employs two words. The first word used for "sin" in this verse is *harmartåno,* which means to miss the mark or to wander from the path. The second word is *ponēria,* which has to do with our natural depravity, picturing someone acting, according to his evil nature. Taken together the words, while obviously referring to some actual wrongdoing, suggest rather the condition that leads to the act itself. The phrase "unto death" means "leading toward death," physical death, that is. In exhorting prayer by a brother in Christ, John envisions a spiritual believer, in tune with the will of God, interposing his petition between the drifting brother and the behavior, which, if continued, will end in death.

John had no doubt that "a sin unto death" could be committed. He had been present in the Jerusalem church, in those very early days, when Peter had passed the sentence of death on Ananias and Sapphira for lying to the Holy Spirit. The time between the sin and the punishment was very short, indeed, although some considerable time might well have elapsed between the time the evil thought was conceived and incubated and the time it was actually done (Acts 5:1–13). The Corinthian church, too, was aware of those who had "fallen asleep" for profaning the Lord's Table (1 Cor. 11:30).

John does not tell us what actually constitutes a sin unto death, but Paul reminds the Corinthians that it was a serious thing to defile God's temple, and that those who did so were in peril of themselves being destroyed. The "temple" is a symbol for both the local church (1 Cor. 3:16–17) and the believer's body, which has become the temple of the Holy Spirit (1 Cor. 6:15–20). On two occasions the Lord Jesus cleansed the Jewish temple in Jerusalem (Matt. 32:12–13; John 2:13–16), and when the Jews continued to defile it, He decreed its utter destruction (Matt. 24:1–2).

Sin is always serious, but there are some sins that call for premature death for a believer, and consequent shame and loss at the judgment seat of Christ.

Next, John focuses on the scope of sin:

"All unrighteousness is sin, and there is a sin not unto death." Obviously, if

---

13. F. F. Bruce, *The Epistles of John* (Grand Rapids: Eerdmans, 1970), 23.

the Holy Spirit smote every believer as He did Ananias and Sapphira, He would make short work of the church. The word used for "unrighteousness" here comes from *adikia* and signifies wrongdoing in general. While the Holy Spirit does not chastise us every time we sin, pointing us rather to the means of cleansing and restoration available to us (1:7–2:1), He is grieved by our wrongful attitudes, acts, and words (Eph. 4:30). Thus, we are well advised to "keep short accounts with God," that is, as soon as the Holy Spirit convicts us of something in our lives that is grieving Him, we ought to put it right at once and not allow it to grow, fester, and become entrenched. Sin has a hardening effect upon us, and the sooner it is dealt with, the better.

3. This world's lord (5:18–19)

John reminds us we are in enemy territory and that we are at war. He speaks first of *the wicked one's defeat:* "We know that whosoever is born of God sinneth not; but he that is begotten of God keepeth himself, and that wicked one toucheth him not" (5:18). "We know" he says, "We know!" The word used for "sinneth" is in the present continuous tense, referring to a continuous course of sin. We know, however, that a consistent pattern of bad behavior is incompatible with the new birth. True, a believer may fall, may backslide, may grieve the Holy Spirit, but that believer is unhappy in that condition and hungers and thirsts after righteousness.

The expression "he that was begotten of God" is generally taken to be a reference to the Lord Jesus. Vine says, "Whereas the perfect tense 'he that hath been begotten' refers to the believer as a child of God, in contrast with those who have not become so, the aorist or point tense 'was begotten' points to a fact in the past and refers to the Son of God, 'the only-begotten from the Father' (John 1:11)."[14] This prepares us for what follows.

The true believer is kept by the power of God, "and that wicked one toucheth him not." The born-again child of God is in the charge of the Son of God Himself, and the Wicked One cannot "touch" that child. The word used for "toucheth" here comes from *haptomai,* meaning "to lay hold of." The only other time John uses this word is in connection with Mary Magdalene, although the word occurs frequently elsewhere (e.g., Matt. 2:3, 15; 9:20–21, 29). When the Lord revealed Himself to Magdalene in the garden, she evidently caught hold of Him, for the

---

14. W. E. Vine, *Vine's Expository Dictionary of New Testament Words,* 1 vol. (London: Oliphants, 1952).

Lord said to her, "Touch me not" (John 20:17). The word used is *haptō*—"Do not be holding me," meaning that the Lord did not want Mary to clutch hold of Him.

Satan is forced to keep his distance from any child of God who is seeking to maintain a victorious life under the protection of the Son of God. No device of Satan can sever the bond between the believer and Christ, no child of God can be seized by Satan and snatched out of the Lord's almighty hand and the hand of His Father (John 10:28–29).

We are not to take, however, the Wicked One lightly. John reminds us of *the Wicked One's domain:* "And we know that we are of God, and the whole world lieth in wickedness" (5:19). The word used for "wicked" here (describing "the wicked one") is *poneros,* from the same root as the word "wickedness." It means "full of labors and pains in working mischief," and that's a good way to describe our enemy.

"The whole world lieth in the wicked one" is John's comment, and such a one is this world's prince (John 1:30) and this world's god (2 Cor. 4:4). But he has been overcome, by the Lord, who faced the combined opposition of the Jews, with all their religious fanaticism, and of the Gentiles, with all their armed might and political power. When put under oath by the high priest, He fearlessly confessed Himself to be "the Christ, the Son of God." Then, to declare Himself far beyond the reach of Caiaphas and his crowd, He added, "Hereafter shall ye see the Son of man sitting on the right hand of power, and coming in the clouds of heaven" (Matt. 26:64). He was quoting from the Scriptures (Ps. 110:1; Dan. 7:13), and informing the Sanhedrin that it had no power at all over Him.

Nor did Pilate, the Roman governor. Pilate was completely baffled, especially by the Lord's refusal to defend Himself. He tried bluster: "Speakest thou not unto me?" he said. "Knowest thou not that I have power to crucify thee, and have power to release thee?" The Lord responded to that—for Pilate's sake, to help him come to a just sentence and to acquaint him with whom he was dealing.

It is the same with God's children in this world, Satan's domain: Satan has no power at all over us and can only touch us when permitted to do so by God, as demonstrated in the book of Job. For Satan, after all, is an usurper on this planet, an alien from outer space. He has seized the world and boasts of his power (Matt. 4:8–11), when in actual fact he is on a leash and can only go where he goes and do what he does subject to the sovereign will of God.

4. This world's lies (5:20–21)
   a. A last word (5:20)
      (1) Two great feats (5:20a–b)

The idiom of Satan's language is the lie. He is the inventor of all this world's false religions, the inspirer of all its false philosophies, and he has a deception suited for everyone. John has the antidote for all that, and in this verse he puts the straightedge of truth alongside Satan's most brilliant lies. To do so, John needs only two words—*know* and *true*—and he hammers them home. Heresy had raised its ugly head—persuasive and pervasive. Soon the last of the apostles would be gone, and who could tell what other lies Satan might invent? John urgently, insistently, again and again brings the church back to foundational certainties. Grasp these and this world's lies become void.

The invalidating of these lies is accomplished through two great feats. The first is *the incarnation of the Son of God:* "And we know that the Son of God is come" (5:20a). About that there can be no doubt at all. John could summon the herald angel to bear witness. He could summon Elizabeth and Zacharias, Mary and Joseph, the wise men from the East, and the shepherds. He could summon aged Anna and old Simon, as well as John the Baptist and all the disciples. He could appeal to the Father and to the Spirit, and he gives witness himself: "The Son of God is come." Significant figures from the prophet Isaiah to the apostle Paul testifies, "The Son of God is come." The second person of the Godhead contracted to the span of a virgin's womb. What a feat! God, who had been manifest in burning suns and blazing stars, has now been manifest in flesh. Let ten thousand false teachers arise to deny it, the truth remains—"The Son of God is come."

The second feat is *the illumination of the sons of God:* "And [he] hath given us an understanding" (5:20b). Our understanding is not based on human reasoning. No, when the unregenerate human mind is brought to bear upon divine truth, it comes up with error. It spawns so-called higher criticism and tears the Bible to shreds—at least to its own soul-damning satisfaction. Or it invents false religions such as the one espoused by Cerinthus.

Our understanding is based on divine inspiration and divine illumination. Thus, when Simon Peter gave his great statement concerning the Son of God, the Lord Jesus immediately said, "Blessed be thou, Simon Bar-Jona: for flesh and blood hath not revealed it unto thee, but my Father which is in heaven." How much Peter was dependent upon divine illumination is evident in his next words, which brought forth the Lord's resounding rebuke: "Get thee behind me, Satan, thou art an offense unto me: for thou savorest not of the things that be of God, but those that be of men" (Matt. 16:16–23).

(2) Two great finds (5:20c–d)

John next affirms a truth, possessed from two perspectives. The first is *a positive truth:* "That we may know him that is true" (5:20c). It is generally considered an asset to know the great ones of this world. But the apostles were singularly unimpressed with that. The all-important One to know is "him that is true," the Lord Jesus Christ. To know Him is to be kept from all that is untrue. Evidently, Cerinthus and his proselytes were in the pursuit of that special knowledge so touted by all the Gnostics. They were not satisfied with Christ—with "him that is true"—so off they went on the broad highway of error that leads, at last, to a lost eternity. "Know him that is true" is John's word. Jesus is the truth. He said so Himself (John 14:6).

Along with this positive truth is *a positional truth:* "And we are in him that is true, even in his Son Jesus Christ" (5:20d). We are, so to speak, centered in Christ. He is all around us, and that's a wonderfully secure place to be—in the Father and in the Son. These are not, mind you, just mystical theological propositions; they are statements of fact. John is describing things that are true. As we pass through a world that is wrapped in lies, we are wrapped in truth.

(3) Two great facts (5:20e–f)

John concludes with *a word about the deity:* "This is the true God," or, as it can be rendered, "This is the real God" (5:20e). John has just referred to the Father as "Him that is true," and to "his Son Jesus Christ." He does not mention the Holy Spirit, but He was present, the One who was revealing these truths and inspiring John to write them down. God the Father, God the Son, God the Holy Spirit—three Persons, one God. This is the true God, the real God.

The gods of the pagans do not faintly resemble Him, nor are the gods of the world's false religions remotely like Him. The gods of the various cults of Christendom are not like Him and are easily exposed as the product of human imagination and, often, of Satanic inspiration.

The real God, the God of the whole Bible, is one God, existing in three Persons, to each of whom are ascribed attributes, qualities, and prerogatives. The

Father, the Son and the Holy Spirit are each distinct from the other, each possessed of deity, each with specific spheres of operation, which operations are said to be wrought by each. The divine names and titles belong properly to the Father, yet the Son and the Holy Spirit bear the same designations. Thus, the Son is called "God" (John 1:1), "the blessed God" (Rom. 9:5), and "the great God" (Titus 2:13). So, too, the Holy Spirit is called "God" (Acts 5:3–9) and "Lord" (2 Cor. 3:17).

The revelation of God as triune is the supreme mystery. The Greeks, with all their intellectual genius, were utterly ignorant of the true nature of God. No unenlightened human mind, in fact, ever envisioned such a mysterious mode of existence as that enjoyed by the triune God as revealed in the Bible. The mysteries inherent in the Trinity are quite beyond the grasp of finite minds. Thus, no mere creature could have invented them.

"This," says John, "is the real God." To know Him and His Son is our greatest safeguard from error.

John follows up this word about the deity with *a word about our destiny:* "This is the true God, and eternal life" (5:20e–f). No other "God" can bestow this gift of all gifts—eternal life. Consider those two words—*eternal life.*

Life! John remembered the words of the Lord Jesus: "I am come that they might have life, and that they might have it more abundantly" (John 10:10). Contrast that statement with the thief who "cometh not but for to steal, and to kill, and to destroy." Cerinthus was just such a thief.

Eternal! To go on living forever and ever in a land of fadeless day where time is not counted by years, where the streets are paved with gold, and where Christ sits at the right hand of God; to go on living beyond the reach of sin and death in a tumult of joy unspeakable and full of glory; to be with Jesus forever and ever; to have a share in all the wonders of the unborn ages in those vast new empires in space that will one day replace this worn-out old rag of a world, all marred and spoiled by sin—such is eternity for the believer.

That's John's last word. But not quite. He has one more thing to say.

b. A last warning (5:21)

"Little children, keep yourselves from idols. Amen." John was living at Ephesus, one of the great centers of idolatry in the Roman world. The chief goddess of Ephesus was Diana, whose image Apollo himself was supposed to have sent down from heaven. Worship of Diana was accompanied by esoteric rites and by the practice of magic, and her adepts guarded the formulas, incantations, and spells that were part of religion. She had been worshiped from time immemorial, was, in fact, old when Alexander the Great halted at her shrine on his way to conquer Persia. A mystic aura surrounded her, and she competed easily with the gods of Greece and Rome and with the dreadful gods of Asia. Ephesus itself was a metropolis, and some of the Jews in the city did a brisk trade in books on magic, to which they appended cabalistic spells of their own.

The Temple of Diana—which rose majestically from a double line of mighty pillars and which had taken two hundred years to complete—was 420 feet long and 220 feet wide. The Ionic pillars soared 60 feet into the air and were adorned with sculptures. One depicted the struggle between Aphrodite and Mars, another captured the dance of the Graces, yet another showed Mercury setting out on a mission from Zeus. All around were gardens, and the great inner sanctuary, the home of the goddess, was adorned with sculptures executed by the greatest artists of Greece, the walls covered with paintings and the trophies of war.

And in the center of it all stood the goddess, her body wrapped in a veil of Persian silk. A giant cupola was suspended in midair above the goddess, held in place no one knew how. The blowing of trumpets announced when the veil would be removed and Diana made visible to the fortunate few, the great ones of the earth, who alone were admitted into the shrine. But people came from the ends of the earth to worship, filling the place with incense and the smoke of sacrifices. As the veil was removed, the worshipers fell prostrate. On a pedestal of black marble she stood, ugly as sin, her body of black ebony, repulsive as a serpent, an Asiatic nightmare. At her unveiling the thousands upon thousands of her worshipers cried, "Great is Diana of the Ephesians." The blind, the lame, the diseased would join the mad rush for the doors, hoping to be healed.

The priests and magicians, tattooed all over, mingled with the multitudes, selling their wares. Small models of the temple and images of the goddess were for sale. And with it all went orgies and vice and all manner of foulness sanctioned as acts of worship.

"Little children, keep yourselves from idols." Idolatry was the prevailing religion, and John—Jew that he was, having an inbred horror of image worship—knew the power of pagan religion. A thousand demons lurked within each image. Many of the Christians had been saved from such idolatry. Sometimes, however, it died hard, and over time it began to creep into the church, and in some quarters has remained entrenched there to this day. Idolatry was the antithesis, the final denial of the worship of "him that is true" and of "his Son Jesus Christ." So John commands, "Keep yourselves from idols."

An idol, of course, is not necessarily made of wood or stone. It may be anything that comes between the soul and God. So the response of all those who echo John's closing "Amen" will surely be,

> The dearest idol I have known,
> Whate'er that idol be;
> Help me to tear it from Thy throne,
> And worship only Thee.

Exploring

JOHN'S SECOND
EPISTLE

Outline

The author calls himself simply "the elder," thus remaining anonymous, as he does in his gospel and other epistles. There can be little doubt, however, as to who he is. In his day, everyone knew who he was—John, the disciple of the Lord Jesus, now a very old man and the last surviving apostle. The word John uses to refer to himself is *presbyteros,* a common New Testament word for one who is a shepherd of a local church. Doubtless, the title was adopted by John, however, as one of endearment. To his flock he was the oldest and wisest shepherd of them all, the last living man who had known the Lord Jesus in the flesh. His fellowship of like-minded believers was made up of his "little children."

This short letter introduces no new teaching. It is concerned, rather, with anti-Christian teaching, which was taking root and needed to be combated. John was particularly concerned because an esteemed Christian sister known to him was unwittingly giving some heretical teachers misguided aid.

The possibility is that this letter was written from Ephesus, but we have no exact information as to when it was written or where John was when he wrote it. It can be divided into four parts.

PART 1: A WORD OF COMMENDATION (VV. 1–4)
    A. The lady as a person (v. 1a)
    B. The lady as a partner (vv. 1b–3)
        1. In the truth of the gospel (v. 1b)
        2. In the triumph of the gospel (vv. 2–3)
    C. The lady as a parent (v. 4)

PART 2: A WORD OF COMMAND (VV. 5–6)
    A. Love demanded (v. 5)
    B. Love defined (v. 6)

PART 3: A WORD OF CAUTION (VV. 7–11)
    A. Danger from the deceiver (vv. 7–8)
        1. How to recognize him (v. 7)
        2. How to regard him (v. 8)
            a. As a threat (v. 8a)
            b. As a thief (v. 8b)

   B.   Danger to the doctrine (v. 9)
      1. Those who abandon the truth (v. 9a)
      2. Those who abide in the truth (v. 9b)
   C.   Danger at the door (vv. 10–11)
      1. Refuse the apostate your hospitality when he comes (v. 10a)
      2. Refuse the apostate your handshake when he goes (v. 10b)

PART 4: A WORD OF CONCLUSION (vv. 12–13)
   A.   What John expected in the future (v. 12)
   B.   What John extended to his friend (v. 13)

"The elder . . . to the elect lady." John carefully hides his identity and that of his addressee. We can only guess why. But because persecution was by no means a thing of the past, John likely had no desire to attract unwanted attention to himself, nor did he wish to expose his friend to enemies of the faith, especially enemies who sat in high places.

PART 1

A Word of Commendation
2 John 1–4

A. The lady as a person (v. 1a)

"The elder unto the elect lady . . ." Some have thought John had in mind the church, either the local church in some area, or the church universal. If this is so, then her "children" are its members. Others take the words literally. The words used for "elect lady," *eklektē kyria,* can be translated "the elect kyria" or even "the lady Electa." Even so, we do not know who she was.

A friend once suggested to me that perhaps John was referring to Mary, the Lord's mother. This raises some interesting speculations. Recall that Mary was John's aunt and James and Jude were his cousins, and if there is anything to my friend's guess, then Mary must have been a very old woman indeed. The title "the elect lady" would suit very well the esteemed mother of the Lord. The same reasons for not mentioning either her or her children by name would hold true and perhaps even more so for himself or for some other distinguished Christian. We can well believe that if word were to reach some in high places that the Lord's mother was alive and active in the church, her life would be in danger. Still, such musing is speculative, because we have no way of proving my friend's suggestion one way or the other. It seems more natural to assume that John is addressing someone else, a woman well known and highly esteemed in church circles.

It is interesting, though, that this epistle, addressed to the elect lady and her children, is written in Greek not in Aramaic. Some see this as proof that the family circle involved was made up of Gentiles, the assumption being that John would have addressed the recipient in Aramaic had that one been a Jew. But that, too, is mere speculation. Most Jews, especially if they had lived abroad and had thus become part of the Dispersion, spoke Greek. Moreover, by the time John wrote this letter, Jerusalem and the temple were no more, the Holy Land was under Roman control, and many Palestinian Jews had been "scattered abroad." In any case, the church was now almost wholly Gentile, the Jews becoming an ever dwindling minority in its fellowship. This letter, then, was intended for the church, not just a single family, although John may not have realized that when he wrote it. But the Holy Spirit most certainly did. He impressed it upon John to write in the universal language rather than in a local dialect.

John begins by expressing his love for this "elect lady," stating his love for her in the truth. John was careful in his choice of words, the word used for love, for instance, being *agapē,* a word not intended as an endearment. When addressing

192

Gaius, however, John used the word for "well beloved"—*agapētos*—the word *beloved* being a special epithet of the Lord's people in the Epistles (see 3 John 1–2). In addressing this Christian woman, John uses no such undue familiarity. He qualifies his *agapē* love for her by clearly stating that he loves her "in the truth" or, as some render it, "in truth"—signifying "in the sphere of truth." Thus, John's greeting was open, honest, and aboveboard, simply stating that he loved this elect lady and her children as all believers are called upon to love other believers—as one who is "of the truth."

Recall that the truth was under attack when John wrote all three of his epistles. It is significant, in this regard, that the Holy Spirit directed John to write this letter to a woman rather than to a man. Although men can be gullible enough, women are often more vulnerable to deception than men are (1 Tim. 2:11–14). John, by addressing a woman, and an honored one at that, and by warning a woman against a plausible antichrist, wanted to put Christian women everywhere on guard.

    B.   The lady as a partner (vv. 1b–3)
        1. In the truth of the gospel (v. 1b)

She is his partner *in the truth of the gospel:* "Whom I love in the truth; and not I only, but also all they that have known the truth" (v. 1b). This Christian lady and her family were not standing alone. They were members of a very much larger family, the family of God. Thus, she had the spiritual resources of the whole church behind her in the never ending battle for truth. Conversely, any retreat, compromise, or error on her part would have repercussions throughout the whole church.

When the Roman legions drew up in battle array against an overwhelming attacking force, they locked their great rectangular shields together against the common foe. The enemy was thus faced with a solid wall of steel against which their arrows, swords, and spears beat in vain. But there could be no breach in that wall. Each soldier had to stand firm. So, too, must this elect lady. She was one with all other believers who, together, made up a solid front against the forces of deception. Let them stand fast in their portion of the battlefield.

        2. In the triumph of the gospel (vv. 2–3)

John continues, stating that this woman is not only his partner in the truth of the gospel but is his partner *in the triumph of the gospel* (vv. 2–3): "For the truth's sake, which dwelleth in us, and shall be with us for ever" (v. 2). We are on the winning side, although it may not seem like it. The church often seems feeble, vulnerable, and ineffective, but lies are eventually shown to be lies and truth triumphs.

Well might James Russell Lowell write,

> Careless seems the great avenger: History's pages but record
> One death grapple in the darkness, 'twixt old systems and the Word.
> Truth for ever on the scaffold; wrong for ever on the throne:
> But that scaffold sways the future; and behind the dim unknown
> Standeth God, within the shadow, keeping watch above His own.

But that is just a mere poet's word for it. We have something better—we have the Lord's own word for it: "On this rock I will build my church; and the gates of hell shall not prevail against it" (Matt. 16:18). Truth is eternal. The tares may flourish for a while, seeming to have triumphed altogether in parts of the harvest field and taken over large portions elsewhere in the field. There is no way we can uproot them, and the Lord was well aware of all that. "An enemy hath done this," He says. The condition is prolonged but not permanent: "Let them grow together [the wheat and the tares, that is] until the harvest." In a coming day "the Son of man shall send forth his angels, and they shall gather out of his kingdom all things that offend, and them which do iniquity; and shall cast them into a furnace of fire: there shall be wailing and gnashing of teeth. Then shall the righteous shine forth as the sun in the kingdom of their Father. Who hath ears to hear, let him hear" (Matt. 13:28, 41–43).

John confirms that the truth "dwelleth" in the believer. The word used for "dwelleth" is *menō*, a favorite word of John's—it occurs forty-one times in his gospel. It means "to abide" or "to remain." The word is used of Paul when, upon his arrival at Rome as a prisoner, he was put under house arrest. Luke says, "Paul was suffered to dwell *[menō]* by himself" (Acts 28:16). Truth takes up its permanent abode in a believer's heart, nor can Satan uproot it.

This is guaranteed: "Grace be with you, mercy, and peace, from God the Father, and from the Lord Jesus Christ, the Son of the Father, in truth and love" (v. 3). Grace, peace, mercy—that's what Satan is up against when he attacks a believer. He may win some tactical battles, but he cannot win the war. *Grace* means that the limitless resources of God's loving-kindness and tender mercy have been harnessed on the believer's behalf. God's unmerited and unbounded favor cuts all the ground from beneath the Enemy's feet. *Peace* means the war is over; it has already been won. As a result of Calvary, Satan's activities are severely restricted (Col. 2:14–15). He can act only by divine permission and under divine supervision and in accordance with the mystery of God's permissive will. *Mercy* means that God will not allow Satan to go any further against us than we are able to bear and that, in each case, a way of escape is provided for us (1 Cor. 10:13).

All this is assured by God the Father and God the Son. John here deliberately equates the Son with the Father as coequal, coexistent, and coeternal. Satan, for all his diligence and resourcefulness, is on the losing side.

C. The lady as a parent (v. 4)

"I rejoiced greatly that I found of thy children walking in truth, as we have received a commandment from the Father." It is always delightful to enter a home where the children are an ornament to their believing parents. It would seem that John had visited this family and his heart had been gladdened by the order and integrity of that home. Now he had moved on, and the joy of that encounter lived on in his heart. Families like this are the joy of any local church. A transparent sincerity adorned this elect lady and her children; they were "walking in the truth." All the characteristics of divinely imparted grace, mercy, and peace, just mentioned by John, were to be found in this home; all energized by "truth and love."

Bunyan's Pilgrim found such a haven when he arrived at the Palace Beautiful. Arriving at the lodge, he rang the bell and requested lodging for the night. The porter summoned an attractive young woman named Discretion, who questioned him to make sure he really was a pilgrim on his way to Mount Zion. Once she was satisfied about that, she invited him in and summoned her sisters Prudence, Piety, and Charity. Before he was invited to supper, he was asked a number of searching questions. Piety was interested in his conversion, Prudence in his progress, and Charity in his family.

What had moved him to become a pilgrim? That was Piety's concern. What had he learned from the Interpreter? What had he learned at the cross? Who, along the way, had helped or hindered him?

How did he now feel about his past life? That was the interest of Prudence. And was he still troubled about clinging remnants of his past life? And why was he now so eager to go to Mount Zion?

But Charity asked the most probing questions. Did he have a family? Why had he not brought his wife and children? Had he done anything to hinder them?

Then came supper, "and all their talk was about the Lord of the hill." That night he was lodged in a large upper room with a view of the sunrise. Before he was allowed to leave the next morning, the sisters gave him a full suit of armor. Then, as a parting blessing, Discretion and Prudence and Piety and Charity helped him on his way, bringing him safely down the dangerous slopes of the Valley of Humiliation. No wonder he was ready to meet the foul fiend Apollyon, who appeared next to bar his path.

The "elect lady" had just such a family. Her ministry was to encourage and help other pilgrims on their homeward way. She already knew Piety and Charity (John would have approved of Bunyan and his *The Pilgrim's Progress*) but needed to make the acquaintance of Discretion and Prudence. John knew them well, and in this letter he introduces her to them.

PART 2

A Word of Command

2 John 5–6

A. Love demanded (v. 5)

And now I beseech thee, lady, not as though I wrote a new commandment unto thee, but that which we had from the beginning, that we love one another." John was about to draw this dear sister's attention to a peril and to a practice that needed to be stopped. Doubtless, she was acting out of the love and generosity of her heart. But love has to be tough as well as tender. John, therefore, precedes his word of caution with a word of command. He takes her back to the foundation of everything Christian—love, love divine, the love of God in Christ, true love, love that shrinks from error and hypocrisy and sin.

His first epistle is an exposition of this love. His gospel is full of it. Love, the noun *agapē*, occurs there seven times; love, the verb *agapaō*, occurs there thirty-seven times; and love, the verb *phileō*, occurs there thirteen times. Love, in other words, shows up in John's gospel no less than fifty-seven times. Christianity is all about love, so for John to insist upon love was nothing new. Jesus insisted upon it. He personified, embodied, incarnated it, and the world has never seen anything like it. Love is the primary way His life is expressed in us by the Holy Spirit (Gal. 5:22), the first evidence of a Spirit-filled life. John reinforces the truth of Christian love with this esteemed believer before injecting the vaccine of, perhaps, unpalatable truth.

B. Love defined (v. 6)

"And this is love, that we walk after his commandments. This is the commandment, that, as ye have heard from the beginning, ye should walk in it." Paul put it this way: "He that loveth another hath fulfilled the law . . . love worketh no ill to his neighbour: therefore love is the fulfilling of the law" (Rom. 13:8, 10). "Working ill," as we shall see, is exactly what the cultists, who were in the habit of visiting this woman, were doing. They were abusing her hospitality, taking advantage of her loving spirit and abounding generosity, and planning, if possible, to do her incalculable harm by subverting her from the truth.

Doubtless, Paul's letters were by this time in general circulation, or at least they were well known and widely quoted. Paul had already addressed the issue John was about to raise: "Now I beseech you, brethren, mark them which cause divisions and offences contrary to the doctrine which ye have learned; and avoid them. For they that are such serve not our Lord Jesus Christ, but their own belly; and by good words and fair speeches deceive the hearts of the simple" (Rom. 16:17–18). The situation was far worse in John's day, and the heretics were even more persistent, prevalent, and poisonous. Paul's commandment can well be included in John's demand that "we [including the elect sister] walk after his commandments," for Paul's words were Holy Spirit inspired and as authoritative as the actual words of the Lord Jesus Himself.

PART 3

A Word of Caution

2 John 7–11

For many deceivers are entered into the world, who confess not that Jesus Christ is come in the flesh. This is a deceiver and an antichrist"—no matter how charming he may be and no matter how golden tongued his or her oratory.

Now we can see why John used the unique title (it occurs nowhere else in the New Testament) for the Lord Jesus—"the Son of the Father" (v. 3). He was putting the emphasis on the great foundation truth of the Christian faith, that the incarnate Son of the living God is the Person through whom the Father has been pleased to reveal Himself to men. The Incarnation will be jettisoned, as a mandatory article of faith, only by those who love not the truth.

There were many such "deceivers" abroad at the end of the apostolic era. John uses the word *planos* to describe them, the word suggesting "impostors," or wandering vagabonds. These people refused to confess the truth of Christ's incarnation, the word used for "confess" being *homologeō*, "to agree" or "to admit." These cultists did not agree with the revealed New Testament doctrine, based upon historical fact, that the person known as Jesus Christ "is come in the flesh," that He was a true human being. The Docetic Gnostics thought that it was outrageous to believe that the infinite God would allow Himself to be born just as all human beings are born, that He would actually become for a time, humanly speaking, a helpless infant, and that He would subject Himself to human limitations. They denied not only the fact of the Incarnation but also its possibility at *any* time, their denial thus including the Second Advent as well.

Deceivers thrive, too, in the twenty-first century. The denial of the Incarnation is common today among liberal theologians. Much modern unbelief stems from the popular acceptance of the mechanistic theory of evolution, which denies the supernatural or any interference on the part of a Supreme Being on the developing order. Thus, it is well to heed John's warnings.

John uses the word *planos* twice in this description of the apostates whose presence was a potential menace to the elect lady. The second time he uses the definite article: "This is the deceiver and the antichrist." As the deceiver, the apostate is the enemy of men; as the antichrist, the enemy of God. The heresies that were surfacing, as the first century drew to a close, were as deadly as any that will be sponsored by the coming Antichrist himself.

2. How to regard him (v. 8)

The false teacher is to be regarded *as a threat:* "Look to yourselves . . ." (v. 8a). The warning is sudden, short, and sharp. "Watch out!" The words ring out all the more clearly from the textual context of praise and congratulation. John evidently knew this elect lady very well and had likely been himself a recipient of her hospitality and generosity. Maybe he had noted at the time her uncritical nature, her eagerness to take everyone at face value.

But such naivete could invite peril. In John's day, traveling was difficult and dangerous (2 Cor. 11:25–27). Inns were few, even when traveling on one of the great Roman roads, and they would be expensive and crowded. Hospitality was a Christian duty. Paul wrote, "Be not forgetful to entertain strangers: for thereby some have entertained angels unawares" (Heb. 13:2; see Gen. 18:1–17; 19:1–3). It is just as possible to entertain devils unawares.

The members of a local Christian fellowship, those who were gregarious and generous by nature, would thoroughly enjoy extending a helping hand to a visiting itinerant preacher. What an opportunity such visits would offer to get to know another brother in Christ. And how much one could learn from conversation around the supper table, not only of the Lord's work in other parts of the world but of the Word of God itself. And what an opportunity to summon in the family, the servants, the neighbors, friends, and fellow believers for some serious after-dinner Bible study.

All well and good, but what if the visitor was one of those "grievous wolves" against whom Paul had warned the Ephesians years before (Acts 20:28–31)? Such men were a threat. No wonder John inserts this blunt warning: "Look to yourselves," that is, "Look out!" On no account was a visiting preacher to be accepted at face value. The word used for "look to" is *blepō,* meaning "to observe accurately" or "to contemplate earnestly." "Use your eyes" or "keep your eyes open" would be one way of putting it. Impostors will, sooner or later, betray themselves. They may be gifted and charming, may drop the names of well-known believers into the conversation, may say many true and helpful things. But out it will come, some subtle, serious error, usually concerning the person of Christ, the ministry of the Holy Spirit, or the inerrancy and inspiration of Scripture.

Such a person, says John, is to be regarded not only as a threat to the family, to the fellowship, and to the faith, but he is to be regarded as *a thief:* "That we [ye] lose not those things which we [ye] have wrought, but that we receive a full reward" (v. 8b). A believer cannot lose his or her salvation but can certainly lose his or her reward. It is a serious thing to be led astray by someone's false doctrine. The New Testament reminds us that all believers must one day stand before the judgment seat of Christ to receive rebukes and rewards. When this prospect is set before us, it is always in sobering language (Rom. 14:10; 1 Cor. 3:11–15; 2 Cor. 5:10). It is a serious thing to lose one's crown, and such a loss is a real possibility (Rev. 3:11).

Those who succumb to false teachers espouse a lost cause and imperil those around him, especially their families, and help lead others astray. They no longer serve Christ but a cult, and they negate a great deal of the good they have done in the past. They become the victims of thieves, they stand in peril of being excommunicated by the body of Christ, and come under the condemnation of many warning passages in the New Testament. Evidently John feared that the kindly, uncritical spirit of the elect lady put her and her family in peril.

  B.   Danger to the doctrine (v. 9)
      1.   Those who abandon the truth (v. 9a)
      2.   Those who abide in the truth (v. 9b)

John now draws a contrast. There are *those who abandon* the truth: "Whosoever transgresseth, and abideth not in the doctrine of Christ, hath not God" (v. 9a); and there are *those who abide* in the truth: "He that abideth in the doctrine of Christ, he hath both the Father and the Son" (v. 9b). One either abides or does not abide in the doctrine. As usual, John makes no room for sitting on the fence.

Truth, then, boils down to doctrine. In the very early days of the church, apostolic doctrine went unchallenged (Acts 2:42). Paul foresaw the day, however, when people would not "endure sound doctrine, but after their own lusts shall they heap to themselves teachers, having itching ears; and they shall turn away their ears from the truth, and shall be turned unto fables"—so he urgently warned Timothy in his last epistle (2 Tim. 4:3). Truth always comes down to doctrine. It was so in John's day, and it was so with Job—the whole book is an answer to this question: "Would Job's theology triumph over his experience; or would his experience triumph over his theology?" Truth came down to doctrine with Martin Luther when he stood before all the massed might of Rome, and truth has come down to doctrine today, as we are inundated with cults that attack all the great fundamentals of the faith and who decry doctrine, claiming it to be divisive and an obstacle to their vision of a global, ecumenical church.

Neither Jesus, nor Paul, nor John, nor any of the other New Testament writers will let us get away with dumping doctrine for the sake of unity and peace. John put it bluntly enough to his friend, the elect lady: "Either you hold to the historic doctrines of the Christian faith, or you don't. If you do, you are a genuine believer, united to the Father and the Son. If you don't, you are deceived 'and have not God.'" Not many these days care to have the issues so cut and dried as that. But John the aged, with a lifetime of experience behind him and eternity opening up before him, had no hesitation in putting it like that. He hoped to see this lady again (v. 12), but at his age he couldn't be sure. At least he would put her—and us—on guard!

    C. Danger at the door (vv. 10–11)
        1. Refuse the apostate hopitality when he comes (v. 10a)

The place to settle matters was at the door, before ever the visitor was able to get into the house. John has two pieces of practical advice: first, *refuse the apostate your hospitality when he comes:* "If there come any unto you, and bring not this doctrine, receive him not into your house" (v. 10a). It ought not take long to find out if a person is sound as to the doctrine of Christ—His deity, His virgin birth, His immaculate life, His miracles and teaching, His atoning death, His resurrection, His ascension, His enthronement, and His coming again. John narrows it down to one issue—the Incarnation: Jesus was either God manifest in flesh, in which case all the rest followed as a matter of course, or else He wasn't—in which case the person denying the doctrine stood self-exposed. Two major cults in our day specialize in going from door to door: the Mormons and the so-called Jehovah's Witnesses. Both cults are heretical with regard to the person of Christ. "Meet them at the door," John says, "don't invite them in—you'll find them hard to get rid of—plausible, persuasive, and persistent. Shut the door firmly in their faces."

        2. Refuse the apostate your handshake when he goes (v. 10b)

That was sound advice. What the gentle and courageous elect lady thought of it we are not told. But John has some more advice: *refuse the apostate your handshake when he goes:* "Neither bid him God speed: for he that biddeth him God speed is partaker of his evil deeds" (vv. 10b–11). A person who comes to one's house professing to be a legitimate evangelist but who is in reality a cultist and an enemy of the faith is a scoundrel and, as such, forfeits the right even to the common courtesy of a greeting or a farewell.

Once the person has been unmasked, and this is to take place at the door, that person must be summarily dismissed. To receive him or her into one's house as though he or she were a believer is to be disloyal, in fact, to the Lord, whom this person denies. It gives the intruder an opportunity to make friends and contacts, exposes one's family members and the local church to false teaching, and helps to confirm the cultist in his errors. It also means that we have personal fellowship in the damage the heretic is doing because, in effect, we are condoning his or her heretical doctrine.

Such mandatory rules sound strange to many these days when compromise, tolerance, and ecumenicalism are considered more important than truth. Many people are so afraid of being labeled "bigots" or "fundamentalists" that they consider such admonitions, even from an inspired apostle, to be harsh, even unchristian, and out of touch with the spirit of the age. The rule still stands. "Don't let them in." "Don't say 'good-bye.'"

PART 4

A Word of Conclusion
2 John 12–13

A. What John expected in the future (v. 12)

John, like the true Christian gentleman he was, did not wish to close his little letter on that unpleasant note. So he adds two concluding remarks. We note *what he expected in the future:* "Having many things to write unto you, I would not write with paper and ink: but I trust to come unto you, and speak face to face, that our joy may be full" (v. 12). Just thinking of this lady and her situation started an avalanche of thoughts tumbling into the old apostle's mind. How much there was to write her about—the evangelical truths found in John's gospel; the rainbow-colored themes of his first epistle; the great eschatological truths now found in the book of Revelation—for surely John had pondered much about the teaching of the Lord Jesus regarding the future and had pored long over the Old Testament prophecies, especially the apocalyptic-type prophecies of Daniel and Zechariah. Or maybe John wanted to be more specific about the particular cultists who had been coming to her door. Perhaps he had in mind a whole treatise on the various popular Gnostic errors raising their hydra heads all over.

We do not know. The task seems to daunt him. He had a better idea. He'd go and see her. He would talk to her "face to face" or "mouth to mouth," just as God spoke to Moses (Num. 12:8). It would help fill his cup of joy one more time. That's what he would do. Maybe the very thought of writing another long letter made him tired. He was an old man. How much better to sit in the elect lady's living room, sampling her cooking, talking over old times and eternal truths, maybe visiting with her delightful children, encouraging the local saints—whether he ever made that trip we do not know. The thought was there, at least.

B. What John extended to his friend (v. 13)

Finally, we note *what he extended to his friend:* "The children of thy elect sister greet thee. Amen." Some think that both sisters were local churches in the neighborhood. It is just as likely that the two women, both elect, both saved, were literal sisters. The children, mentioned here, in that case would be nephews or nieces of the "elect lady," and their mother possibly was away at the time John wrote. As a final gesture of goodwill toward the elect lady, whom he did not wish to hurt in any way, he extended these personal greetings to her—just another demonstration of John's love and tenderness in his old age. The old "son of thunder" (Mark 3:17) was gone. In his place was a gentle man who much preferred to throw the aura of the rainbow around any place where might be seen a forbidding sky.

Exploring

JOHN'S THIRD EPISTLE

Outline

There are similarities and contrasts between John's last two letters. The second letter was sent to a woman, the third to a man; the second urges against receiving false messengers, the third warns against rejecting true messengers; anonymity marks the second letter, naming of individuals highlights the third; the second letter warns against being too soft, the third against being too hard; one warns against the deceiver, the other against the dictator.

These three letters of John are very touching. We get a picture of the aged apostle, concerned about the inroads of apostasy in the church, writing his impassioned first epistle. He adds, as it were, a postscript by writing another letter. Then he adds one more. Brevity is the hallmark of all three letters, the first being about 2,350 words; the second only 245; the third, fewer still, a bare 219—only a little more than 2,800 words in all. We get a picture in this of John's feeling for the desperate urgency of the situation. He puts down his pen, picks it up again, puts it down again, picks it up again, and puts it down a third time. He is the last of the apostles and he is old. The times are uncertain; Nero has gone but Domitian will soon pick up Nero's policy of persecution. Error is abroad; tares are growing profusely, springing up everywhere among the wheat, and Christians are squabbling.

So John writes and writes and writes. His last two letters are mere memos, but the Holy Spirit urged him to write them, breathed into them, saw to it that they were preserved, brought them into the divine library, added them to the Book as almost His very last word. We should certainly not make the mistake of underestimating their importance simply because they are brief. In the things of God, as we learn from the so-called "minor" prophets, it is a mistake to measure the man by the size of his manuscript; the Holy Spirit doesn't always inspire long books in order to convey vital beliefs. Weighty things can often be stated in a few dynamic words—"I love you," for instance, or "Don't touch," or "Exit," or "Help!" We certainly don't expect a drowning man to express his urgent need in flowery paragraphs.

PART 1: THE VIRTUOUS PASTOR (vv. 1–4)
    A. John's devotion to him (v. 1)
    B. John's desire for him (v. 2)
    C. John's delight in him (vv. 3–4)

Because of
1. The reputation Gaius had (v. 3)
2. The relationship Gaius had (v. 4)

PART 2: THE VISITING PREACHER (vv. 5–8)
   A.   Recognizing him (v. 5)
   B.   Refreshing him (vv. 6–7)
       1. A privilege extended (v. 6)
       2. A principle extolled (v. 7)
   C.   Receiving him (v. 8)

PART 3: THE VAINGLORIOUS POPE (vv. 9–11)
   A.   His pride (v. 9)
   B.   His presumption (v. 10a)
   C.   His practice (vv. 10b–11)
       1. Condemned (v. 10b)
       2. Contrasted (v. 11)

PART 4: THE VALUED PARTNER (v. 12)

PART 5: THE VIGILANT PRESBYTER (vv. 13–14)
   A.   He had so much to say (v. 13)
   B.   He was coming that way (v. 14)

Five men! And an interesting collection of men they are and all connected with one local church. Taken together, they form a cameo of any one of a hundred churches in our land today.

PART 1

The Virtuous Pastor
3 John 1–4

"The elder unto the wellbeloved Gaius, whom I love in the truth." Gaius was evidently a person of some prominence in the local church where he resided. He was a man with a pastor's heart, a true shepherd of the sheep—in glaring contrast with the man in the church who fought for position and authority.

John begins the letter by telling of his *devotion to Gaius:* "the wellbeloved Gaius, whom I love in the truth" (v. 1). The name *Gaius* was common enough in the Roman world. F. F. Bruce says it was one of a dozen and a half names from which Roman parents could choose a *praenomen* for one of their sons. We meet the name several times in the New Testament besides here: a Gaius of Corinth (Rom. 16:23; 1 Cor. 1:14), who was Paul's host when he was in that city, sent greetings to the church at Rome, and was one of the few people Paul baptized in person; a man of Macedonia by the name of Gaius, who was with Paul at Ephesus (Acts 19:29) at the time of the Ephesian riot; a Gaius of Derbe (Acts 20:4), who was Paul's traveling companion when, after the Ephesus riot, Paul made his way to Jerusalem. Some think that "Derbe" should read "Doberus" and that the last two named are the same individual. We have no way of knowing whether the Gaius addressed by John was one of these but it could well be. In any case, he was a man much loved by the aged apostle John.

B. John's desire for him (v. 2)

"Beloved, I wish above all things that thou mayest prosper and be in health, even as thy soul prospereth." In the Old Testament, one's spiritual prosperity could be measured by one's material prosperity. The Old Testament blessing was "the blessing of the LORD, it maketh rich, and he addeth no sorrow with it" (Prov. 10:22). Job was rich. When, under the assaults of Satan, he was beggared and bereaved, broken in health, and regarded with scorn by his wife, his friends lost no time in judging him by this criterion (Job 1:1–5; 8:6). Abraham was rich (Gen. 13:2; 24:34–35). Jacob was rich (Gen. 30:27, 43; 31:4–9). Solomon was rich (1 Kings 3:5–14; 10:14–29). The Old Testament rule equated godliness with prosperity (Ps. 1:1–3).

The New Testament blessing is quite different. What constitutes blessedness in this age is spelled out in the Beatitudes of the Sermon on the Mount (Matt.

5:1–12). God makes no guarantee to us that He will give us wealth and health if we walk in His ways. In the Old Testament, God's people were an earthly people and were promised a literal kingdom on earth (Gen. 12:1–3). The conditions under which they would be prospered as a nation were spelled out in the Palestinian Covenant (Deut. 27–30), were incorporated by Moses in his great farewell song (Deut. 31:30–32:47), and are echoed in many of the Psalms (Ps. 78, for instance). We, by contrast, are God's heavenly people and our blessings are positional, spiritual, and eternal (Eph. 1–3).

A brand of false teaching is very popular today, encouraging us to "name it and claim it." Those who listen to the siren voices of these "evangelists" are fed a "gospel of prosperity" that promises health and wealth to those who respond to the message. When the promises fail to materialize and followers get sick or lose their jobs or disaster strikes, they are cynically told that either they do not have enough faith or else there must be sin in their lives. This entire religious philosophy is based on ignorance. Calvary has changed everything, including a change of dispensations. Failure to recognize that gives rise to many modern delusions.

Here, however, John's wishes for Gaius arise from benevolence. There is, after all, nothing particularly blessed about being poor, just as there's nothing particularly blessed about being rich. Solomon prayed, "Give me neither poverty nor riches . . . lest I be full, and deny thee, and say, who is the Lord? or lest I be poor, and steal, and take the name of my God in vain" (Prov. 30:8–9). So John prayed that Gaius might "prosper and be in health." John may have felt that Gaius could handle money and use it wisely and well in the cause of the kingdom. God always has some of those around. Possibly John knew that Gaius was not well off and in poor health. Regardless, he was a key person in his local church and one who was "rich toward God." Thus, it stands to reason that an improvement in his material and physical situation would benefit him and everyone else. It's one thing for an aged apostle, with a heart full of compassion and love, desiring that a key church member's physical and material circumstances might improve, and to pray to that end. It's quite another thing, this modern arrogance of demanding that God heal this person and enrich that one.

    C. John's delight in him (vv. 3–4)
        1. The reputation Gaius had (v. 3)

John mentions the *reputation* of Gaius: "For I rejoiced greatly, when the brethren came and testified of the truth that is in thee, even as thou walkest in the truth"

(v. 3). It would seem that John hears good reports about Gaius, that he was standing up for the truth. The false teachers who were knocking at the door of the elect lady would receive short shrift at the door of Gaius. He would have the ugly truth out of them in no time and send them away with a warning to steer clear of his flock.

But more than that—Gaius had a reputation not only for standing for the truth, he had a reputation for walking in the truth. His conduct endorsed his creed. It is one thing to have one's doctrine correct; it is something else to practice what we preach. Gaius had the reputation of incarnating truth in life.

2. The relationship Gaius had (v.4)

John mentions also the *relationship* of Gaius: "I have no greater joy than to hear that my children walk in truth" (v. 4). The word "my" is emphatic and can be rendered "my own children." Evidently Gaius was one of the people whom John himself had led to Christ. Such people are the soul winner's trophies. Thus, Paul could write ecstatically to the saints at Philippi: "My brethren dearly beloved and longed for, my joy and my crown . . . my dearly beloved" (Phil. 4:1). It is a great joy to lead someone to a saving knowledge of the Lord Jesus Christ. It is an even greater joy to get word that they are growing in grace and increasing in the knowledge of God and that they have become useful members of the body of Christ.

PART 2

The Visiting Preacher
3 John 5–8

A. Recognizing him (v. 5)

B eloved, thou doest faithfully whatsoever thou doest to the brethren, and to strangers." John is still commending Gaius, but he shifts the focus slightly. He has in mind now the itinerant evangelist, sometimes a man not well known, who can use all the help he can get. Gaius had a reputation of being a friend to all such, evidently regarding as a sacred duty to extend help and hospitality to visiting preachers. And he was faithful in discharging this duty, recognizing all such. The well-known visiting preachers and those he had never met before—one and all found a warm welcome with Gaius. The strangers, of course, would be put to the test at the door, but once their credentials were verified, they would be invited in, their feet washed, a guest room put at their disposal, and an extra plate put on the table.

B. Refreshing him (vv. 6–7)
1. A privilege extended (v. 6)

John now points to *a privilege extended,* underlining the importance of ministering to those who have given their lives to ministering to others: "Which have borne witness of thy charity before the church: whom if thou bring forward on their journey after a godly sort, thou shalt do well" (v. 6).

Gaius evidently seized every opportunity to show the love of Christ to these visiting preachers, and they appreciated his hospitality, telling of his helpfulness wherever they went in their travels. Gaius himself appears to have been a very ordinary person. His name means "of the earth," and as we would put it, he was a "down-to-earth" sort of person. The Lord could have said of him what He said of the woman in the house of Simon of Bethany: "She hath done what she could" (Mark 14:8). Gaius had a true pastor's heart, noted not only because he championed the truth but also because his heart was full of love. The Lord has many such. In many years of traveling across Canada and the United States and to other countries, I have been royally helped by many a present-day Gaius. Great will be their reward in heaven.

2. A principle extolled (v. 7)

John points also to *a principle extolled:* "Because that for his name's sake they went forth, taking nothing of the Gentiles" (v. 7). These visiting preachers deserve to be helped. John had in mind those who had no visible means of support, those who lived by faith, looking to the Lord to meet their needs, determined to accept financial aid from other believers, not from the unsaved.

When I was a boy growing up in Britain, my father had a small automobile business. He bought and sold and repaired cars, had a garage, a workshop, a showroom, and some gasoline pumps. He was not a wealthy person, but we lived comfortably. Then came the war. Overnight his business was practically wiped out. The government commandeered private cars for the military, spare parts vanished off the market, gasoline was severely rationed. The only people who could drive cars were those on essential war work. Still, my father struggled on, and the Lord saw to it that he had sufficient customers—farmers and the like— so that we survived.

And he was a true Gaius. His hospitality was proverbial. One missionary family sat at our table every Sunday for years, despite the stringent food rationing. I can think of a number of traveling preachers who headed for my father's workshop whenever they were passing through town. Two of them, particularly, stand out in my mind. Both of them were poor, both had ramshackle old cars, always in need of repair work, always nearly out of gas. And both of them always seemed to arrive at mealtime. Neither of them was sent away empty. My father fixed their cars for them and, out of his own small allowance of gas, filled up their tanks. My mother performed miracles, multiplying loaves and fishes so that these preacher friends could go on their way well fed. And my dad always left a sizable wad of banknotes in their hands with his parting hand-shake. Often, we had a Spartan meal or two afterward. But that was my dad. He ought to have been called Gaius. Great is his reward now in heaven, and great is my mother's reward as well.

C. Receiving him (v. 8)

"We therefore ought to receive such, that we might be fellowhelpers to the truth." It is the responsibility of believers to support those who are full-time workers in ministry. There is no place in the New Testament for the practice, common enough in our day, of shamelessly begging for money. Saint and sinner alike are besieged with requests to give to this "ministry" and that.

We are the ones whom God calls upon to be His "fellowhelpers," receiving and supporting those who have given themselves to the ministry. The word used for "fellowhelper" is *sunergos,* and Paul used it of Apollos, one of his colleagues in the Lord's work: "We are laborers together *[sunergos]*," he said (1 Cor. 3:9). Paul planted, Apollos watered, God gave the increase—and an army of people like Gaius lent a helping hand.

PART 3

The Vainglorious Pope
3 John 9–11

A.   His Pride (v. 9)

There was a Gaius in this particular church, but there was also a Diotrephes. Gaius was always willing to receive those who loved and served the Lord; Diotrephes was the opposite. "I wrote unto the church," John says to Gaius, "but Diotrephes, who loveth to have the preeminence among them, receiveth us not."

It would seem that John had written to the church, but the letter was intercepted and destroyed by this man Diotrephes. He evidently was a man of considerable influence in the church, possibly with a following, and liked to control everything that went on in the church. It's possible that Diotrephes liked to monopolize the pulpit and that he felt threatened by the aged apostle. John may have written to the church, urging the willing reception of some of John's preacher friends, and that was the last thing Diotrephes wanted. Perhaps John had said something in the purloined letter about a proposed visit to the church, something Diotrephes wanted even less than visits from run-of-the-mill evangelists. It was a bold move to destroy an apostolic letter. John was not about to let him get away with it. Hence, this letter to Gaius. Diotrephes would not be able to intercept *his* mail.

B.   His presumption (v. 10a)

"Wherefore, if I come, I will remember his deeds which he doeth, prating against us with malicious words." Diotrephes, in other words, wanted to be the local pope, setting himself up in the church as an ecclesiastical despot. He had evidently wormed himself into a position of such power that he felt he could launch a diatribe against John.

John denounces the man's pride and presumption, and what he calls his "prating," in Greek *phluareō,* meaning "to talk nonsense." But Diotrephes' nonsense was malicious nonsense, and he had arrogated sufficient power to enforce it, using exclusivism as his weapon. Moreover, he was malicious, the Greek word means "depravity" and has to do with the active wickedness of an evil nature. The depravity of Diotrephes, then, was very serious, bad enough to be malicious toward anyone, especially a fellow believer, even more so against one of God's anointed apostles, and supremely so against the aged apostle John, the very last of them. What pride and presumption!

C. His practice (vv. 10b–11)
   1. Condemned (v. 10b)

He is *condemned:* "And not content therewith, neither doth he himself receive the brethren and forbiddeth them that would, and casteth them out of the church" (v. 10b). Diotrephes, it seems, had sufficient power and enough of a following that he was able to excommunicate people who disagreed with him. Anyone wanting to be received into his church, whether as a member or as a visitor, had to pass his inspection and interrogation. It made no difference whether or not a person knew and loved the Lord. What mattered was whether they knew and bowed to Diotrephes. Doubtless, this man would claim he was keeping the church pure, protecting the people from the possible inroad of heretics. In actual fact, he was simply protecting his preserve.

We do not know why Diotrephes disliked John. Possibly, John had once had dealings with him, perhaps he was jealous of John's position and power, John's past and his popularity, and even his personality. In any case, Diotrephes was not above making malicious remarks about John.

   2. Contrasted (v. 11)

Diotrephes is not only condemned, he is *contrasted.* John comes back to Gaius: "Beloved, follow not that which is evil, but that which is good. He that doeth good is of God: but he that doeth evil hath not seen God" (v. 11). Again, there appears John's typical contrasting absolutes. The inference is that Gaius did good and was of God; Diotrephes did evil and had no vision at all of God.

Evidently the situation was becoming critical, so much so that John, old as he was, entertained the thought of coming in person to deal with it (v. 10). It is interesting to compare Paul's "if I come" (2 Cor. 13:2) with John's. Paul wanted the people at Corinth who were attacking him and toward whom he had displayed such patience and long-suffering to know that if he did come they would get a taste of his power—and an apostle wielded mighty power (Acts 5:3–11; 1 Tim. 1:19–20). The same kind of veiled threat can be detected in John's "if I come," a sound like the distant rumble of thunder, muffled and no immediate peril, but present nonetheless. It would be a bad day for Diotrephes if the "Boanerges" (Mark 3:17) in John ever reawoke. The Holy Spirit would have to do the awakening now, but that would only make it even more terrible.

We do not know whether or not the spirit and ambition of Diotrephes received

224 of John's warning. We do know that, eventually, it arose in all its carnal and worldly power and flourished, in later centuries, into full clerical and papal domination of the church.

a check by John's warning. We do know that, eventually, it arose in all its carnal and worldly power and flourished, in later centuries, into full clerical and papal domination of the church.

PART 4

The Valued Partner

3 John 12

It would not be necessary for Gaius to stand alone. John was sending him a like-minded colleague, Demetrius, doubtless John's postman, the man who carried this brief letter to its destination. It was no use sending it through the usual channels, for it would only suffer the same fate as his previous letter—Diotrephes would seize it and tear it up. By sending it directly to Gaius, by the hand of a chosen messenger, it could be kept out of the clutches of the enemy. More—Demetrius could strengthen the hand of Gaius.

Satan overreached himself by having his vassal destroy the earlier letter from John. That letter was now replaced by a Spirit-breathed, Holy Spirit inspired New Testament epistle, and not even Satan himself could destroy this letter. Its destiny was to become part of the Bible, a permanent memorial to the triumph of truth and a deathless warning to all Diotrepheses of this world—they are really fighting against a God who always wins in the end.

As for Demetrius, he had John's complete and unqualified endorsement. Everybody who knew him bore witness to his integrity. Moreover, if "the truth" here can be capitalized and personified, then he had the highest commendation of all—the backing of Him who Himself is the truth (John 14:6). How kind of John to send such a man as Demetrius, to support such a man as Gaius, against such a man as Diotrephes!

PART 5

The Vigilant Presbyter
3 John 13–14

A.   He had so much to say (v. 13)

And so the end of the little memo refers to John himself. He had introduced himself to Gaius as "the elder" (*presbyteros*—not an official title), and throughout this entire memo breathes the spirit of a man who was not just old but who was a true elder, a true shepherd of God's people. As such, John tells Gaius two things in closing. First, he had *so much to say:* "I had many things to write, but I will not with ink and pen write unto thee" (v. 13). He said almost the same thing to the elect lady (2 John 12). Face-to-face communications are usually more satisfactory than those sent by mail.

B.   He was coming that way (v. 14)

Second, since he had so much to say—to Gaius, to Diotrephes, to the church that allowed itself to be bossed and bullied by such a tyrant—then, let Gaius and everyone else be alerted, he was *coming that way:* "But I trust I shall shortly see thee, and we shall speak face to face. Peace be to thee. Our friends salute thee. Greet the friends by name" (v. 14).

The situation in the church where Gaius lived was an aberration, nor must Gaius think for one moment that he stood alone. John was coming. Gaius had many friends in the circle of fellowship where John was, and John had many friends in the circle of fellowship where Gaius was, closed though that circle may have been by the outrageous behavior of Diotrephes. Gaius did not have to fight and could, therefore, be at peace.

"Greet the friends by name!" This expression, John's last epistolary word, occurs only once elsewhere in the Bible—Jesus, as the Good Shepherd, tells us that He calls His own sheep "by name." Perhaps John felt his position as the last of the apostolic shepherds. He had been acting, after all, as a true shepherd of the sheep in writing this memo. As a true shepherd he planned to come to this distressed flock and deal with their false shepherd. In the meantime, let the flock of God know—they are being remembered, one by one, as distinct individuals, personally and by name.

Gnosticism Unveiled

Elgin Moyer

Several heresies crept into the early Christian church, one of the most inimical and formidable being Gnosticism.[1] The roots of Gnosticism lie in pre-Christian times and made their way into the Christian era by way of Jewish philosophers who were injecting foreign religious and cultural elements from the pagan world. Lars P. Qualben says, "In these foreign elements, taken over and cultivated on Jewish and Christian soil, the germ of Gnosticism must be sought. Left to themselves and allowed to develop on native soil, these foreign elements would not of themselves have constituted a Gnosticism. But when the Jews mixed these elements with Jewish and Christian ideas and molded the whole thing into a religio-philosophic system, a Gnostic movement resulted." Philip Schaff says, "Gnosticism is the grandest and most comprehensive form of speculative religious syncretism known to history. It consists of Oriental mysticism; Greek philosophy; Alexandrian, Philonic, and cabalistic Judaism; and Christian ideas of salvation, not merely mechanically compiled, but as it were, chemically combined." Farrar says, "There were Jewish Gnostics, like the Ebionites and the pupils of Cerinthus; and pagan Gnostics; and Syrian Gnostics, like Bardesanes; and Zoroastrian Gnostics, like Manes. There were ascetic Gnostics, like Basilides; and licentious Gnostics, like the Nicolaitans and Carpocrates. There were Gnostics who taught and believed insane nonsense, like the Cainites and Ophites; and Gnostics of high culture and vivid imagination like Valentinus. There were Gnostics whose Christianity was merely a feeble graft on Judaism, like the Nazarenes; and Gnostics who, like Marcion, flung aside the Old Testament with abhorrence, and saw in the Jewish Jehovah a malignant demiurge. [*Webster:* In some Gnostic systems, a demiurge was an inferior, not absolutely intelligent, deity, the creator of the world, identified by some with the creator God of the Old Testament, and distinguished from the supreme God.] But all these sects claimed the possession of a *knowledge,* which they often represented as secret and traditional; and their views were all swept together under the name *Gnosticism,* for which an antidote was needed." Farrar further says that this antidote was provided by the Alexandrian school of Christianity in the third and fourth centuries. The Alexandrian fathers, too, claimed for themselves the name *Gnostic* but said they were *Catholic* or *Christian* Gnostics. Since their teaching and influence were distinctly Christian, however, they are not to be considered as a part or branch of the Gnostic heresy.

---

1. Taken from *Great Leaders of the Christian Church,* by Elgin Moyer (Chicago: Moody, 1951), 36–41. Used by permission.

Gnostic teaching found a seedbed in Alexandria, a great cosmopolitan center, where Greek, Jew, Egyptian, Roman, and Oriental met and fused their philosophies and cultures. In fact, this great center of learning became the hotbed of early Jewish Gnosticism and a disseminating center from which this strange new teaching penetrated Christian churches in many parts of the Christian world. Different localities offered various interpretations of Gnosticism. In Samaria was one particular brand; in Syria, another; in Asia Minor, another, and so on. Cerinthus, Basilides, Valentinus, and Saturninus were Jewish heretics who had received their Gnostic tenets in part from Philo Judeas, a learned Jew of Alexandria (20 B.C.–A.D. 40). Yet each of these men developed his own particular views and interpretations, becoming prominent leaders of late first-century and early second-century Gnosticism. Their various systems harassed and threatened the ancient church much as rationalism has done for the church of modern times. Gnosticism reached its greatest influence and power and became a formidable enemy of the expanding Christian church of the second century, much as Judaism and Judaistic sects had threatened the existence of the church in the preceding century.

Already in the first century, however, it had gained such strength that both Paul and John saw its impending threat to the church and sought to fortify the churches against its inroads in their day. Paul perhaps referred to this sinister teaching when he said to the elders of Ephesus, on the occasion of his last meeting with them, "Take heed therefore unto yourselves, and to all the flock, over which the Holy Ghost hath made you overseers, to feed the church of God, which he hath purchased with his own blood. For I know this, that after my departing shall grievous wolves enter in among you, not sparing the flock. Also of your own selves shall men arise, speaking perverse things, to draw away disciples after them" (Acts 20:28–30). In John's later years, as the only surviving apostle, he remained strong in his defense of the gospel against Gnosticism. Doing so was one of John's chief pastoral concerns, and it may have been the immediate urgency that prompted him to write his three epistles.

The name *Gnosticism* is derived from the Greek word *gnosis* meaning *knowledge*. Hence the system becomes a system of knowing, or in religious or theological language, a system that proclaims salvation by knowledge. The question may arise in one's mind, however, as to whether Gnosticism should really be called a religion at all. As it originally appeared, it may be defined, rather, as a system of speculative thought, a heretical philosophy of religion, or a mythological theosophy. Yet its adherents clung to it with strong religious fervor.

The Gnostics gradually built their speculative philosophy on the foundation of Christian doctrine, thus giving it a greater appeal and plausibility. To them Gnostic Christianity comprised essentially a superior knowledge, and Gnostics fancied themselves the sole possessors of the intellectual, esoteric, philosophical religion that made them genuinely spiritual men. They deemed themselves the intellectual aristocracy and considered all others as mere men of the soul and of the body. Salvation or the end of life, they claimed, lay in the knowledge of these psychic, esoteric, spiritual theories or fantasies. By endeavoring to fathom and explain the profundities of God and His universe, and by syncretizing the diversified views of many leaders from different centers of thought, culture, and religion, these Gnostics devised for their cult a most complex and confusing religio-philosophic system. Perhaps the best summary of the essence of Gnosticism may be stated in the words of Philip Schaff: "It is an attempt to solve some of the deepest metaphysical and theological problems. It deals with the great antitheses of God and world, spirit and matter, idea and phenomenon; and endeavors to unlock the mystery of the creation; the question of the rise, development, and end of the world; and of the origin of evil. It endeavors to harmonize the creation of the material world and the existence of evil with the idea of an absolute God, who is immaterial and perfectly good. This problem can only be solved by the Christian doctrine of redemption; but Gnosticism started from a false basis of dualism, which prevents salvation."

Some of the tendencies of the Gnostics were to substitute the irrational for the supernatural, and prodigy for miracle. They greatly mutilated the Bible, eliminating parts or all of the Old Testament, and certain parts or even whole books of the New Testament, interpreting what they retained according to their own fancies and appealing to multitudes of apocryphal documents for further teachings. Marcion, an influential leader of one of the outstanding branches of Gnosticism in the second century, selected only eleven of the twenty-seven New Testament books as the New Testament canon. He ingeniously blended the Gnostic philosophy more definitely with the Christian doctrine of the New Testament, thus making his teachings all the more insidious and dangerous.

Although many variations of Gnosticism existed, the teachings common to nearly all of them are (1) dualism—the assumption of an eternal antagonism between God and matter, or spirit and matter, (2) the demiurgic notion—the distinction between the demiurge, or alleged creator of the world, and the true God, (3) Docetism—the human element in the person of the Redeemer as mere deceptive appearance.

Rather than an organized group or church, Gnosticism was a philosophic movement finding its adherents both inside and outside the church. Says Schaff, "The aim was to resolve Christianity into a magnificent speculation; the practical business of organization was foreign to their exclusively intellectual bent." Gnosticism, then, was a body of thought rather than a body of believers, having, nonetheless, great influence upon the church, presenting itself as a real enemy to the church for two or three centuries.

Paul and John, especially the latter, earnestly opposed the heresy in the first century. Ignatius, Irenaeus, and other first- and second-generation disciples of John carried on the warfare into the second century.

Along with Gnosticism in the Christian church, Judaism also should be mentioned as an early heretical movement. It greatly agitated the early church, Judaizing representing an insidious tendency, even from the days of the early Jerusalem church. The Council of Jerusalem settled the matter in principle but not in fact, and Judaistic leanings and even sects arose through the years.

Following the fall of Jerusalem in A.D. 70, groups of Jewish Christians formed called Nazarenes. They tried to be at the same time both Jew and Christian, but the more distinctly Christian element among them gradually merged into, and became an integral part, of the Christian church. The more distinctly Jewish element, the Ebionites and other similar sects, continued to hold to their Mosaicism, becoming less and less Christian. About the fourth century they finally lost their identity as separate religious groups.

Another Judaistic group, the Elkasaites, mixed pagan teaching with their Judaism. They, too, finally became extinct as a movement.

Beside the Judaistic and Gnostic heresies of the first century, several other sects agitated the church, but these ran their course in the first century or shortly thereafter. Among these were the Ophites, Nicolaitans, Simonians, and Docetists, all of which were tinged more or less with Gnostic teaching and with other heathen philosophies.

Explore the

BIBLE

in greater depth with the
John Phillips
Commentary Series!